LIVING WITH GRIEF

■

COPING WITH

PUBLIC TRAGEDY

EDITED BY
MARCIA LATTANZI-LICHT AND KENNETH J. DOKA

Foreword by Jack D. Gordon, Chairman, Hospice Foundation of America

HOSPICE FOUNDATION
OF AMERICA

Brunner-Routledge

This book is part of Hospice Foundation of America's
Living With Grief® series.

Support has been provided in part by the Foundation for End of Life Care.

© 2003 Hospice Foundation of America®

This book is part of HFA's *Living With Grief*® series.

Ordering information:

Brunner-Routledge
29 West 35th Street
New York, NY 10001

To order by phone, call toll-free: 1-800-634-7064
Or send orders on a 24-hour telefax: 1-800-248-4724
www.routledge-ny.com

For bulk quantity orders call Hospice Foundation of America: 800-854-3402

Or write:
Hospice Foundation of America
2001 S Street, NW #300
Washington, DC 20009
800-854-3402
www.hospicefoundation.org

Managing Editor: Judith Rensberger
Copy Editor: Pat Tschirhart-Spangler
Cover Design: Patricia McBride
Typesetting and Design: Pam Page Cullen
Cover Photo: Mario Tama/Getty Images

Library of Congress Cataloging-in-Publication Data

Coping with public tragedy / edited by Marcia Lattanzi-Licht and Kenneth J. Doka ; foreword by Jack D. Gordon.
    p. cm. -- (Living with grief)
    Includes bibliographical references.
  ISBN 1-893349-04-7 (pbk.)
1. Disasters--Psychological aspects. 2. Disasters--Social aspects.
3. Crisis intervention (Mental health services) I. Lattanzi-Licht, Marcia E. II. Doka, Kenneth J. III. Series.

BF789.D5C67 2003
155.9'35--dc21

                                     2003001429

■ DEDICATIONS ■

*To Mike Licht, my love and my strength, and to
Steven Lattanzi, my son and my delight.*

—Marcia Lattanzi-Licht

*In loving memory of Catherine Sanders, a wonderful
colleague whose pioneering work and life illustrated
the transforming power of grief.*

—Kenneth J. Doka

*For all whose lives have been touched by public tragedy,
and in appreciation of all first responders.*

—Marcia Lattanzi-Licht and Kenneth J. Doka

Contents

■ FOREWORD ■

Jack D. Gordon
Chairman, Hospice Foundation of America

The year 2003 is a momentous one for both the hospice movement and Hospice Foundation of America. It is the 20th year of the Medicare Hospice Benefit. In 1983, Congress formally recognized the importance of compassionate care for the dying by institutionalizing hospice as a reimbursable service. One of the core services of hospice is the commitment to ongoing bereavement counseling to the family. In fact, hospice is the only Medicare benefit that continues service to the family for up to a year after the death of the patient.

In the 20 years since the start of the Medicare benefit, and because of the growing societal importance of bereavement services, hospices have become an important community resource on grief and bereavement. Maintaining a high level of quality in grief counseling, spiritual care, and emotional support is difficult to attain. To assist in that, Hospice Foundation of America provides as one of its central services innovative free or low-cost educational opportunities for grief counselors.

The year 2003 also finds HFA celebrating the 10th anniversary of the *Living With Grief®* teleconference series, of which this book is the companion volume. The application of bereavement services has evolved in many ways over the past decade, and we at HFA are proud that this series has been a part of that evolution. When we select a topic for each year's teleconference and accompanying book, a key consideration is how we can help hospices broaden their community outreach. I believe that hospice has many contributions to make to a community, primarily as the basic resource for bereavement counseling, but also as a major influence in increasing patient autonomy in the health system.

This year's topic, *Living with Grief: Coping with Public Tragedy*, also is designed to give local hospices an opportunity to make known their capabilities in helping their communities when terrible events occur. The chapter by Marcia Lattanzi-Licht reviews hospice participation in a number of community disasters. It is a record in which everyone involved in the hospice movement can take pride.

From television, radio, and daily newspapers, we get detailed and sometimes graphic accounts of the results of natural disasters such as hurricanes, tornadoes, and forest fires, as well as man-made disasters such as multiple shootings, auto accidents, and, of course, the devastating terrorist attacks that occurred on September 11, 2001.

These events affect everyone, because there is always the thought, there but for the grace of God, go I. So when we deal with such events, we are concerned about the feelings and thoughts of everyone including, obviously, family and loved ones. That is what makes this topic such a difficult one to understand. We bring our own experiences, as well as our own attitudes toward life and death, to the attempt to understand what has happened. What we bring is not only our impression of the event, but also the memories and fears that it stimulates. Because everyone's experience is different, we have to think hard to arrive at a common basis for discussing how we can help others and ourselves.

It is the Foundation's hope that a careful reading of this book will provide readers with a better understanding of the nature of this kind of trauma. Ideally, we would never again have to face this problem, but we know that is not possible. Being better prepared can only make the aftermath less disrupting for everyone affected. ■

■ ACKNOWLEDGMENTS ■

In times of public tragedy, we are reminded of the importance of relationships. We appreciate anew the love and friendships that at other times we may take for granted. This is why it is critical to acknowledge with thanks those who nourish our work and enrich our lives.

Both of us wish to thank our authors, who met tight deadlines to make this book a reality.

We also wish to acknowledge Hospice Foundation of America and its dedicated staff. We thank Jack D. Gordon, chairman, and David Abrams, president, for supporting the development and publication of this and all previous volumes in the *Living With Grief*® series. Special thanks also go to Sophie Berman, vice-president and chief fiscal officer.

Judith Rensberger, senior program officer, served well as the book's managing editor, capably assisted by Kate Viggiano, continuing education coordinator. We also thank Jon Radulovic, communications director (and HFA teleconference guru), Lisa Veglahn, program consultant, Donna Hines, administrative associate, and Bertha Ramirez, accounting assistant.

We thank Patricia McBride for the cover design, Pam Page Cullen for typesetting and page design, Patricia Tschirhart-Spangler for copy editing, Helen McMahon for proofreading, and Anthony Sullivan for photo research.

We offer special thanks to Cokie Roberts for her continuing commitment to Hospice Foundation of America's annual teleconferences on grief and bereavement. The 2003 teleconference, for which this is the companion book, is Cokie's tenth year as moderator.

Marcia Lattanzi-Licht thanks her husband, Mike, for his love, understanding, support, and wisdom. The material in this book touches on personal as well as public tragedy. The experience of Marcia's daughter Ellen's tragic death has shaped Marcia's understanding and commitment to this work. Ellen's energy and bright spirit guide her still. Marcia's son, Steve, has been a continuing source of joy, encouragement and love. Marcia greatly values all they have learned together.

Marcia also acknowledges her network of family, friends and colleagues in Boulder, Colorado, and across the country. She thanks them for their continuing friendship, support and feedback. Special thanks go to Galen Miller, Chuck Corr, Barbara Bouton, Stephen Connor and Nadine Reimer Penner. Finally, Marcia wishes to acknowledge the courage of the first responders and victims' families with whom she has had the honor of working. They continue to live and love in spite of tragedy and disaster.

Kenneth J. Doka acknowledges his family. The pleasure of finishing this book was surpassed only by his delight in learning that his son and daughter-in-law, Michael and Angelina Rooney, are expecting a baby in June. Ken also acknowledges his godson, Keith Whitehead; sister, Dorothy McCoy; brother, Frank Doka, and their families. Very special thanks go to Kathy Dillon.

Ken also acknowledges the support and encouragement of several good friends and neighbors: Eric Schwarz, Larry and Ellie Laterza, Scott and Lisa Carlson, Lorraine and Tom Carlson, Jim and Mary Millar, Lynn and Joel Miller, Don and Carol Ford, Margot and Paul Kimball, Allen and Gail Greenstein, Fred and Lisa Amori, and Dylan Rieger. All are there to share the great joys and private tragedies of life.

Finally, we both wish to acknowledge all those who touched our lives in tragedy. By sharing their pain, they teach us all.

Marcia Lattanzi-Licht and Kenneth J. Doka
3 January 2003

PART I

Dimensions
of Public Tragedy

Events such as the assassination of President John F. Kennedy, the shootings at Columbine High School, Hurricane Andrew, the Oklahoma City bombing and 9/11, while different in many ways, all generated similar public responses. In each there were public outpourings of grief, spontaneous memorialization, collective actions, and attempts to find meaning. Yet not every traumatic event generates so public a response. Automobile crashes are a common cause of death, yet rarely do they generate strong attention. Why do certain events capture the attention of the public, arousing intense grief, while others do not?

In his opening chapter, Kenneth Doka focuses on that question. He first identifies ten interrelated factors that can define a traumatic event as a public tragedy. He also describes the role of the news media in framing public perceptions of that event. Dr. Doka then discusses how hospice can remain a major source of grief support in a community, even as emergency services leave and the focus of the news media turns elsewhere.

Other chapters in this section provide case examples from selected public tragedies. Sherry Schachter offers a first-hand account of providing assistance at Ground Zero. She reflects on the effects that 9/11 had on those already grieving, such as patients with life-limiting illnesses and newly bereaved individuals. Dr. Schachter also reaffirms the need to address the care of professionals who assist those directly affected.

In his examination of Hurricane Andrew, which devastated south Florida in 1992, Rick Eyerdam offers an in-depth account of the impact of a natural disaster. His chapter is a cautionary tale; it reminds us that traumatic events can outpace contingency plans and that community organizations and government agencies should frequently reassess their disaster plans.

In his chapter, Larry Beresford reviews the events of the shootings at Columbine High School in 1999, and reflects on some of the lessons learned. As is often the case, the scope of the event overwhelmed local resources. Yet President Clinton's call for grief counselors generated an extraordinary response and created a new problem—how to evaluate and effectively make use of all the individuals and resources that suddenly became available.

Finally, William Lamers reminds us that not every public tragedy is necessarily massive in scope. We may so identify with certain public figures that their deaths, especially when violent or unexpected, affect us to a surprising degree. Dr. Lamers notes that the outpouring of grief and public ritual can provide a release for those dealing with more personal losses. ■

CHAPTER 1

What Makes a Tragedy Public?

Kenneth J. Doka

- Greg Harris and Dylan Klebold opened fire at Columbine High School in Littleton, Colorado, killing 13 of their classmates and teachers before turning the weapons on themselves.

- In July 1999, the small plane piloted by John F. Kennedy, Jr., and carrying his wife and sister-in-law failed to land at its Cape Cod destination. An extensive search yielded the wreckage and the bodies of the three occupants.

- A tornado touched down on a small community in upstate New York. Slamming into an elementary school, it took the lives of seven children.

- On September 11, 2001, terrorists hijacked four planes. In attacks on the World Trade Center and the Pentagon, approximately 3,000 persons died.

All four of these illustrative events were different. All four had very different death tolls. Each had different causes and consequences. Yet each was a very public tragedy—the focus of national attention and mourning. In each there were extensive media coverage, considerable public attention, and debate.

This raises a critical question. What causes certain events to be perceived as a public tragedy? Kennedy's plane was not the only small plane to crash nor was Columbine the only school shooting. Yet these events were raised to a level of public attention not shared by every other event. Deaths and disasters touch the lives of others daily. Everyday, hundreds or thousands of individuals experience personal, private tragedies. When and why does a tragedy become public?

DISASTER, TRAUMA, AND PUBLIC TRAGEDY

It is surprising that while there is much literature on specific public tragedies—witness the books published about 9/11—there is little written about public tragedy sui generis. There is considerable research on trauma and disaster. Trauma results when individuals directly experience extraordinary events that actually threaten survival (Janoff-Bulmen, 1992). These events, Janoff-Bulmen (1992) reminds, shatter our assumptions, that is, our underlying model of a safe, meaningful, and benevolent world.

Disasters are collective traumas. Barton defines disasters as "a collective stress that occurs when members of a social system fail to receive the expected conditions of life from their social system due to external or internal sources" (1970). Raphael, in her classic study, also notes that disasters test assumptions; they usually are overwhelming events that test the adaptational responses of communities or individuals beyond their capability and lead, at least temporarily, to massive disruptions of function (1986). Both Raphael (1986) and Barton (1970) acknowledge that disasters can be sudden, as a tornado, or gradual and prolonged, as in a famine or drought. Raphael describes the circles of impact ranging from those totally affected to those partially affected to those outside who might, at best, experience vicarious involvement. She also suggests those distinct roles individuals may play in a disaster: victims, rescuers, and helpers. Rescuers, for example, might be emergency personnel—intimately involved in search and recovery efforts (1986). Helpers may include medical personnel as well as those who bring supplies to the effected area. We might expand Raphael's typology, making a distinction between victims who succumb to death or injury and survivors who are, at least physically, unscathed. We might also include "hidden victims." These may encompass family members or others who experience loss in a disaster. For example, 9/11 left not only families mourning the dead, but also thousands who were unemployed.

While the literature of disaster can inform a discussion of public tragedy, it is critical to remember that the concepts are not identical. Not every disaster is necessarily a public tragedy. For example, the famine stemming from civil war in the Nigerian breakaway province of Biafra in the late 1960s aroused strong public interest. There were television specials and a major rock concert—all raising public attention, interest, and financial support. Yet only the victims and the relief agencies that attempt to alleviate the suffering notice other famines. Why is one famine a public tragedy worthy of international assistance when another goes unnoticed?

Nor is every public tragedy a disaster. Car fatalities, unfortunately, are not unusual. Few, unless the toll is massive, are perceived as public tragedies. Yet the death of Princess Diana clearly was perceived as public tragedy.

DEFINING A PUBLIC TRAGEDY

The American sociologist, C.W. Mills, once made a critical distinction between "private troubles" and "public issues" (1963). To Mills, private troubles had to do with an individual's character or circumstances; public issues transcended the individual. For example, someone can drink too much, at some point, though, the fact that too many people drink too much raises a public issue: how does a society deal with alcoholism?

There is a critical question that arises from Mills' work. How do private troubles become transformed into public issues? There are many private troubles common to a large number of individuals that never are addressed by the larger society. How do individuals transform private problems into public issues? Consider, for example, drinking and driving. For many years, individual families faced a private problem. Someone driving under the influence of alcohol caused a crash that killed a family member. Yet these individuals, sometimes repeat offenders, received minor sentences. Eventually, one mother turned her private grief into activism and formed the group, Mothers Against Drunk Driving. That made drinking and driving a public issue, ripe for social action.

There are numerous tragedies each year, ranging from plane and car crashes to natural disasters to acts of terrorism or violence. Of these numbers, how do some become defined as public tragedy, worthy of attention and action?

FACTORS INFLUENCING THE PUBLIC PERCEPTION OF TRAGEDY

As individuals sort through varied events, there are factors that influence public perception. These factors determine not only whether or not an event will be defined as a public tragedy. They also determine ways that individuals will perceive a tragedy and react and respond to it.

Scope

A significant factor in the perception of tragedy is scope. In any tragedy, there are circles of persons affected—victims, helpers, rescuers, survivors, family and friends, even those indirectly affected (e.g., those experiencing layoffs or dislocation). The larger the scope, the more likely a tragedy will be defined as a public one.

Moreover, large-scope tragedies demand a different response. When a tragedy affects a large number of people, it tends to overwhelm local resources. For example, the shooting at Columbine High School affected so many that local resources were insufficient to handle the needs of grieving and traumatized students and families. Individuals, too, may be overwhelmed by the multiple losses that they experience.

Yet the deaths of Princess Diana, John F. Kennedy, Jr., or Prime Minister Rabin remind us that scope is only one factor. Even small-scope events can become defined as public tragedy.

Identification

We identify with individuals to different degrees. The suicidal deaths of cult members, for example, may not engender as much personal identification as the random victims of a terrorist attack. We may not see ourselves, or even family members, as likely to join a self-destructive cult, but we do identify with the pain of individuals mourning the deaths of those who simply went to school or to work.

Part of identification involves an assumption of risk. Even in risky sports, for example, participants will evaluate the deaths of other participants, offering far less sympathy for a death that others perceive as due to the assumption of unnecessary risks (Doka, Schwarz, & Schwarz, 1990). Thus, the deaths of military personnel may draw less attention than that of noncombatants.

The process of identification is complex. We may identify with Princess Diana not on the basis of her unique status but on shared experiences. Many, for example, mourned not so much the death of a princess as that of a young mother. We may identify with public figures because their lives were so public. We all watched John F. Kennedy, Jr., grow from toddler to adult. The point is that the greater the identification with the victim or victims, the greater the likelihood that the death will be defined as public tragedy.

Social Value

Every society has assumptions of social value. This means that in any given society, certain individuals or members of a class may have greater attribution of social worth than other individuals or different groups of people. This attribution of social value in any given society can be influenced by a number of variables, including race, age, social class, position, role, or family.

The greater the social value of the victims, the more likely an individual's death will be perceived as a public tragedy. For example, youth has a positive social value. The killings at Columbine sparked more attention than a similar shooting might have caused had it been at a nursing home. The deaths of individuals of such a high social value as Princess Diana, John F. Kennedy, Jr., or other celebrities or public figures are often perceived, in and of themselves, as public tragedy. It is important to recognize that as attributions of value change, so might the original perceptions of the tragedy. While the assassination of Israeli Prime Minister Rabin was considered a great public tragedy, the subsequent breakdown of peace efforts, in some ways a consequence of his death, has given his death even a greater pathos.

Consequences

This suggests another factor: the greater the consequences resulting from a tragic event, the more likely that event will be perceived, even retrospectively, as a public tragedy. The terrorist attacks of September 11, 2001, are mourned not only for the horrific loss of life but also for a national loss of a sense of safety, and an increased sense of vulnerability. These events are likely to lead to significant and structural changes in security systems. Should these changes erode civil liberties, that, too, will be mourned and contribute to the attribution of tragedy.

Duration

The duration of a tragedy also affects public perception and evaluation of an event. Most tragedies, such as 9/11, take place within a relatively short period of time—hours or days. Others, such as a famine or drought, may unfold over a much longer time. Duration may have a mixed effect on whether or not an event is perceived as public tragedy. Events, such as a famine, that unfold over time can allow both recognition and organized efforts for support. Conversely, such events may fuel a sense of powerlessness that tax public interest.

The Natural-to-Human-Made Continuum

In an earlier work, (Doka, 1998), I described six factors that influenced responses to violent loss. These factors also affect responses to public tragedy. One of the most significant involves causality. We sometimes think about causality in terms of whether a tragedy is due to natural or human action. In fact, such a distinction is artificial. Most acts have, at least, some degree of human intention or omission. Some, such as the attacks of 9/11, are clearly on one end of this continuum—definitely the result of human action. Others, such as Hurricane Andrew, fall toward the natural end of the continuum. These tragedies result primarily from forces of nature—hurricanes, tornadoes, or earthquakes. Yet even here there may be elements of human involvement. For example, a number of years ago, I went to the Red River Valley of North Dakota to assist in the recovery efforts following the floods. The Red River is one of the rare rivers that flow north. Yet towns over the Canadian border were not flooded. The Canadian government had built a series of dams and dikes to control the floodwaters. The U.S. government had not because its cost-benefit analysis suggested that the likelihood of a devastating flood was remote, a once-in-500-years event. Even here, human decision making played a role.

This continuum affects public perception of tragedy in two ways. First, in rare cases, assumptions of cause, including assumptions of risk, may limit public sympathy and identification. There is little public sympathy for persons who cause tragedy. For example, enraged parents and supporters destroyed two markers placed by a church for all the adolescents and adults who died at Columbine. They wanted no symbol for the students who caused 13 deaths. Similarly, there might be less sympathy for victims of tragedy who are perceived to have had a role in their fate, whether as a result of a suicide pact or as a consequence of choosing to live in a flood plain.

Second, responses to tragedy may differ. Disasters more on the natural end of the continuum may threaten one's spirituality, evoking themes of unfairness, and even generating anger toward God. Those caused by human intention or indifference may direct anger toward others, either as perpetrators or scapegoats.

Degree of Intentionality

Another critical continuum is the degree of intentionality (Doka, 1996). Some tragedies clearly are due to the willful acts of another person. Others may involve the unintentional actions of another human being such as a train engineer inadvertently throwing a wrong switch. Still others, such as a pure natural disaster, may involve little or no human action or intention.

Intention affects public perception of tragedy in several ways. Events perceived as random are more likely to generate identification with victims. In such cases it reminds others that they all share risk—a collective there but for the grace of God go I. When someone or some group is perceived as intentionally causing the tragedy, however, there will be a different social response. The individual or group will be held responsible and face the collective wrath. One of the dangers of public tragedy is the tendency to scapegoat or assign blame on the innocent. For example, in the middle ages, European communities assigned blame for the plague pandemic to various groups—dissenters, heretics, Jews, or lepers—even as they too died of the disease. Assigning blame has social value beyond simply providing a convenient target for public anxiety and anger. By assigning blame, an illusion of safety and preventability can be maintained. It fosters a sense of control.

Degree of Expectedness

Traumatic events and disasters fall as well along a continuum of expectedness (Doka, 1996). Some events, such as a flood, may be predictable. For example, it was possible to predict the cresting of the Red River and ascertain the areas in danger. As a result, despite considerable damage to property, no one died in the flood. Other events, such as the Oklahoma City bombing are unpredictable. The more unpredictable an event is, the more likely it is to be perceived as a public tragedy. There will be retrospective analysis and reassignment of blame. The thought that an event such as 9/11 could not be predicted threatens any perception of future safety.

Degree of Preventability

Related to the degree of expectedness is the degree of preventability. Events such as a tornado may have limited degrees of preventability. Yet even here, blame may be appointed. For example, years ago I worked with a school that was hit by a tornado, killing seven children. In the aftermath, there was considerable debate. Were the walls properly reinforced? Was it wise to bring the children to the cafeteria during the tornado watch? In other circumstances there may be even greater debates. After Columbine, for example, there were questions about whether or not the perpetrators' parents, friends, or teachers could have prevented that tragedy and the larger debates ranging from the culture of adolescence to the availability of guns.

Generally, the more unpreventable an event is, the more likely it will be perceived as tragic. Nonetheless these debates serve a critical function in public tragedy. Not only do they help define the tragedy, they serve to mediate it. The policies and practices, the lessons learned that emerge from tragedy may prevent future tragedies and reestablish a sense of safety. More importantly, they provide meaning and purpose to the tragic event—a form of "benefit finding" that mitigates grief.

Perception of Suffering

A last element that influences the definition of an event as a public tragedy is the perception of suffering. In some events, such as a plane explosion, survivors may take comfort that victims died instantly, unaware of danger or death. In other situations, not knowing whether family members suffered or being aware that they did may trouble individuals. The attacks on the World Trade Center are full of horrific images of individuals making a final phone call describing the carnage and death. Meanwhile, other survivors are haunted because they cannot reconstruct a coworker's or family member's last moments. The greater the perception of suffering, the more likely an event will be perceived as public tragedy.

HOW DOES A TRAUMATIC EVENT BECOME A PUBLIC TRAGEDY?

Public tragedies, it is clear, are more than simply traumatic events. A traumatic event becomes a public tragedy when there is a collective definition of that event as a significant calamity. This appraisal of any given event is likely to be idiosyncratic, but it involves some combination of the factors of scope, identification, social value of the victims, consequences, duration, causation, intentionality, predictability, preventability, and perception of suffering. Some combination of these factors will arouse public perception of the event, focusing attention and eliciting societal responses and collective actions.

In defining an event as a public tragedy, it is critical to remember the definition of the word *public*—a group of people with a shared interest. Most tragedies have many publics. For example, 9/11 affected victims, families, survivors, rescuers, military, airline employees, residents of metropolitan New York and Washington, Americans generally, and others throughout the world. Most of these publics shared a definition of the event as an unparalleled and horrendous tragedy. Yet each of these publics was affected differently by the event—some directly, others more indirectly. As time goes on, the interests in the event also will differ. Within the first year, there already has been conflict among some of these publics about the future of the site, the appropriateness of memorials, and the disbursement of funds.

This concept explains as well the differential responses to a tragedy. Some publics or groups may be totally unaffected. For some, the death of Princess Diana was a major tragedy. For others, it was sad and unfortunate but of no major significance to their lives.

ROLE OF THE NEWS MEDIA

The news media play a critical role in defining public tragedy. They report what happened, describe its significance, and suggest social action. Beyond these functions, the news media influence in other ways. By the very allocation of time and space in coverage, the news media help frame the perception of the tragedy. While there may be debate about the degree to which the news media shape or reflect public interest, the amount of coverage testifies to the importance of the event. The fact that 9/11 pre-empted regular television and radio programming and dominated the print media for days was a continuing reaffirmation of the significance of the tragedy.

The news media also create identification. Barton (1970) cites an example of a headline in a Catholic newspaper, early in the 20th century. The headline read, "Tornadoes Strike Southwest, No Catholics Killed." Moreover, the news media select spokespersons, often from among victims or families, thereby validating their role and helping shape public sympathy and response.

CONCLUSION

One of the clichés of public tragedy is that life will never be the same after one. For some individuals, life does not change; they resume the basic rhythms of their lives as the immediacy of the tragedy recedes. But for others, life really does change. Those immediately affected must cope with their losses and grief. For them, basic assumptions of life may be shattered. The world no longer seems benign. This may lead to a sense of anxiety and fear. Individuals may also experience a spiritual crisis. They may feel that their lives now have no purpose or goals, or that their constructs—the ways they view the world—are bankrupt, that their spirituality is threatened. For many survivors, tragedy leaves a terrible imprint. On a larger scale, some tragedies can fracture a community, creating conflict and division. This, too, can contribute to an individual's sense of loss (Eriksen, 1976).

Yet for others, this may lead to attempts to reconstruct a sense of order, to rebuild shattered assumptions. Sometimes these attempts themselves are illusionary. In an earlier book, Jack Gordon and I (2000) described the phenomenon of "resonating trauma," in which people focus their generalized anxiety on a specific "expected" event. For example, following 9/11, rumors abounded that there would be a major attack on a shopping mall on October 31. When these attacks failed to materialize, persons could once again feel safe.

Other attempts to reconstruct may be far more resilient. In the aftermath of a tragedy, some persons may experience considerable growth. They may have a changed sense of self—seeing themselves now as stronger. They may reprioritize relationships, developing and enhancing ties with others. Individuals may experience a sense of existential and spiritual growth (Calhoun & Tedeschi, 2001). They may find new purposes, goals, and meanings, develop more resilient constructs, and even find secondary gains in their experience of loss such as new skills or insights that mitigate grief (Davis & Nlen-Hocksima, 2001).

Collectively, too, public tragedy can strengthen even as it injures. There may be a new collective unity and sense of purpose. In time, tragedies may lead to collective actions that create new policies and change the social order. The horror of the Triangle Shirt Factory fire not only shocked a nation but also created support for legislation to improve occupational safety.

Grief, collective or individual, can generate growth. This process takes time, however, and that is why hospices, community mental health centers, and funeral grief programs are so critical. They remain in the community long after disaster relief agencies have left, donations have ceased, and public attention has turned to a new tragedy. ■

Kenneth J. Doka is a Professor of Gerontology at the Graduate School of The College of New Rochelle and Senior Consultant to the Hospice Foundation of America. Dr. Doka has written or edited 16 books and published more than 60 articles and book chapters. He is editor of both Omega *and* Journeys: A Newsletter for the Bereaved. *Dr. Doka was elected President of the Association for Death Education and Counseling (ADEC) in 1993. He was elected to the Board of the International Work Group on Dying, Death and Bereavement in 1995, and served as chair from 1997 to 1999. ADEC presented him with an Award for Outstanding Contributions in the Field of Death Education in 1998. In 2000 Scott and White presented him an award for Outstanding Contributions to Thanatology and Hospice. Dr. Doka is an ordained Lutheran minister.*

REFERENCES

Barton, P. (1970). *Communities in disaster: A sociological analysis of collective stress situations.* Garden City, NY: Doubleday.

Calhoun, L., & Tedeschi, R. (2001). Posttraumatic Growth: The Positive Lessons of Loss. In R.A. Neimeyer (Ed.) *Meaning reconstruction and the experience of loss.* (pp. 157-172). Washington, DC: The American Psychological Association.

Davis, C., & Nlen-Hocksima, S. (2001). Loss and meaning: How do people make sense of loss? *American Behavioral Scientist 44*, 726-741.

Doka, K.J., Schwarz, E., & Schwarz, C. (1990). Risky business: observations on the nature of death in hazardous sports. *Omega 21*, 215-224.

Doka, K.J., (1996). *Living with grief: After sudden loss.* Washington DC: Hospice Foundation of America.

Eriksen, K.T. (1976). *Everything in its path: Destruction of community in the Buffalo Creek Flood.* New York: Simon & Schuster.

Gordon, J.D., & Doka, K.J. (2000). Resonating trauma: A theoretical note. In K.J. Doka (Ed.) *Living with grief: Children, adolescents, and loss.* (pp. 291-293). Washington, DC: The Hospice Foundation of America.

Mills, C.W. (1963). *Power, politics and people: The collected essays of C. Wright Mills.* New York: Oxford Press.

Raphael, B. (1986). *When disaster strikes: How individuals and communities cope with catastrophe.* NY: Basic Books.

Thomas, W.I. (1937). *The unadjusted girl.* Boston: Little Brown.

CHAPTER 2

9/11: A Grief
Therapist's Journal

Sherry R. Schachter

INTRODUCTION

The events of 9/11 have changed many lives in many ways. Specialists in posttraumatic stress disorder (PTSD) note that the terrorist attacks on the World Trade Center affected not only those individuals who lost loved ones but the population of the entire tri-state area (Gordon, 2002). It is still too soon to fully comprehend the effects of the trauma because acts of terrorism resulting in mass casualties have a wide impact (Office for Victims of Crime, 2000; Doka 2002). Traumas resulting in massive killings, property destruction, and long-term unemployment will challenge the structure of the community in which they occur (Williams, Zinner, & Ellis, 1999).

Statistics from the United States Department of Labor (2002) note that approximately 368,000 persons worked within a few blocks of the World Trade Center, more than 500,000 worked within the area cordoned off by emergency officials responding to the attack, and about 700,000 worked in the southern quarter of Manhattan. In the report, *Extended Layoffs in the Fourth Quarter of 2001*, issued February 13, 2002, the Bureau of Labor Statistics found that as of December 29, 2001, there had been 408 extended mass layoffs, involving 114,711 workers, directly or indirectly attributed to the attacks. Thirty-three states reported extended mass layoff activity related in some way to 9/11. Among the workers laid off because of the terrorist attacks, 42 percent, or 44,756 workers, had been employed in the scheduled air transportation industry. An additional 28 percent, or 32,044 workers, had been employed in hotels and motels.

These statistics, however staggering, do not fully explain the devastation or help us comprehend how many lives and families will be forever affected by this tragedy. As of August 15, 2002, the number of deaths confirmed by the New York City coroner's office and the U.S. Department of Defense was 2,872, including those for whom a death certificate was issued although no body was recovered. The United States lost 2,106 individuals; New York City lost 1,127 (including 343 firefighters, 37 Port Authority police officers, and 27 police officers). Most were men whose average age was 40. (Spektor, 2002)

The aim of terrorism is to traumatize and immobilize a population through threats, physical destruction, killing, and creation of widespread panic, suffering and chaos. For survivors, witnessing the murder or catastrophic injury of large numbers of people as they go about the routine tasks of daily life creates a sense of horror and vulnerability that may last a lifetime (Turman, 2002).

Clinicians and researchers suggest that bereaved persons whose loved ones have been murdered are at higher risk for complicated grief reactions and posttraumatic stress disorders (Figley, 1995; McCann & Pearlman, 1990; Rando, 1993; Redmond, 1989). One study, conducted by the New York Academy of Medicine from mid-October to mid-November 2001, focused on Manhattan residents and the prevalence of acute posttraumatic stress disorder and depression since 9/11 (2002). Adults were randomly sampled and asked about their exposure to the events of 9/11 and any subsequent psychological symptoms. Of the 998 adults sampled, 7.5 percent met criteria consistent with a diagnosis of PTSD and 9.7 percent reported symptoms of clinical depression. These findings suggest that approximately 67,000 people experienced PTSD and 87,000 were depressed during the time of the study.

THE RUSH TO HELP

Just hours after the attacks on the twin towers and the Pentagon, the Pennsylvania Medical Society sent an e-mail requesting medical volunteers willing to travel to New York and Washington. By evening, more than 1,000 physicians, nurses, and emergency medical personnel had responded. By the following day, more than 2,000 volunteers were in New York and Washington. Two days after the attacks, the Pennsylvania Medical Society again e-mailed its membership to report that nearly 4,000 volunteers had signed up. Similarly, the New York State Medical Society reported that it had far more volunteers than survivors to care for. What officials needed was not physicians to care for the wounded, but pathologists to identify the dead. Across the country, health care workers expressed frustration and a sense of inadequacy, wishing they could have done more.

The sense of helplessness was certainly acute at New York City's Memorial Sloan-Kettering Cancer Center. That Tuesday morning at the Center was typically busy. I was in the middle of morning rounds in our Pain and Palliative Care Service. My pager beeped insistently; it was my husband trying to let me know what was happening. Everyone ran to the windows and then to the television set. Families and staff crowded into hospital day rooms or stayed in patients' rooms and watched the events with them on television. The remainder of the day I spent talking with and supporting our dazed staff, many of whom had missing husbands, fathers, and friends.

The next night after work, some of the staff went to help out at Ground Zero. We had no idea if we would be allowed past the barricades or if we would be sent back, but we needed to go. We brought blankets, gauze pads, bottles of saline, bandages, gloves and, most important, face masks.

A New York City police officer gladly arranged transportation for us. City streets were deserted and the absence of traffic was eerie. Smoke filled the sky as the fires blazed and the wail of sirens pierced the night. We had to stop at barricades four times for police checks of our identification before we arrived at Stuyvesant High School, where a makeshift medical center was set up.

As we walked amid the rubble, the smell was sickening and the smoke so thick we had to don the face masks. We passed many disabled police cars and other vehicles, which were burned, partly crushed, and covered with inches of debris. It seemed as if we were walking through a battle scene on a movie set. Searchlights lit up the area as if it was daytime. It was overwhelming to see so many people: police, firefighters, national guard, and construction workers. The search dogs, beautiful German Shepherds, wore booties on their feet to protect them from the rubble. All were busy with a mission; though exhausted and covered with layers of dust they were determined to find survivors. The streets were set up with booths dispensing water, drinks, and snack foods. There were ambulances and emergency trucks from all over the area.

The high school had been turned into a makeshift hospital. Stations were set up to treat rescuers with eye irritations and other injuries. Behind a sign reading "Respiratory Stations" there was a large triage area with army cots lined up and IVs ready for use. Another area was staffed with psychiatrists, psychologists, and social workers.

We worked informally with rescuers who arrived dazed and shocked by the gruesome sights they had seen: bodies and body parts, but no survivors. Nurses and physicians worked in the medical triage area, caring for wounded rescue workers. Most were treated for dehydration, bruises, and broken bones. Still, no survivors were found. Upstairs, a large area had been set up with tables of food and refreshments. Another area was set aside for rescuers (including the rescue dogs) to get massages for their weary bodies. Workers came in, stayed briefly, then returned to their rescue efforts, still hopeful. Volunteers washed floors and carried boxes of supplies.

At 3 a.m., exhausted, we were driven home by two police officers. Outside the barricades, people thronged the streets. There were flags on parked cars, and people waving flags and banners that said: "Thank you, YOU are our heroes" and "The City thanks you." People were applauding, shouting, "Thank you, God bless you." Not far away, both sides of the streets were lined with refrigerated trucks waiting to bring human remains to the medical examiner.

Over the following months, I returned to the neighborhood of Ground Zero many times. I debriefed rescuers, helped families go through hospital lists of emergency admissions, worked with the Red Cross and the firefighters. There were military boats with guns in our rivers, national guard units on the streets, and military planes in our skies. Pictures of missing loved ones are still seen throughout the city, tacked on lampposts, fences, and buildings. American flags wave from cars, hang from windows, and are placed in backpacks; men and women are wearing flag pins on their lapels; the front of every firehouse and police station is filled with flowers, cards, and other mementos.

LAYERS OF BEREAVEMENT: PUBLIC TRAUMA, PERSONAL LOSS

Emotionally we are in a different place now than we were at the time of the attacks, and our needs have slowly changed. As an attending grief therapist at Memorial Sloan-Kettering Cancer Center, the focus of my work is facilitating bereavement support groups. Each week I facilitate four to six groups for people whose spouses or partners have died, adults whose parents or siblings have died, and parents whose adult children have died. All the deaths are from cancer. At the time of the attacks, five of my groups were in progress, and several participants actually worked at the World Trade Center.

Initially, all bereavement groups were canceled. The groups were on hold while my hospital, along with others in New York City, vacated all available meeting rooms to free up space to treat injured survivors of the disaster. As we now know, very few survivors were found.

It was several weeks before the bereavement groups resumed. Once the telephone lines could be used for nonessential calls, there was a flurry of calls back and forth between the group members and myself. Of immediate concern were several members working that day at the World Trade Center. All were alive, but some had been injured and hospitalized. One group member, a young man whose sibling died from esophageal cancer, not only worked at the World Trade Center but also lived in the area. He could not be accounted for. His home telephone line (along with thousands of others in the city) was down; he couldn't be reached by e-mail. It was late September before we learned that he was safe.

After the bereavement groups resumed, I observed several changes in the reactions of the group members. There was a shift in the bereavement themes they had previously identified as important. Before 9/11, individuals in the group for bereaved spouses focused on their sadness, their roles as caregivers, and their loneliness now that their partners had died. Among women whose parents have died from cancer, themes that generally arise include feelings of abandonment, guilt, unfinished business, anger, and uneasiness with role changes within the existing family structure. The women in our group also described problems with their siblings related to rivalry and inheritance. After the terrorist attacks, these themes shifted as group members focused on the overwhelming grief in the city. It was difficult for them to refocus on their own grief. They talked about the events of 9/11, where they were, and how they personally were affected.

With the exception of two group members who were hospitalized, we were fortunate: no one in the group had lost a family member in the attacks. Several group members were displaced from their work environment. A few were working out of their homes and in time, several commuted to temporary office space in nearby New Jersey.

Members of the group exhibited increased anxiety and several developed panic attacks; three had exacerbation of existing panic behaviors. After some time they were better able to describe their own feelings and soon were able to refocus on their individual grief. They often expressed intense anger at not feeling supported in their grief by friends or co-workers.

JUGGLING WITH GRIEF: THE MEMBERS SPEAK

Jane, a widow of many years, was grieving the death of her mother from breast cancer:

> Although I'm 62 years old I still miss my mother. It's like a double
> whammy. When she died in August I couldn't believe it; it was
> such a shock. She had been battling and surviving breast cancer
> for almost 20 years. My friends didn't support me when she died.
> People would say: "she was 84 years old and lived a full life." They
> couldn't understand where I was coming from, and after a while I
> stopped trying to explain. Since 9/11 it has been even harder. People
> make me feel ashamed. After all, they're right when they say to me,
> "Look at all the youngsters who were killed; their lives were just
> beginning. Your mother lived a full life, what more do you want?"
> I don't know what to tell them.

Kathleen's husband died of pancreatic cancer on September 10. Mourners could not get to the funeral home the next day, and Kathleen felt guilty. "I know it sounds silly, but I worried about him being alone without any family with him. I've been closed down since the attack. I can't watch the news or listen to the radio. I don't want to know or read anything about the war." Kathleen often described the cornerstone of her family's belief system as rituals and their religious beliefs. "People who attended the funeral talked only about the attack, and my husband wasn't given the respect he deserved."

At 35, Annette is an only child and estranged from her alcoholic father who lives out of state. At the time of the attack her mother was at home dying from leukemia. Annette had no friends or support, explaining that she devoted herself to caring for her mother who actually died two weeks after the attack. Because of her mother's deteriorating condition they didn't talk about the attack and didn't watch television. Shortly after her mother's death Annette became withdrawn and terrified. The events of 9/11 plagued her during the day as well as at night in her dreams. Although Annette had a history of panic attacks (the last one was seven years prior) she had been managed well on medications. After her mother's death, however, the panic attacks resumed and she found it increasingly difficult to leave her apartment and was unable to return to work.

Ana Marie was shocked when her 80-year-old husband died suddenly on September 13. Although he had prostate cancer and had been hospitalized for sepsis, he was tolerating his radiation treatment and seemed to be doing well. Then he died after a sudden heart attack. Ana Marie believes that watching the events unfold on television caused his heart attack. She also feels that the staff was more interested in watching television then in caring for her husband. She ruminates on thoughts that her husband was devastated by the events and that this was the last thing he heard and saw before he died.

Susan is a 25-year-old dental hygienist whose 50-year-old father died of a brain tumor in early June, months before the terrorist attack. "I live in Staten Island where many of the residents are firefighters. Just when I thought I was getting over the trauma of my dad's death, I was bombarded with daily reminders. The sounds of bagpipes are a daily occurrence along with the streets being lined with firefighters. Sometimes I see two or three funerals a day. It brings it all back to me."

THE YEAR SINCE

As we approached the one-year anniversary of 9/11, we wondered if the general population (i.e., those whose loved ones have not been killed) is experiencing a different or second wave of grief. Statistics indicate that many crisis hot lines have seen an increase in the amount of calls received. LifeNet, a crisis hot line providing supportive services and referrals for both mental health and substance abuse, had seen an average of 3,000 calls a month prior to 9/11. By December the calls had reached 5,000 a month; by January they had reached 6,600. Currently LifeNet is averaging 250 calls a day (Gordon, 2002). Project Liberty, a program begun shortly after 9/11 by the Counseling Service of the Fire Department of New York (FDNY), previously had averaged 300 new cases in any six-month period. Since the attack on the World Trade Center (where 343 firefighters died), the FDNY has served more than 3,000 new cases (FDNY, personal communication, October 18, 2002).

John Draper, the psychologist who directs LifeNet reported: "the farther we get from 9/11, the support that people depended on to get through the crisis has faded . . . it's not just those who lost family members or fled for their lives who are having a terrible time: the collateral damage to the entire tri-state region has been brutal" (Gordon, 2002).

One additional effect has been the recent announcement that hundreds of firefighters have retired since 9/11 (*The New York Times*, 2002). The department is facing the loss of some of its most senior commanders and most experienced front-line firefighters. Fire Commissioner Daniel Nigro reported that 661 firefighters retired between January 1 and July 26, 2002, compared with 274 who retired during the same period in 2001.

CARE FOR THE CAREGIVERS

In general, professionals are at a high risk for developing stress responses because of their intimate involvement with traumatized people. Those involved with responders or, in the aftermath of the attack, working with survivors or victims are at greater risk. They listen to the horror stories of fear, pain, and suffering, which in turn causes pain and suffering in the clinicians. This phenomenon is known by various terms: *burnout, compassion fatigue* (Figley, 1995), *vicarious traumatization* (McCann & Pearlman, 1990; Pearlman & Saakvitne, 1995), or *secondary traumatic stress* (Stamm, 1995). All describe the profound psychological distress that can result from exposure to the traumatic experience of the client. Ochberg (1988) differentiates between traumatization and victimization, noting that traumatization refers to natural disasters, whereas victimization results from acts of human cruelty.

Doka described the phenomenon of disenfranchised grief as "the grief that persons experience when they incur a loss that is not, or cannot be openly acknowledged, publicly mourned or socially supported" (1989, p. 4). In essence, society gives the survivor permission to grieve and sets the rules and defines not only who has the legitimate right to grieve, but where, when, and for how long. Doka explored three factors contributing to disenfranchised grief: (1) the loss is not recognized, as with prenatal deaths, abortions, or adoptions; (2) the griever is not recognized, for example, the mentally disabled or the elderly; and (3) the relationship is not recognized, as when the death is that of an ex-spouse, co-worker, or lover in an extramarital affair.

A parallel to these categories is exemplified by the bereaved individuals and the mental health professionals caring for them whose personal grief may have been disenfranchised as a result of the terrorist attacks. Neimeyer and Jordan describe the concept of empathic failure as "the failure of one part of a system to understand the meaning and experience of another" (2002, p. 96). They illustrate the notion that disenfranchised grief can arise in any situation and has multiple levels. Similar to the work by Corr (1993; 1998) and others (Kohut, 1977; Wolf, 1988) who describe contemporary societies and their impact on an individual's support during grief, Neimeyer and Jordan describe how important transitions can go unnoticed by others. Clearly the events of 9/11 at times overshadowed an individual's grief, especially grief resulting from cancer. For these bereaved individuals, their grief was largely unrecognized, or if recognized initially, was soon minimized in comparison with the outpouring of support given to the larger community.

Have the events of 9/11 changed the way we practice or our sensitivity in listening to our clients? Do our own judgmental feelings overshadow and constrict our degree of empathic listening or change the therapeutic empathic environment?

For many, the rescue effort has had a price. Although returning to business or the chores of ordinary life events has been difficult for many New Yorkers, some have witnessed first hand how much can be accomplished through teamwork and resiliency. Although much healing still lies ahead, communities have come together in symbolic and practical ways to help one another in our healing journey. ■

Sherry R. Schachter has worked at Memorial Sloan Kettering Cancer Center for 20 years. She is Assistant Attending Grief Therapist, Pain and Palliative Care Service, and she holds a secondary appointment in the Department of Psychiatry and Behavioral Sciences. Dr. Schachter works with individual patients and families and facilitates bereavement support groups. She chairs the section on Professional Standards and Ethics of the Association for Death Education and Counseling. Dr. Schachter is a member of the International Work Group on Death, Dying and Bereavement.

REFERENCES

Corr, C.A. (1998). Enhancing the concept of disenfranchised grief. *Omega: Journal of Death and Dying*, 38, 1-20.

Corr, C.A. (1993). Death in modern society. In D. Doyle, G.W.C. Hanks, & N. MacDonald (Eds), *Oxford Textbook of Palliative Medicine* (pp. 28-36). Oxford: Oxford University Press.

Doka, K.J. (Ed). (1989). *Disenfranchised Grief: Recognizing hidden sorrow*. Lexington, MA: Lexington.

Doka, K.J. (Ed). (2002). *Disenfranchised Grief: New directions, challenges, and strategies for practice*. Champaign, IL: Research Press.

Feuer, A. & Wilson, M. (September 11, 2002). Threats and Responses: The Firefighters; Its Ranks Depleted, A Weary Fire Department Is Trying to Regroup. *The New York Times*.

Figley, C.R. (Ed). (1995). *Compassion fatigue: Coping with secondary traumatic stress disorder in those who treat the traumatized*. New York: Brunner/Mazel.

Gordon, M. (2002, March 18). Living in the shadow: Six months later (pp. 23-26). *New York*.

Kohut, H. (1977). *The restoration of the self*. New York: International Universities Press.

McCann, L., & Pearlman, L. (1990). Vicarious traumatization: A framework for understanding the psychological effects of working with victims. *Journal of Traumatic Stress*, 3, 131-149.

Neimeyer, R.A., & Jordan, J.R. (2002). Disenfranchisement as empathic failure: Grief therapy and the co-construction of meaning. In K.J. Doka (Ed.) *Disenfranchised grief: New directions, challenges, and strategies for practice* (pp. 95-117). Champaign, IL: Research Press.

New York Academy of Medicine. (2002). *NYAM researchers find depression, post-traumatic stress disorder prevalent in NYC after September 11 Attack*. Retrieved September 9, 2002 from http://www.nyam.org/news/032602.shtml

Ochberg, F.M. (1988). *Post-traumatic therapy and victims of violence*. New York: Brunner/Mazel.

Office for Victims of Crime. (2000). *Responding to terrorism victims: Oklahoma City and beyond* (Publication No. NCJ 183949). Washington DC: US Department of Justice.

Pearlman, L.A., & Saakvitne, K.W. (1995). *Trauma and the therapist: Counter transference and vicarious traumatization in psychotherapy with incest.* New York: Norton.

Rando, T.A. (1993). *Treatment of complicated mourning.* Champaign, IL: Research Press.

Redmond, L. (1989). *Surviving: When someone you love was murdered.* Clearwater, FL: Psychological Consultation and Education Services.

Spektor, A. (2002). *September 11, 2001 Victims.* Retrieved August 15, 2002, from www.September11victims.com

Turman, K.M. (2002). Panel Discussion: 9/11 Revisited. *The 6th Gathering of Women in Thanatology.* Cullowhee, NC.

U.S. Department of Labor, Bureau of Labor Statistics. (2002, February 13). Extended layoffs in the fourth quarter of 2001. Retrieved February 17, 2002 from www.bls.gov

Williams, M.B., Zinner, E.S., & Ellis, R.R. (1999). The connection between grief and trauma: An overview. In E.S. Zinner & M.B. Williams (Eds.), *When a community weeps: Case studies in group survivorship* (pp. 3-17). Philadelphia: Brunner/Mazel.

Wolf, E.S. (1988). *Treating the self.* New York: Guilford.

CHAPTER 3

Hurricane Andrew

Rick Eyerdam

In 1992, Hurricane Andrew killed 23 people in South Florida, about the same number who would have died over a tropical Florida summer weekend among the elderly, critically ill, accidental deaths, murder victims, and vehicle accident victims. Andrew didn't cause great death, but it did bring to a screeching halt a half million lives. Andrew and its aftermath grabbed the residents of South Florida and spun them around.

It ripped away homes and shredded lives like trees, demolishing prized possessions and permanently disrupting normal routines. Though only 23 were killed in Florida by the impact of the storm, studies suggest that at least 30 percent of the people who felt the brunt of the storm believed that they were going to die; they believed they would be blown away, drowned, or crushed by their own homes or those of their neighbors, propelled by the howling wind (Ironson, Wynings, Schneiderman, Baum, Rodriquez, Greenwood, Benight, Antoni, LaPerriere, Huang, Klimas, & Fletcher, 1997).

MEET HURRICANE ANDREW

On Sunday, August 16, 1992, the storm called TD-3 was followed only through satellite observation. When the first reconnaissance flight entered the wall of TD-3 early Monday morning, the one-day lapse in close surveillance brought a surprise: by 8:00 a.m., Andrew had earned his name; the western hemisphere's first tropical storm of 1992. By August 19, however, Andrew was an air mass in disarray, battered by a rival weather system on its way to England; it seemed to be on the verge of dying.

By dawn of August 21, Andrew had traveled less than 15 degrees latitude and about the same distance of longitude. Sitting virtually still for several hours, the storm had conserved its energy while drawing strength from the warm ocean currents. Soon, Andrew was in motion again, organized, and showing every sign of growth to hurricane status.

The State of Florida Emergency Operations Center (EOC) opened on Thursday with four staff members working on computer models. At that time Andrew seemed to be on a north-by-northwest course that would probably take it into the Mid-Atlantic states in the next five or six days. Hurricane watches are posted a minimum of 36 hours before a storm can possibly strike the target area. Warnings usually go up 24 hours in advance of a predicted landfall. There were days left for preparation, if all went as it seemed.

What happened next took everyone by surprise. Heading north by west, Andrew bumped into the Bermuda high and made a hard left. The turn raised the prospect that the storm could strike Islamorada in the Florida Keys. By Saturday morning, Andrew was already a minimal hurricane moving at a remarkable 17 miles per hour. There was then little question the storm would strike somewhere on the Florida peninsula.

At 5:45 p.m. on Saturday, just in time for prime time newscasts, hurricane watch flags—a black square in a red background—were hoisted from Titusville to Key West. At that moment, 36 hours before the ultimate landfall, the odds were highest—20 percent—that Andrew would come ashore along the densely populated Dade and Broward county line.

COMMUNICATION BREAKDOWN

Exacerbating the crisis was the near complete breakdown in communications caused both by poor planning and by storm damage. The telephone bank, the most critical component of the Dade County EOC, was completely inadequate for the level of disaster Andrew brought. A dozen different emergency functions including a two-line computer notification system for special needs citizens, communications and dispatch for police, dispatch for fire rescue and the National Guard, rumor control, and the 911 system for Dade County were all on the same rotary phone switches. When the hurricane watch was posted at 5:45 p.m. on Saturday, the volume of incoming calls jammed the lines, and the phones did not stop ringing for the next week.

As a result of the failure to plan, for the first few critical days of operation it was impossible to make an outgoing call without several failed attempts. The volume of incoming calls also caused the switch to roll over and crash the 911 system. The poorly planned phone system meant that no one could call into the EOC to report on needs, request assistance, or find out where to go with critically needed supplies and volunteers. It made the isolation of the victims all the more intense.

At the region's 79 movable bridges, State Department of Transportation crews stood by, awaiting orders to lock them down. State law says that all bridges under the control of the DOT get locked down when the wind reaches 39 miles per hour, but the law does not say where the wind must reach 39 miles per hour, for how long, who decides that the wind has reached the required level, and who makes the announcement. In the meantime, the bridges, over which a massive evacuation was being conducted, opened and shut at the demand of hundreds of boaters attempting to move their craft to safety. Since Andrew was a smaller diameter storm than usual, its 39-mile-per-hour winds did not arrive until the storm was almost on top of Florida. Since the winds did not reach 39 miles per hour as expected, the evacuation of the coastal areas was hampered by the constant raising of the bridges to allow pleasure craft to venture inland for protection.

Meanwhile, 517,000 residents from the Keys and flood-prone areas and those who did not feel safe at home clogged the mainland highway system. No one expected either the volume of traffic or the delays caused by automatic coin-operated tollbooths. It took a complaint from the local weather man for the state to realize that taking tolls along the turnpike system meant risking the lives of thousands of evacuees. Long after the decision should have been made, the tollbooths were opened for unfettered passage.

At 7 p.m. no one was allowed across the causeways onto Miami Beach. Thousands of elderly residents remained in their condominiums, unwilling or unable to evacuate, hoping that the more recent projected storm track across South Dade and the Keys would come true. Since the phones had jammed at the EOC immediately after the watch was sounded, the EOC was not able to make phone calls and warn special needs individuals to pack and eat a meal and await further notice. Likewise, when the evacuation order came at 9 a.m. on Sunday, EOC was not able to notify special needs patients that someone would be coming within six hours as prescribed in the county evacuation plan.

At 7:30 p.m. Fort Lauderdale International Airport closed, and at 9:30 p.m. Miami International Airport closed, stranding hundreds of tourists who had been forced out of their hotels by the evacuation warnings. At the Fontainebleau Hotel, where the majority of the guests were European, few spoke enough English to know what the hurricane watch meant. Few paid attention to the darkening weather forecasts until hotel staff told them they had to leave and should not expect to find rooms south of Orlando.

The deaf and hearing-impaired were worse off than the non-English speaking tourists. The Federal Communications Commission requires that, in order to inform the hearing impaired, all emergency information be provided over television in the form of a "crawler"—a written message along the bottom of the screen to accompany any voice message and pictures. Tyrone Kennedy, the founder of the Deaf Services agency in Dade County, recalls that the system worked well until the hurricane watch was changed to a hurricane warning. At the moment of greatest need, television stations stopped using the crawler because the messages were thought to be too complex to be reduced to writing.

By 10 p.m. most shelters in South Florida were filled to overflowing, and there was still little tangible indication of the storm's growing power. The fearful winds did not begin until midnight. By that time the limited order that had prevailed dissolved in the deepening gale. Mental patients without essential psychotropic drugs or the trained professionals to manage them were dropped in the midst of families hiding from the storm. Elderly patients who had not been moved from their beds in years were loaded on buses and dumped at hospitals.

At 4 a.m., the entire power grid serving South Florida collapsed, leaving 4 million people in the dark, cut off from the comfort of fans or air conditioning and the assurance of television. Channel 6's 1,500-foot-tall broadcast tower had been erected with the latest in safety procedures because it was a key communication link between the Keys, South Dade, and the rest of the world. At least a dozen telephone and radio relay stations were installed on the tower as well as the radio communications network for law enforcement and emergency services. At around 4:30 a.m., the mighty tower began to bow in the wind, and at the height of the storm it could no longer withstand the blow. Its three-inch-diameter cables snapped with a retort like a mortar round exploding and it toppled to the ground, deafening a 350-square-mile area.

When the Channel 6 television tower buckled, local law enforcement was left with no radio tower. Cell phone technology was very new at the time and the police had only a few cellular phones, which were useless in the jammed airwaves caused by the collapse of the Channel 6 tower and several other relay stations. With four districts to control and important emergency information to dispense, the police chief was left with one radio frequency that matched no other nearby law enforcement station or agency.

At 4:57 a gust that might have been as high as 178 miles per hour raked the Hurricane Center building in Coral Gables. As the wind increased, the National Hurricane Center's hurricane-proof radar antenna was blown off the building by the gust, leaving the center virtually blind and deaf. Its rooftop wind gauges were also destroyed but remained in place with a final reading of 164 miles per hour.

South Dade is a relatively new area, much of it built in the past 30 years using technologically advanced materials. Everyone who builds in the path of hurricane is expected to build to withstand a typical storm of 120-mile-per-hour winds and 15 inches of rain. Andrew was anything but typical; its sustained wind velocity was estimated to be anywhere from 140 miles per hour to 180 miles per hour. In its path, air conditioning units and antennas became projectiles. Virtually every place an air conditioning unit was attached a gaping hole was left behind, exposing the facilities to torrential rains and devastating winds. The rains poured into the duct work and filled the ceilings, then the walls, ending the usefulness of all electrical and communications equipment located in the walls, then turning elevators into wells and stairs into waterfalls. It took almost a week before the world learned about the experiences of those hiding in the hospitals, apartment buildings, migrant camps, trailer parks, and bungalows of far South Dade County.

THE DISASTER AFTER ANDREW

Anyone who had not visited South Florida prior to Hurricane Andrew would have a difficult time appreciating the shock that came with the dawn. The landscape was totally altered. Things that could never be seen before through the dense, lush, tropical foliage now loomed large enough to touch on the horizon. Any trees left standing were withered and leafless. No bushes of consequence survived. All signage was damaged. The streets, avenues, driveways, and parking lots were strewn with downed trees, drywall board, lumber, and aluminum. Many buildings were only empty shells.

As Andrew roared through, its rain was substantial but insignificant when compared to the wind. In the days following the storm, however, the rain was devastating—soaking possessions laid bare by the wind and turning the suburbs into a shambled fleet with flapping blue sails.

When the victims of Andrew and their would-be rescuers emerged from shelter in the morning they found unimaginable damage. It took four months for the toll to be tallied, but on that hot and soggy Monday no one could have known that 92 percent of the power grid in South Florida needed reconstruction, with 1.4 million or 84 percent of Florida Power and Light customers in Dade without power. It would take 34 days before power was restored to 100 percent of the Dade County homes that could accept it. Most people went longer than two weeks without power to cool their home, preserve their food, or heat their water. At night the darkness was total and remained total with 7,300 street lights down and 21,000 wooden power poles snapped and needing replacement. About 24,000 homes were unable to accept power even after it was restored a month after the storm because the damage to those homes was so extensive.

Into the lurch came relief workers and emergency personnel from other parts of the county and the state. Emergency personnel from the area were disoriented because they could no longer rely on street signs and landmarks to find their way through South Dade. So it was no surprise that emergency personnel who arrived from Broward County or other areas to the north and west were confounded. Even those who knew their way were confronted with a maze of blocked streets and dead ends.

Under the Stafford Act, the Federal Emergency Management Agency (FEMA) cannot come into play until after the governor of a stricken state requests the President to declare a major disaster. This is defined as a finding on the part of the governor that the scope of the problem is beyond the state's ability to respond. This rule anticipates that local agents of the state will be able to promptly make an assessment of their needs. After Andrew, that was beyond the immediate ability of the residents in South Florida, since there were no communications, no open roads, no power, and no way to conduct an orderly aerial survey. In addition, the phones that worked were jammed.

At 10:45 am, Monday, August 24, 1993, Florida Governor Lawton Chiles declared a state emergency and called in the National Guard, which arrived in some strategic locations by noon. The National Guard units were called in not so much to dig in the debris for survivors or to clear the roads, but to counteract the lawlessness that began even before the winds subsided. It was a frantic lawlessness and violence that stifled any other efforts to save the wounded, locate the dead, or help those in need of food and water. Mother Nature had issued a credit card to every malefactor in this huge impoverished area of South Dade that was filled with crime and despair before the passage of Andrew.

By the afternoon of the first day television shots came back from the only helicopters available—those from television stations. They, of course, were not doing a systematic survey of the disaster and routes of ingress and egress. They were looking for dramatic images, concentrating on the damage to the coastline and the looting of the posh malls. The images were spectacular, but they bypassed Homestead, Naranja, Perrine, and Florida City, tiny, poor cities that had been completely obliterated.

The rescue effort was further complicated by staffing shortages at the Red Cross shelters. Emergency medical technicians and paramedics who might otherwise have been available to relieve those on duty during or after the storm were pinned down in the shelters as thousands of injured and soaked people fled their demolished homes for the only place they could find help. Since the public health nurses and private duty nurses hired by Dade County failed to show up, the EMT personnel were desperately needed at the shelters.

At 6:00 p.m. President George Bush arrived at Miami International Airport and traveled south Interstate 95 to view the damage. The visit took no more than two hours, including a nationally televised speech. In three hours Bush was back in the air, and South Florida was designated a federal disaster area.

At the Red Cross shelters in South Dade, the normal pattern following a natural disaster was reversed. Instead of reduced occupancy, the numbers increased dramatically. Those families who saw their houses destroyed around them fled to the already crowded hurricane shelters. There was nowhere else to go. But the shelters were not designed to house refugees after a storm and were already running out of water and food.

Those families that had weathered the storm in the shelters, hearing of the devastation, were anxious to get home to learn the fate of their homes, pets, and valuables. Rather than requiring them to stay in the shelters for a few days, thereby reducing the logistics of public health and safety, the shelter managers were glad to be relieved of some of their burden, and, since supplies were short, no effort was made to send the families home with the supplies of food, water, and protective gear that most of them would immediately need. The flow of families returning to their destroyed homes in South Dade immediately became a law enforcement problem: how to distinguish the tattered homeowners from the looters.

The official fire department incident log shows the progression of injury types encountered in the first few days. On Day One, the first two cases were cardiac, the next a childbirth. Many of the earliest calls were for individuals having trouble breathing. All day long the maternity calls continued. By midday, individuals who had lost their medication began to experience seizures, the number of slip and fall injuries increased as people attempted to climb through debris. As night approached, the number of mugging victims increased as did the number of auto accidents, and, in one bizarre hour, apparently after the shock of the storm had worn off and desperation set in, there were three suicide attempts.

By August 26, tons of supplies, hundreds of would-be-helpers, and a host of agencies were prepared to rush into South Dade, if only they had somewhere to go and armed guards to protect them from the looters. Security beyond the military encampments was a problem since few buildings that could be locked were left standing and even fewer were solid enough to prevent looting at night and drenching during the day. So many crimes were being committed that the police standing order was to respond only to assaults, murders, and armed robberies that were in progress. Within 24 hours, the first contingent of 2,000 federal troops arrived.

A new estimate put the storm's toll at 22 people dead, 63,000 homes destroyed, 175,000 people left homeless, and 1 million without power. Kate Hale, drowning in failure, noticed that the one way to get a problem solved in the midst of the chaos was to bring in a live action news team. Within hours, whatever problem the news media highlighted was on its way to being solved.

The 18th Airborne Division, with 20,000 troops on standby since Monday, was finally released that evening. At 9:15 the next morning an Army C-5A was on the ground amid the remains of Homestead Air Force Base disgorging Rangers in humvees to restore order and set up kitchens. Within 24 hours, a million rolls of toilet paper and 4,000 portable toilets were being unloaded on the dock at Dodge Island. It was the end of the beginning and the beginning of the end.

TAKING THE TOLL

According to research produced by the Florida International University (FIU) International Hurricane Center and Institute for Public Opinion Research, the storm altered the landscape in less obvious ways. According to Internal Revenue Service data analyzed as part of an unfinished FIU study and cited by the *Miami Herald* on the 10th Anniversary of Hurricane Andrew, one of every 16 families—a total of 40,000 families, or 83,000 people—moved out of Miami-Dade. "Especially in Homestead, we saw the disappearance of much of the middle class, and a lot of what we call Anglo flight," sociologist Betty Hearn Morrow, co-director of Florida International University's Laboratory for Social and Behavioral Research, told the *Herald* (Merzer, Brecher, de Vise, Yardley, Henderson, Fields, & FIU International Hurricane Center and Institute for Public Opinion Research, 2002, August 19).

During the first 12 months after Andrew, Miami-Dade saw a decline in population for the first time since 1860. Many people moved north about 40 miles to Fort Lauderdale's western communities in Broward County, which absorbed 80 percent more residents than had arrived during the preceding 12 months.

Insurance money provided a quick fix for those who financed homes and cars. But the poor who had no insurance got poorer. Reported in the FIU study, between 1990 and 2000, the median household income declined by 15 percent in Leisure City, 28 percent in Florida City and 41 percent in Naranja, according to inflation-adjusted statistics gathered for the U.S. Census. The FIU survey and its analysis of Census Data found that 43 percent of the non-Hispanic whites who relocated within six months of the storm moved to Broward or points farther north while 12 percent of the blacks and 9 percent of the Hispanics who relocated shortly after the storm left Miami-Dade. Between September 1992 and September 1993, 12,000 Miami-Dade families moved north to Broward County's southwestern suburbs of Miramar, Pembroke Pines, and Weston. The data suggest that many took their insurance settlements and bought in areas where the storm's damage was not visible and future storm damage was perceived to be less likely. But the data also show that out-migration continued long after Andrew (Morrow, 2002).

A CHALLENGE: REBUILDING HEALTH CARE

After Andrew, an ad hoc mental health system sprang into place where mental health services had previously been nonexistent. When Hurricane Andrew wiped out the physical landscape it also leveled the health care landscape of South Florida as well, providing an opportunity and a challenge to start over again, especially in the delivery of primary care and mental health services.

Andrew destroyed or severely damaged the few existing public health care centers, including Perrine, Doris Ison, and Martin Luther King Health Centers. In their place, ad hoc health care facilities blossomed only to wilt as the damaged traditional systems returned to action. With expectations raised by the sudden outpouring of medical assistance, hurricane victims flocked to hospitals and clinics for treatment and follow-up care for the wide range of traumas inevitable during extended hurricane cleanup. As the frustrations that followed the storm ramified, anger built within the victims without an appropriate vent. Guilt, fear, loss, and anguish dominated the emotions of the victims, creating a festering psychological sore that no one had prepared to treat, let alone prevent.

Into the mix of victims and rescuers came highly paid but uninsured construction workers and their families who put enormous demands on the already stressed system. These workers were essential to the rebuilding, and their right to access the local health care system was undeniable, yet their unpaid medical bills were not regarded as a consequence of the hurricane and, therefore not eligible for federal underwriting. Because of this, Homestead/SMH Hospital, which treated many of them as walk-ins at its emergency room, was forced to go to the state to offset $18 million in unanticipated costs associated with post storm clients.

Perhaps the most successful interim program spawned by Andrew was the mental health and social service delivery program established by Sara Herald. Herald, an attorney and pro bono advocate for children and families, assumed the unfilled position of Disaster Relief Coordinator for the Alcohol, Drug Abuse and Mental Health section at the Florida Department of Health and Rehabilitative Services District XI. Since the agency had no plans for post hurricane service, she assembled a team of social workers, public health nurses, psychologists, and volunteers and launched a door-to-door program that became the definition of successful outreach. Her teams stayed in the same neighborhoods, tracking the progress of the same families, providing a wide range of preventive help, from public assistance to drug counseling to family planning.

Herald and Dr. Evelena Bestman were among many South Floridians who made presentations at the 15th Annual National Hurricane Conference, which was dedicated to lessons learned from Hurricane Andrew. Dr. Bestman, a University of Miami psychologist, told the delegates that the National Association for Psychology had organized a group of psychologists who arrived in South Florida within the first week after Andrew, the first time any such effort on the part of mental health professionals had been attempted. "Pre-Andrew, mental health had a slow evolution into the disaster arena," Bestman recalled. "This is the first time, maybe in history, that mental health was put into the disaster relief program. We were given a real presence, but the key question is, What is mental health in disasters?" Dr. Bestman asked at the time (Eyerdam, 1994, pp. 119-120).

"There was a tendency to call it post disaster dysfunction. The percentage of emotional problems in families is very deceptive. They don't stop at the moment people answer the questionnaires. It is a process or planning and learning and of training. The whole field of mental health is an evolutionary field," Bestman said prophetically in the months after the storm. "We are a bit primitive, but in Dade County it is moving because of what Sara Herald is doing and her model comes closer to what we need to be thinking of" (Eyerdam, 1994, pp. 119-120).

Appearing before that first Hurricane Andrew Conference, Herald recalled her introduction to mental health and social services, government style:

> I was working on getting aid for foster kids and getting foster kids relocated and the stuff that I normally do. And I got a call, two weeks post storm. I got a desperate phone call to come in and be the disaster relief coordinator. Does that kind of tell you the kind of planning that we had going on for alcohol, drugs or mental health? There was no plan. And the federal government couldn't find anybody at the state level or at the county level who was in charge in alcohol or mental health. So what you had was a whole bunch of very well-meaning individuals and group social services and community-based organization and university personnel and doctors and psychologists and counselors who were coming into town, and absolutely no coordination.

And the irony of this is that the only stream of funding, at the federal level, that is absolutely guaranteed in the case of a natural disaster, is money for mental health. Can you believe it is the only one that anybody could have told you, six months before the hurricane, that you were going to get [a grant] after a hurricane? It is a recognized part of the Stafford Act, therefore, everyone could have been guaranteed mental health services if we had had a plan.

I brought in people like Evelena Bestman, over 150 people who provided substance abuse and mental health services, both in the public and private sectors, and we developed a plan for the community health team….We took a holistic approach. Most of the people we were dealing with were well. They were not mentally ill. They were well, but they were having to deal with extraordinary stress. And if you help them create linkages and let them vent to you and get crisis counseling done at their door, then you reduce the risk that they will become mentally ill. (Eyerdam, 1994, pp. 119-120)

Herald reviewed the mental health system when she came on the scene and found that although there was a plan for the mentally ill, there wasn't adequate shelter for them. Also lacking were mental health care givers, a serious situation for the length of time needed for recovery from the storm. While prescriptions were available for physical illnesses and injuries, no mental health medications were available immediately, a situation with lasting effect: six months after the storm, the mental health centers that serve the indigent populations were out of mental health medications because they had exhausted their medication fund. Herald recalled, "You had people who got prescriptions for $60 medication, then they could not get the medication and they were decompensated. Then how did we treat them? We put them in a crisis stabilization unit at significantly higher cost than the 60 bucks the medication would have cost. We are paying to have the hospital or Medicare, or whatever they qualified for, because we did not get them the $60 they needed to function." Herald's recommendation was that "[These individuals] need to be sheltered and medicated so that they can remain stable at a time when there is a greater likelihood that they will be decompensated anyway" (Eyerdam, 1994, pp. 119-120).

It is clear from any review of the literature that the need for immediate, organized intervention following major disasters has been accepted as a fundamental tenet and built into most action plans. Dozens of conferences have discussed Hurricane Andrew and what was learned from it. The world is better prepared for all kinds of disasters because of what the residents of South Florida endured.

Rick Eyerdam is an expert on natural disaster planning and mitigation. He researched and wrote When Natural Disaster Strikes: Lessons from Hurricane Andrew, *the official report of the South Florida Health Planning Council on Hurricane Andrew and what it revealed about the health care delivery system in South Florida. Mr. Eyerdam has won more than two dozen journalism awards. He has served as an adjunct professor of communications at Florida International University where he taught writing and editing. Mr. Eyerdam is currently a consulting editor for Southern Boating and Yachting Publications and for Boating Industry International.*

REFERENCES

Eyerdam, R. (1994). When Natural Disaster Strikes: Lessons from Hurricane Andrew. Washington, DC: Hospice Foundation of America.

Ironson, G., Wynings, C., Schneiderman, N., Baum, A., Rodriquez, M., Greenwood, D., Benight, C., Antoni, M.H., LaPerriere, A., Huang, H., Klimas, N., & Fletcher, M.A. (1997). Posttraumatic stress symptoms, intrusive thoughts, loss and immune function after Hurricane Andrew. *Psychosomatic Medicine, 59,* 128-141.

Merzer, M., Brecher, E.J., de Vise, D., Yardley, W. Henderson, T., Fields, G., & the Florida International University's (FIU) International Hurricane Center and Institute for Public Opinion Research. (2002, August 19). Lives uprooted, many fled. *The Miami Herald,* p. A1.

Morrow, B.H. (2002, April). Community rebuilding since Hurricane Andrew. Paper presented at the 2002 National Hurricane Conference, Orlando, FL.

CHAPTER 4

Looking Back at Columbine

Larry Beresford

When two high school students opened fire on their classmates at Columbine High School in Littleton, Colorado, at 11:21 a.m. on April 20, 1999, they ignited an intense, unprecedented, nationwide outpouring of public anguish. Entering the school with an arsenal of shotguns, automatic weapons, grenades, and homemade bombs, Eric Harris, 18, and Dylan Klebold, 17, killed 12 classmates and a teacher, wounded 24 others, some permanently, and then took their own lives in 15 minutes of mayhem that reverberated around the world. The killers also planted homemade pipe bombs in and around the school, which failed to detonate but would have multiplied the killing many-fold.

Afterward, crime investigators and commentators sought to extract a reason why from the killers' journals, videotapes, and other evidence left behind—without truly explaining how their teenage alienation, frustration, and rage could have led to such bloodletting. The Columbine shootings culminated a series of high-profile incidents of classroom violence during the previous three years, including multiple-fatality shootings in Moses Lake, Washington, on February 2, 1996; Bethel, Alaska, February 19, 1997; Pearl, Mississippi, October 1, 1997; West Paducah, Kentucky, December 1, 1997; Jonesboro, Arkansas, March 24, 1998; and Springfield, Oregon, May 21, 1998.

Although Columbine has been described as the single worst act of school violence in U.S. history, a more deadly attack occurred in the village of Bath, Michigan, on May 18, 1927, when a dynamite blast shattered one wing of the Bath Consolidated School, killing 37 children and two teachers. The dynamite had been planted by a member of the school board, Andrew Kehoe, 53, embittered over school taxes and the impending foreclosure of his farm. Kehoe had planned the bombing for months, stringing wires and hiding hundreds of pounds of dynamite in the school basement. The blast made the front pages of newspapers nationwide and resulted in an outpouring of donations to rebuild the Bath school (Ellsworth, 1927).

Yet Columbine gripped America in a way that previous incidents had not, while leaving unprecedented emotional scars on Littleton. News media exposure and the community's outpouring of grief were unequaled until the terrorist attacks of September 11, 2001, a tragedy that upped the ante once again in the stakes of public grief. What made the events at Columbine so singularly horrifying in the public imagination may hold clues or lessons for those who seek to understand and prevent future public tragedies in our nation's schools—and for those who are in the business of responding to the community grief generated by such events.

"What happened in Littleton pierced the soul of America," President Bill Clinton said at a one-year anniversary memorial service at Columbine High School. "Though a year has passed, time has not dimmed our memory or softened our grief at the loss of so many whose lives were cut off in the promise of youth" (Griego, Kurtz, & Abbott, 2000).

HOW BAD IS SCHOOL VIOLENCE?

After the series of school shootings that culminated at Columbine, television coverage had seared into the public consciousness images of suburban schools roped off with police tape and paramedics pushing critically injured children and adolescents on gurneys. Yet despite the impression they left of escalating school violence, data from sources such as the National Center for Education Statistics of the U.S. Department of Education, the National Criminal Justice Reference Service of the Department of Justice, and the National School Safety Center at Pepperdine University suggest that overall school-related violent deaths are actually decreasing in this country, albeit slowly.

In contrast to the deliberately planned killing spree unleashed at Columbine, school administrators are more likely to deal with students bringing guns or knives to campus to settle scores with specific individuals, to show off, or to protect themselves in an environment they perceive as hostile (Sheley, 1999). The most common school crime is theft, and teachers can be targets of violence from students, but overall rates of crimes committed in schools decreased throughout the 1990s (U.S. Departments of Education and Justice, 2000). The percentage of high school seniors injured in an act of violence at school—with a weapon or without—was lower in 1996 than it had been 20 years earlier (Wirt, 1998).

A report issued by the Justice Policy Institute of the Center on Juvenile and Criminal Justice concluded that the chance of a child being killed at school is about one in a million (Donohue, Schiraldi, & Ziedenberg, 1998). More than twice as many Americans are killed annually by lightning strikes. These data are cited not to trivialize the schoolhouse shootings, but to put them in a larger context of the real nature of violence directed at children.

Approximately 4,500 American children are killed every year in intentional shootings (homicides or suicides), which is the equivalent of a Columbine massacre every day of the year. Homicide is the second leading cause of death in school-age children, but less than one percent of such killings are associated with schools (Kaufman, Chen, Choy, Ruddy, Miller, Chandler, Chapman, Rand, & Klaus, 1999). In fact, as in Bath, Michigan, young people are more likely to be victims of violence perpetrated by adults than to kill: 90 percent of children under 12 and 75 percent of those aged 12 to 17 who are homicide victims were actually killed by an adult (Donohue, Schiraldi, & Ziedenberg, 1998). Meanwhile, one out of 13 children and adolescents under the age of 19 attempts suicide each year. The high-profile school shootings thus may be misdirecting public policy toward safeguarding schools, even though more serious threats to children lie elsewhere, the Justice Policy Institute report argues.

WHAT MADE COLUMBINE UNIQUE?

The response to the Columbine tragedy was unprecedented for an act of public violence—and unsurpassed until the September 11 terrorist attacks. Why did Columbine grip the public imagination so strongly? Beyond the fact that it involved such a large number of deaths, the public grief reaction to Columbine was shaped by a number of other elements, according to Marcia Lattanzi-Licht, a nationally prominent expert on grief and loss and co-editor of this volume. Based in nearby Boulder, Colorado, Lattanzi-Licht was active in grief counseling and first-responder debriefing efforts in Littleton in the wake of the shootings and thus had a close vantage point of the unfolding public grief.

First of all, there was the sheer scale of the reaction. Before law enforcement officials could even secure the school building, local telecommunication systems were gridlocked by proliferating emergency calls, while traffic in the area was jammed by arriving parents, onlookers, and journalists. News media presence and coverage were massive in the days and weeks following the shootings, to the point where some in the community came to resent the journalists' role in sensationalizing and inflaming public grief.

A memorial service held five days after the shootings drew an estimated 70,000 people to a nearby shopping center. Spontaneous memorials sprouted in Clement Park, adjacent to the school, including thousands of messages sent from around the country, makeshift shrines, floral bouquets, photographs, and stuffed animals. An estimated 200,000 people visited the park before those memorials were dismantled. The local Red Cross distributed 15,000 navy blue and silver ribbon lapel pins, representing Columbine's school colors, as a way for the community to show solidarity with the victims. The tragedy also generated a tremendous outpouring of generosity and donations as well as political activism aimed at limiting easy access to deadly handguns. A campaign headed by Tom Mauser, father of a student slain at Columbine, led to passage of four bills by the Colorado legislature to control handgun access.

Turnout by mental health professionals, trauma volunteers, and other first-responders was also unprecedented. An estimated 150 counselors were on the scene in the early days, and more than 1,600 people received counseling from the Jefferson Center for Mental Health and its hastily formed adjunct agency, Columbine Connections.

Another important aspect of the reaction was the way the shootings shattered illusions of safety in Littleton, a well-to-do community, and at Columbine High, a suburban public school where such terrible things "just don't happen." The disbelief and horror mounted as additional information was released about the killers' deliberate arsenal building and suicidal intent. Yet, as senseless as the carnage was, there was something shockingly familiar about the reports of school bullying and cliques and the adolescent angst from which this incomprehensible act sprang.

At the same time, the tragedy was deeply personalized for many law enforcement officials, journalists, grief counselors—and members of the public—who had school-age children of their own and thus could easily imagine the danger faced by the students at Columbine.

The tragedy also generated a powerful need to assign blame—beyond the two actual instigators—along with widespread controversy and second-guessing about how the incident was handled, especially regarding the length of time it took for law enforcement personnel to enter and secure the school building after the shooting began. Criticism targeted SWAT team procedures as well as an apparent missed opportunity for authorities to intervene prior to the killing based on reported violent content and threats contained on Harris's personal website.

The massive Columbine archives housed on the web page of the Denver *Rocky Mountain News* (2002) identify at least 16 lawsuits filed in federal court arising from the shootings, specifically naming the killers' parents, the school district, Columbine Principal Frank DeAngelis, the Jefferson County Commissioners, the Sheriff's Department, a sheriff's deputy accused of inadvertently killing a student with "friendly fire" (ultimately disproved by the forensic evidence), national video game manufacturers, and even the therapist of one of the killers.

The incident had other fallout as well. Months after the shooting, the mother of a 17-year-old girl who was slain at Columbine committed suicide. Another student killed himself shortly after the first anniversary. Some first responders on the scene that fateful day have since left the profession and most of the teachers working at Columbine have left the school. A prominent local minister quit his Lutheran congregation 16 months after the shooting, citing stress over the incident and controversy within the congregation over his outreach to the Klebold family.

Parents of a teenager named as a potential suspect, but later formally cleared, launched a recall campaign against Sheriff John Stone. Some non-Christians in Littleton reacted to the strongly fundamentalist Christian tenor of some memorial activities held in the community. Parents of the slain children also objected to an upbeat "Take Back the School" pep rally held at Columbine on the first day of the new school year four months after the shooting. Further controversy erupted over what form a permanent memorial to the victims should take, particularly what should be done with the school library, where most of the victims died. There was even conflict over a display of decorative hand-painted tiles mounted in the school, also intended as a memorial.

Such divisions are not unusual in the highly charged atmosphere that follows such a public tragedy. A comparable fictional portrait of a community deeply divided by a school-related tragedy can be found in Russell Banks' novel *The Sweet Hereafter* and the Atom Egoyen film based on the novel.

BACKLASH AGAINST NEWS MEDIA
AND GRIEF PROFESSIONALS

Two key themes in contemporary culture that were intensified in the wake of the Columbine shootings are widely expressed concerns about the role of the news media in high-profile public tragedies and the emergence of a backlash against grief professionals.

Journalists were accused of oversaturation in their coverage, of invasiveness in filming the immediate grief reactions of students on the scene, and of reporting inaccuracies, including a number of widely repeated statements about Harris and Klebold that were later found to be untrue. A local television crew pursuing follow-up Columbine stories months later reported being showered with angry epithets and even snowballs.

Columbine demonstrated anew how graphic footage on television can reopen old wounds for the survivors of similar previous tragedies. It also challenged journalists to balance the needs and interests of those most immediately affected by the news event, especially the grieving families, with those of the wider audience. Analysis of Columbine coverage on the Poynter journalism review website notes two ways that the tragedy altered Denver area news organizations. The first is a renewed sensitivity toward the community to which the news organizations belong. The news organizations reportedly are also more open to seeking out varied views around the newsroom and using more teamwork in covering such events (Lavin, 2002).

Obviously, attempts to stonewall journalists' pursuit of a high-profile news events such as Columbine can backfire and create the impression that important news is being withheld from the public. Those managing a public crisis are better served by striving to provide good, accurate, timely information to the media and taking advantage of teachable moments to educate journalists—and through them the public—about the complexities of the issues involved. Officials at Columbine attempted, with some success, to be responsible gatekeepers of media access by limiting coverage of the first day of the next school year to only pool reporters. They designated a perimeter line that reporters could not cross, recruited a "human chain" of parents and volunteers wearing badges to greet arriving students and shield them from the cameras, and paired reporters and photographers with school district escorts.

Even more than at previous public tragedies, there was a huge deployment of mental health and grief professionals on site at the school. A police psychologist was positioned at the scene 30 minutes after the shooting started. Also participating in immediate crisis intervention and counseling for students, parents, and faculty, and critical incident stress debriefing for other first responders were the Victims Services Unit of the Jefferson County Sheriff's Department, the Colorado Organization for Victim Assistance and the Red Cross.

Debriefings, which give those at the scene of a traumatic event the chance to discuss their reactions with a trained counselor, were offered to individual police officers, SWAT team members, and school resource officers—especially those who had viewed the carnage inside the school building and emerged visibly shaken. Eventually hundreds of other individuals and dozens of agencies were involved in offering grief counseling, many of them volunteers who just showed up and offered to help. Coordinating all of the support people was a challenge for those managing the response and points to the importance of bringing response efforts under tighter control.

A new theme in the national discourse about public grief emerged in commentaries on Columbine, focused on the purported overabundance, intrusiveness, and self-seeking qualities of some grief counselors—epitomized by a *New Yorker* magazine cartoon comparing grief counselors to hovering buzzards. A *Time* magazine article published soon after Columbine asserted that the value of support offered by grief professionals on site at such events is "up for debate" (Labi, 1999).

Psychologist Sally Satel has written recently in other prominent publications about the commodification of the grief "industry" and the "busloads" of grief counselors who show up at public tragedies. "Forced ventilation makes little sense for those whose ordinary style is to remain calm, maybe too calm for some people's tastes," she argues, questioning the profession's assumptions that grief work is always necessary and that talking about trauma in its immediate aftermath is always helpful (Satel, 1999; Satel & Sommers, 2001).

It is not within the scope of this chapter to address the concerns raised by Satel and other critics. Grief professionals should be aware, however, that similar concerns surfaced in the wake of 9/11 and are likely to come up again in the future. "There were far too many helpers at Columbine," Lattanzi-Licht said in a telephone interview (2002). "Perhaps we need to look at our own egos and motivations. Do we all need to be at the front lines of a public tragedy, even when there is more help than is truly needed?"

Careful community planning for future crises can address who will be in charge at the scene of a crisis, who will be called first to provide crisis intervention support, who else in the community can be mobilized to help, how crisis responders will be credentialed, who will serve as the gatekeeper, and how spontaneous offers of help will be managed in appropriate proportions. Questions of training, professional competence, and supervision also need to be addressed.

OTHER LESSONS

The importance of community planning remains an important lesson from Columbine and other recent public tragedies. Crisis response planning is an ongoing challenge for communities. The shootings in Littleton and the 9/11 attacks remind us that conventional crisis planning may not go far enough in preparing for such unimaginable, extreme situations. Responding to community needs for support and counseling after the news media go home and public interest starts to fade is another challenge. The real healing from a high-profile public tragedy, and the emergence of the need for counseling and support, may take years.

The Columbine experience also underscores how school violence directed at children can be traumatic for teachers. Helpers also need to be aware that suicides, divorce, drinking, and reckless behavior can all rise after a major community tragedy, according to the National Education Association's (NEA) online Crisis Communications Guide & Toolkit (NEA, 2002). In some highly charged situations, teenage suicide has become "contagious." The NEA toolkit is designed to help schools respond to issues that can arise in the aftermath of an incident like the Columbine shooting. The toolkit contains specific suggestions for setting up memorial donation funds, managing spontaneous memorials and donations, creating permanent memorials, and managing benchmark anniversary dates—all of which were challenges for school authorities at Columbine.

Since the shootings, many suggestions have been offered for how to prevent similar tragedies in the future. Some of these address the problem of teasing and taunting directed at students who are different, as well as the code of silence under which peer pressure discourages reporting violent threats by students. Two specific ideas highlighted on the Internet suggest the range of possibilities now being explored.

In January 2002, the state of North Carolina asked its 2,042 public schools to assemble emergency kits with school blueprints, maps of evacuation routes, rosters of students and staff, coordinates for landing a helicopter on the premises, codes to shut of alarms and power, and contact information for key personnel—all of which were sorely lacking at the Columbine crime scene. The state program also includes funds for the distribution of lock boxes, cell phones, and instructional videos on managing crises (*Teacher Magazine,* May 2002).

The Dallas, Texas, school system has placed nine Youth and Family Centers on or near public school campuses for its 150,000 students (Bush & Wilson, 1997). Developed in 1995 in partnership with Parkland Health and Hospital System's Community-Oriented Primary Care Division and the Dallas Mental Health-Mental Retardation Agency's Child and Adolescent Services Division, the innovative program is staffed for intensive mental health services designed to promote academic success, resiliency, and self-sufficiency for students and their families. It offers medical care, intensive mental health counseling, and 24-hour crisis intervention. The program has achieved high satisfaction ratings from parents and school principals. More than half of the participating students with behavior problems measurably improved from fall to spring while nearly half of those referred with attendance and academic problems also showed notable progress by the following spring.

Ultimately, preventing school violence is the most meaningful answer to the tragic events illustrated by Columbine. If schools across the country can learn from such tragedies and apply that knowledge to make sure they aren't repeated, that will be Columbine's lasting legacy. If not, we need to remember that the healing from such public grief can take forever. As Columbine High School's principal, Frank DeAngelis, told the *San Diego Union Tribune* in the wake of another school shooting, "It will never be back to normal. You don't go through such a tragedy and return to what it was before" (Gembrowski, 2001). ■

Larry Beresford is a health care journalist and editor specializing in the economic, policy, administrative, clinical, and human implications of care at the end of life. He is the author of The Hospice Handbook: A Complete Guide *(1993: Little, Brown & Co.) and a contributor to numerous hospice publications and health care trade magazines. He has also contributed his writing and editing skills to the annual bereavement books produced by the Hospice Foundation of America. He lives in Oakland, California, with his wife Rose Mark, a special education teacher.*

REFERENCES

Bush, M.J., & Wilson, C.S. (1997). Linking schools with youth and family centers. *Educational Leadership* 55(2).

Columbine: Hope from heartbreak. RockyMountainNews.com. Retrieved October 2002 from http://www.rockymountainnews.com/drmn/columbine.

Donohue, E., Schiraldi, V., & Ziedenberg, J. (1998). *School house hype: School shootings and the real risks kids face in America.* San Francisco: Justice Policy Institute of the Center on Juvenile and Criminal Justice. Retrieved from http://www.cjcj.org/jpi/schoolhouse.html.

Ellsworth, M. (1927.) *The Bath School Disaster* . Bath, MI: M. Ellsworth (out of print). Retrieved from http://www.msu.edu/~daggy/tbsd/tbsd-t.htm.

Gembrowski, S. (2001, March 25). Shots on campus: Easing the 'worst nightmare.' *The San Diego Union-Tribune.*

Griego, T., H. Kurtz, H., & Abbott, K. (2000, April 21). We have made it through the first year. *Rocky Mountain News.*

Kaufman, P., Chen, X., Choy, S., Ruddy, S., Miller, A., Chandler, K., Chapman, C., Rand, M., and Klaus, P. (1999). *Indicators of school crime and safety.* Washington, DC: U.S. Departments of Education and Justice. NCES 1999-057/NCJ-178906. Retrieved from http://nces.ed.gov or http://www.ojp.usdoj.gov/bjs/.

Labi, N. (1999, May 17). The grief brigade. *Time,* 99.

Lavin, R. (2002). Not business as usual. Poynter.org. Retrieved October 2000 from http://www.poynter.org/offthenews/042100index.htm

National Education Association. (2002). Being diligent: Moving beyond crisis. In *Crisis communications guide & toolkit.* Retrieved from http://www.nea.org/crisis/b3home2.html.

Satel, S. (1999, April 23). An overabundance of counseling. *The New York Times.*

Satel, S., & Sommers, C.H. (2001, October 15). Good grief: Don't get taken by the trauma industry. *Wall Street Journal.*

Sheley, J.F. (1999). Controlling violence: What schools are doing. In S.G. Kellan, R. Prinz, & J.F. Sheley (Eds.), *Preventing school violence: Plenary papers of the 1999 Conference on Criminal Justice Research and Evaluation.* Washington, DC: National Institute of Justice.

Survivor mentality. Current Events. (2002, May). *Teacher Magazine.* Retrieved from http://teachermagazine.org/tmstory.cfm?slug=08safety.h13.

U.S. Department of Education & Department of Justice. (2000). *Annual Report on School Safety.* Washington, DC. Retrieved from www.ed.gov/offices/OESE/SDFS/publications.html.

Wirt, J. (1998, November). Indicator of the month: Student victimization at school. Washington, DC: National Center for Education Statistics, U.S. Department of Education. Retrieved from http://nces.ed.gov/pubsearch/pubsinfo.asp?pubid=1999002.

CHAPTER 5

When a Public Figure Dies

William M. Lamers

INTRODUCTION

When President John F. Kennedy was assassinated, I was on active duty as a psychiatrist in the Medical Corps of the U.S. Navy. As word of the tragedy was confirmed, our staff gathered to share observations, try to understand what had happened, and speculate on what might happen next. There was a great deal of anxiety in the first hours; some coupled news of the assassination with fears related to the Cuban missile crisis. In the midst of the confused messages we were hearing, one staff member rose to say he was going to call his broker to tell him to sell everything in his account. He had just heard that the stock market was in rapid decline and he feared he would lose all his investments. I suggested that he tell his broker to buy stocks instead, explaining that the panic would be resolved after the weekend when a state funeral and public mourning would restore faith in the government and reverse the sharp slump in the stock market.

Several weeks later I received a call from a member of the San Francisco Stock Exchange. He had heard about my suggestion to buy stocks when most others were selling. He wanted to know the basis for my recommendation. I told him that I was familiar with the dynamics of grief and that I trusted that a public state funeral would help restore confidence in the government. Looking back on the incident, I am led to speculate on the therapeutic benefit of observing and even personally participating in public mourning following the death of notable persons.

This chapter focuses on the phenomena that accompany and follow the death of a public figure. It explores some of the similarities and differences between the death of a loved one and the death of a distant, unrelated public figure and examines some variables that determine the intensity of response to the death of public figures.

CATEGORIZING DEATHS

Death can be categorized in a number of ways. For example, deaths may be divided into two general categories. The first involves the deaths of loved ones, family, friends, and co-workers. The second includes persons unrelated to the survivor, who are deemed public figures because of their prominence in politics, entertainment, society, or some other area of public endeavor. Death can also be categorized based on the perception of its appropriateness, determined largely by the age of the deceased. The death of a child or young person is usually perceived as inappropriate because he or she has not yet experienced the fullness of life. The death of a productive person or leader in mid-career may also be deemed inappropriate. Deaths can also be categorized as to their cause. In the United States today, 90 percent of deaths are anticipated due to a prolonged illness or the result of injury. Only about 10 percent of deaths in the United States today are unanticipated. They commonly result from injuries, acute incurable illnesses, or violence (murder or suicide). Grief following the death of a public figure often results from an unanticipated death due to some type of violence: accident, murder, or suicide.

GRIEF AT A DISTANCE

The death of a public figure allows grief at a distance. The grieving person did not know the deceased yet may weep openly and have many of the psychological symptoms and behavioral changes that accompany grief following the death of a loved one. In some cases, the death of a public figure may even offer opportunity for individuals to confront earlier, unresolved losses.

The grief that follows death of a public figure usually resolves spontaneously, without serious behavioral or psychological sequelae. It creates a need for information about the facts of the death coupled with a desire to view the televised funeral events. While observing the funeral, the distant observer learns more about the life of the deceased, observes the grief of those intimately associated with the person, and, during funeral ceremonies, has an opportunity to synchronize his or her own grieving with that of mourners physically present at the services.

It is common to hear people speak of where they were when they learned of the death of a certain public figure. This was not always the case; before the advent of the telegraph, news traveled slowly by horseback, rail, or boat. The coming of the radio compressed the size of the world in terms of the dissemination of news. Television added another dimension that was later augmented by the development of instant replay. It was bad enough to learn of the 9/11 tragedy; it was even more stressful to watch the airliners strike the buildings and then watch the buildings collapse, over and over again. Likewise, we have seen the assault on the Waco compound and the Oklahoma City bombing multiple times. We have not become inured to the tragic deaths of thousands. Nor have we become desensitized to the unanticipated violent deaths of public figures. If anything, living in a digital generation of instant replay and satellite news coverage has sensitized us to the news of tragic deaths. We seem to wait upon the next event tragedy and bring to it our unresolved feelings from the last such event.

CASE IN POINT: DIANA'S DEATH

The fifth anniversary of the death of Diana, Princess of Wales, brought a flurry of news media attention to her life and death. A television program devoted to her entitled, "The Shrine," focused on the impact her violent death had on a variety of people. Several persons reported feeling guilty since her death. They felt that their curiosity during her life prompted the paparazzi to pursue her and that this was somehow linked to her untimely death. The husband of one of the couples interviewed made the unusual statement, "We felt guilty when we left her," as if to say that they had a personal role in her demise. His statement gives a measure of the distortion that can be found in persons grieving the loss of a public figure.

The death of the Princess of Wales offered a focus for many persons to identify with her. She was the outsider who entered the dream-like magic kingdom, became a princess, and was then rejected by her husband and his family. She was the benevolent fairy tale character who hugged children with AIDS and campaigned against land mines. She was the shy bulimic who was repeatedly photographed for tabloid front pages. She was the private person whose every move was public in life and in death.

Alec Guinness (1999), who knew the princess over many years, wrote of his response to learning of her death and offered a prediction that has come true:

> This Sunday morning I heard the appalling news of the death in
> Paris of the Princess of Wales, Mr. Dodi Fayed, and their driver.
> One forgets how much she has entered our national consciousness.
> For 16 years the media have kept us aware of her daily; and even
> now, when the poor woman's life has been snatched away, I doubt
> they will let her die.

The emotional response of strangers to the death of public figures often appears to be out of proportion to the personal loss. The public figure who died was not a loved one in the family sense of the word. This was a stranger, a person we would most likely never meet, much less get to know. Most of what we knew of the public figure was gathered by the news media and presented to us in exaggerated form over an extended period. We may have idolized the person, we may have had great personal respect for him, or we may have identified with her for the way she triumphed over adversity. Diana had the added cachet of becoming royalty by marriage only to be disenfranchised by divorce. The British public took her to their hearts and sided with her in their antipathy toward some members of the royal family. Thus, the princess's death brought to the surface an outpouring of feeling not only for her untimely, tragic death, but a growing residual resentment toward royalty in general. In a sense then, the outpouring of grief upon her death appears to have been augmented by antipathy toward those who it was believed had treated her badly, from royalty to the news-hungry public.

RESPONSES TO DEATH OF A PUBLIC FIGURE

Public responses to the death of a famous person vary considerably. Some deaths evoke intense, prolonged reactions while others receive only passing attention. The Princess of Wales and Mother Theresa died within a few days of each other. Both were world-famous public figures, but the contrast in media response, ceremony, and public outpouring of grief between the two events was striking.

The unanticipated or violent deaths of young public figures (the Princess of Wales, John Lennon, and John F. Kennedy, Jr.) and the untimely assassinations of young leaders (John F. Kennedy, Robert Kennedy, and Martin Luther King, Jr.) evoke massive outpourings of public grief accompanied by extensive, continuing news coverage. By contrast, the anticipated, nonviolent death of an older public figure after a full life elicits considerably less public response than those still in the midst of life who die a violent death. Examples of this latter group include Mother Teresa and Great Britain's "Queen Mum."

One death that has evoked a particularly enduring and unusual response was that of Elvis Presley. It is now almost 25 years since Elvis Presley died, but it is not unusual to hear that he has been sighted in one country or another. There is a certain amount of folk humor in these sightings. Yet there is also another side to the sightings: there are people who cannot accept that Elvis ("The King") is dead. Several factors contribute to this phenomenon. Because his death was not anticipated, the public was not prepared for the fact that he could or would die at that time. He was relatively young and seemed to have the invulnerability we assign to heroes. He was creative, surprising us with his music, compositions, his style, and flair. He was an icon for several generations. There was something inherently poignant about him and his life story. The public's sense of loss was compounded by learning the circumstances of his last weeks and months. Disbelieving the reality of his death was a way of trying to convince ourselves that the sordid circumstances of his later personal life were not really true.

An interesting variant on denial of death occurred early in the last century in the lyrics of a labor movement song by Alfred Hayes (Killibrew, 2002). Joe Hill was an immigrant laborer and musician whose songs and simple lyrics galvanized hitherto unorganized workers in their struggles to unite. Hayes evoked the spirit of Joe Hill in a song that itself came to life a second time when Joan Baez sang it before an audience of 300,000 at the 1969 Woodstock Festival.

> I dreamed I saw Joe Hill last night,
> As live as he could be.
> Said I, "Joe Hill, you're ten years dead."
> "I never died," said he.
> "I never died," said he.

FUNERAL RITUALS AND PUBLIC FIGURES

The funeral is an organized, purposeful, flexible, time-limited, and group-centered response to a loss (Lamers, 1959). In earlier societies, funerals consisted of several distinct stages that extended for months to a year. The funeral of a leader in earlier societies evoked participation of the entire community with those related to the deceased most closely involved. Eisenbruch (1984) details the sequence of rituals in a number of earlier societies from rituals of separation to later rituals of transition (dealing with the spirit world), and final rituals of integration that served to release the community from the period of formal mourning and restore social order.

The funeral serves social as well as personal and public health functions. It helps to resolve any uncertainty about the fact that a death occurred. Identification of the body of the deceased has become a legal requirement in funeral practice. When a public figure dies identification is an important element in the funeral. Because many deaths of public figures are the result of violence (gunshot wounds or violent accidents), formal identification is done in private by a person familiar with the deceased. When there is no public viewing of the remains, the probability increases for a small minority to have suspicions about the identity of the deceased. Over time, these suspicions may support fantasies that the person is still alive.

RITUAL AT A DISTANCE

The funerals of public figures also allow for ritual at a distance. I learned this after the assassination of President Kennedy. Earlier that week, a mother had brought her young daughter to the Child Psychiatry Clinic because of the sudden onset of behavioral problems for no apparent cause. A brief history revealed that her husband had been killed recently in Vietnam. A month previously the body was returned to California for burial. The daughter was not allowed to attend the funeral for her father. She began to experience disturbed behavior only after the funeral, not upon learning of her father's death.

I had only one session with the daughter; it was the day before President Kennedy's assassination. The day after the assassination, I received an urgent message from the mother. Her daughter had run away. She wanted to know if I had any idea what had happened to her daughter based on my one session with her. I admitted that I had no idea but asked her to stay in touch with me.

I later learned that the daughter had gone to the home of a friend and had persuaded the friend's mother not to let anyone know she was there, including her own mother. The daughter spent all weekend plus Monday watching the televised progression of funeral-related activities, including the final dramatic procession to Arlington National Cemetery and the formal burial ceremony. The mother called me after the daughter returned and told me that her daughter had said, "I'm all right now. I know what happened to my Daddy." The televised continuum of rituals for the President provided the daughter with an explanation (and passive participation) previously denied her by her mother.

CONCLUSION

Recent tragedies ranging from domestic terrorism to the threat of open conflict have sensitized us to the fact that each one of us and our loved ones are vulnerable. Violence is part of our everyday life. We see and hear it on the nightly news, read about in newspapers and magazines, and encounter it in discussions with family, friends, neighbors, strangers, and co-workers. In fact, I suspect we have been exposed to more tragic stories, especially on television, during the past year than at any time in our history. In the current atmosphere, death of a public figure takes on new considerations: what was the cause of the death? Who was responsible for the death? In what way are we more vulnerable because of the death of this public figure?

Current losses, whether personal or public, make us aware that grief does not occur in a vacuum. Each new loss reminds us of prior losses and sensitizes us to further losses yet to come, including our own dying and death. The current rise in interest in caregiving is partly a reflection of the changing demographics of aging and the economics of healthcare, but it is also a reflection of the fact that we have grown apart. We have lost a sense of community in terms of caring for one another on local national and international levels. The death of a public figure causes us to fear for our safety and that of our loved ones. It reminds us of our continuous vulnerability. For some, it triggers memories of the vulnerability to annihilation that we first sensed during the Cold War.

Thoughts of vulnerability and fears of annihilation are not new. Tribal societies experienced the same anxieties on the death of a leader or warrior. Some, like the Nilgiri (Habenstein & Lamers, 1956) in southern India, tried to disguise their vulnerability by conducting only a partial funeral lest a neighboring tribe see their loss as a sign of weakness. The Nilgiri held a brief "green funeral" soon after a death and a common "brown funeral" annually for all who had died during the year. One fascinating aspect of their customs held that a child conceived by the widow before the brown funeral was considered to be the child of the deceased man.

Many people experience a sense of personal vulnerability after the untimely death of a leader and public figure. They feel moved to do something to acknowledge the loss, to express a common sentiment and participate in meaningful ceremony. If we have learned anything from recent public tragedies and deaths of public figures, it is that we need to work together to seek improved ways to support one another in dealing with loss. ■

William M. Lamers, Jr., MD, is one of the first physicians to develop a hospice program in the United States with the Hospice of Marin in northern California in the mid-1970s. He helped establish the first program to train people to develop hospices and served as the chair of the Standards and Accreditation Committee of the National Hospice and Palliative Care Organization. Dr. Lamers is the author of many books on hospice care as well as on grief and bereavement. He is currently Hospice Foundation of America's Medical Consultant.

REFERENCES

Eisenbruch, M. (1984). Cross-cultural aspects of bereavement. A conceptual framework for comparative analysis. *Cross-cultural Medicine and Psychiatry 8*, 283-309.

Guinness, Alec. (1999). *A positively final appearance.* London: Penguin Books.

Habenstein, R., & Lamers, W. (1956). Funeral Customs the World Over. Milwaukee: Bulfin.

Killibrew, M. (2002). "I never died." In *Joe Hill: Songs of Hope.* Retrieved September 17, 2002 from http://www.pbs.org/joehill/voices/article.html

Lamers, W. (1959, May). Psychological reactions to loss. *The Director*, 29-32.

Lamers, W. (2000). Televised deaths of notable persons. *Journal of Pharmaceutical Care in Pain and Symptom Management.*

◼ PART II ◼

Responses to Public Tragedy

From the venal to the heroic, public tragedy brings out a range of responses. In some cases, violence and looting have followed tragedy. In other cases, there has been an outpouring of support. Tragedy seems to bring forth our best and worst efforts.

In his overview, Charles Corr asserts that the multiple losses associated with tragedy create a "bereavement overload." The trauma associated with tragedy challenges our assumptions about our perspectives, faith and philosophies. Dr. Corr, a pioneer in the development of task models in grief, here delineates the major tasks made necessary by public tragedy.

Dana Cable and Terry Martin address the effects of public tragedy on first responders. They point out that the line between first responders and victims can become blurred in a tragedy. Rescuers are at risk for physical injury, secondary traumatization, and death. The authors note, however, that interventions should be selected carefully. They introduce the idea, developed later in the book by Louis Gamino, that some models have achieved widespread acceptance despite a lack of supporting evidence. The authors remind us that one size does not fit all.

Paul Dolan, of ABC News, discusses another group of professionals who are among the first to arrive at the scene of a tragedy—reporters. In covering the news, they will shape public response and may even influence the grief reactions of victims and their families. Because a sensitive media response can facilitate grief (and a negative response can complicate it), Dolan discusses journalistic codes of ethics and lays out the rules of engagement. He also offers advice for grief counselors who encounter the news media. Finally, he advises organizations to specify in their disaster plans both contact persons and access policies for reporters who cover public tragedies.

The illuminating chapter by Janice Harris Lord, Melissa Hook and Sharon English reminds us of another critical aspect of grief and public tragedy— the impact of spiritual beliefs. The authors provide an overview of the theological understanding of tragedy from the perspective of each of five major religions. They also offer practical advice, reminding professionals to listen and learn, and to remain sensitive to individual interpretations of spirituality.

Finally, Elizabeth Bradley and LaVone Hazell describe the public service roles and responsibilities that funeral directors assume in the context of public tragedy, and they advocate for recognition, validation and support.

Taken together these chapters reinforce a critical point about responses to public tragedy. The line between rescuers and survivors can become very thin. Effective policies will minister sensitively to all those traumatized by the event, whatever their roles. ■

CHAPTER 6

Loss, Grief, and Trauma in Public Tragedy

Charles A. Corr

Public tragedies challenge us in our efforts to understand what they involve and in our desire to help those whom they affect. In this chapter, we examine some key elements that are typical of the experiences of those affected by public tragedies. Among these, the most prominent are loss, reactions to loss (grief), trauma, and reactions to trauma. Situating public tragedies in this context helps to clarify the nature, implications, and effects of public tragedy. With this clearer understanding, we can develop a task-based approach to helping that considers the efforts of individuals and communities as they cope with public tragedy and adapt to a changed world.

Loss

Readers of this book already know that loss in everyday life takes many forms. Public tragedies involve loss whose impact is felt broadly across a community or the general public. Their immediate effects go beyond those that fall primarily upon an individual, family, or friends. The scale of loss and destruction is larger than that of an individual loss. In addition, these events often involve a strong element of surprise and shock.

Public tragedy also reminds us that a single loss can affect different members of a community in distinctively different ways. That is, of course, also true of losses experienced by smaller social groups. When one member of a family dies, the impact of that death will be experienced by all of the surviving members of the family, and the experience will have some common factors, but it will also be different for each survivor.

Nevertheless, public tragedies impress themselves on their victims in ways that have special qualities. Some public tragedies may be completely unexpected and stunning, such as those involving:

- Sudden death

- An assassination

- A terrorist assault, or

- A tornado or earthquake

Other public tragedies may provide time and notice for a community to make more or less successful attempts to resist the full horror of the anticipated outcome. These public tragedies might include those arising from:

- A hurricane

- Flooding resulting from a gradual buildup of heavy rain

- A large-scale wildfire

- The well-publicized kidnapping of a child who is later found to have been assaulted and killed

In all of these examples, the key variables are not whether the tragic events are natural phenomena or human-induced—although those qualities can add to the elements of the tragedy—but how the event comes about and how members of the community are affected by its results.

Because of the size and diversity of a public community, any tragedy that affects that community is especially likely to resonate with its members in different ways. How any public tragedy impacts individuals within the community will depend on such variables as their proximity to the events, their attachments to the primary victims of the events, the way in which the losses occur, and their own personal circumstances at the time.

In both individual losses and public tragedies, primary losses are most often accompanied by secondary losses. For example, the death of a husband is not just the loss of a spouse and lover for the wife. It also involves the loss of a helpmate, a supporter, a person who shares in parenting responsibilities, or someone who may have been an annoying critic or even an abusive partner. The loss sets up ripples of associated losses that will eventually touch on all aspects of the relationship and the life together that the survivors had shared with the deceased individual, and it may take some time for all of these secondary losses to come to the fore and be fully appreciated. So too, the implications and the secondary losses arising from a public tragedy may be varied, diverse, and not immediately evident at the time of the principal loss.

A further aspect of loss in public tragedy and in many other private situations is suggested by Shakespeare's observation that "when sorrows come, they come not like single spies, but in battalions" (*Hamlet,* IV, v: 78). Loss is frequently not experienced as an isolated phenomenon; more typically, survivors experience many primary losses simultaneously or closely following one another. That led Kastenbaum (1969) to coin the phrase "bereavement overload," which he used to indicate the many losses that elderly persons often experience when their peers and others die in rapid succession. In the case of public tragedies, bereavement overload applies to the multiple losses that they embrace, as, for example, when all of the members of a family are killed together in an automobile accident or when there are multiple losses and many different types of losses encountered in the crash of an airliner. Experiences on September 11, 2001, are a paradigm of multiple losses, embracing as they do many different types of deaths, injuries to many at the sites, widespread destruction of property and treasure, and the loss of a sense of innocence and security on the part of many who could never have imagined such terrible events.

GRIEF

Every significant loss in the life of a human being can be expected to generate a grief reaction. When one suffers a significant loss, one experiences grief. The word grief signifies reaction, both internally and externally, to the impact of a loss. The term arises from the grave or heavy weight that presses on bereaved survivors (*Oxford English Dictionary,* 1989). Not to experience grief for a significant loss is an aberration. It suggests that there was no real attachment prior to the loss, that the relationship was complicated in ways that set it apart from the ordinary, or that one is suppressing or hiding one's reactions to the loss.

The term *grief* is often defined as "the emotional reaction to loss." One needs to be careful in understanding such a definition. As Elias noted, "broadly speaking, emotions have three components, a somatic, a behavioral, and a feeling component" (1991, p. 117). As a result, "the term *emotion,* even in professional discussions, is used with two different meanings. It is used in a wider and in a narrower sense at the same time. In the wider sense the term *emotion* is applied to a reaction pattern that involves the whole organism in its somatic, its feeling and its behavioral aspects. . . . In its narrower sense the term *emotion* refers to the feeling component of the syndrome only" (Elias, 1991, p. 119).

Grief clearly does involve feelings, and it is certainly appropriate to think of the feeling dimensions of grief. Anyone who has experienced grief or who has encountered a grieving person is familiar with the outpouring of feelings that is a prominent element of most grief reactions. Yet, it is also important to recognize that reacting to loss is not merely a matter of feelings. Grief is broader, more complex, and more deep-seated than this narrower understanding of emotional reactions to loss might imply (Rando, 1993).

Grief is experienced and expressed in numerous ways (Corr, Nabe, & Corr, 2003; Worden, 2002). These include physical, psychological (affective/cognitive), behavioral, social, and spiritual dimensions, represented by

- Physical sensations, such as hollowness in the stomach, a lump in the throat, tightness in the chest, aching arms, oversensitivity to noise, shortness of breath, lack of energy, a sense of depersonalization, muscle weakness, dry mouth, or loss of coordination

- Feelings, such as sadness, anger, guilt and self-reproach, anxiety, loneliness, fatigue, helplessness, shock, yearning, emancipation, relief, or numbness

- Thoughts or cognitions, such as disbelief, confusion, preoccupation, a sense of presence of the deceased, or paranormal (hallucinatory) experiences

- Behaviors, such as sleep or appetite disturbances, absentmindedness, social withdrawal, loss of interest in activities that previously were sources of satisfaction, dreams of the deceased, crying, avoiding reminders of the deceased, searching and calling out, sighing, restless overactivity, or visiting places and cherishing objects that remind one of the deceased

- Social difficulties in interpersonal relationships or problems in functioning within an organization

- Spiritual searching for a sense of meaning, hostility toward God, or a realization that one's value framework is inadequate to cope with this particular loss

These many dimensions of grief reactions are as evident in the different ways in which individuals react to personal loss as they are in the ways in which communities react to public tragedies.

TRAUMA

In a sense, any death or significant loss can be perceived as traumatic by those left behind. In a more precise usage, however, the term, *trauma* refers to situations that are outside the range of normal human experience and that include certain objective elements, such as "(a) suddenness and lack of anticipation; (b) violence, mutilation, and destruction; (c) preventability and/or randomness; (d) multiple death; and (e) the mourner's personal encounter with death, where there is either a significant threat to personal survival or a massive and/or shocking confrontation with the death and mutilation of others" (Rando, 1993, pp. 568-569).

Many aspects of this more precise sense of the word can be found in certain experiences of an individual as, for example, in cases of rape or incest. Our concern in this chapter, however, is with the trauma of public tragedies. Here, trauma may take many forms. For example, as the International Work Group on Death, Dying, and Bereavement (IWG, 2002) has noted in its discussion of disasters, a traumatic event may

- Be human-induced (e.g., torture, terrorism, or war-related atrocities) or natural (e.g., serious accidents, earthquakes, hurricanes, tornadoes, or floods)
- Arise from a deliberate or nondeliberate act
- Apply to a local, national, or international community
- Range in duration from less than a single day to a much longer period of time
- Be relatively small, medium, or large in the scale of deaths, injuries, and/or property damage that is involved

In addition to its many diverse forms, another important aspect of trauma is the impact that it has on those whom it most closely affects. In addition to those who might die in a pubic tragedy, trauma has a distinctive impact on those left alive. Psychologists and traumatologists have come to identify this distinctive impact by pointing out that traumatic events have a tendency to shatter our assumptive worlds.

Janoff-Bulman (1992) described an assumptive world as "a conceptual system, developed over time, that provides us with expectations about the world and ourselves" (1992, p. 5). She argued that the most fundamental of these assumptions are "the bedrock of our conceptual system" and are those "that we are least likely to challenge" (1992, p. 5). In particular, Janoff-Bulman suggested that the most fundamental assumptions held by most people in their assumptive worlds are likely to be of the following types:

- "The world is benevolent," a conviction that is typically applied both to people and to events—especially to one's own limited world and future expectations, if not to the world at large

- "The world is meaningful," a conviction that there is a relationship between a particular person and what happens to that person, and that this relationship is characterized by justice (moral persons deserve positive outcomes, while misfortune is most appropriate for those who are corrupt) and control (we can influence what happens to us or there is some other principle of control [e.g., God] that influences outcomes in an appropriate way), which means there is order and comprehensibility in the world rather than randomness and absurdity

- "The self is worthy," a conviction that one is essentially good, decent, and moral in character, as well as wise and effective in one's actions

Janoff-Bulman conceded that everyone may not hold these three beliefs, but she argued that they are at the foundation of many individual world outlooks even when the individuals in question do not think this is what they believe. She also contended that such assumptions are broad and adaptive, but not foolhardy, because they "afford us the trust and confidence that are necessary to engage in new behaviors, to test our limits" (1992, p. 23). Traumatic events challenge the most fundamental convictions in our assumptive worlds.

REACTIONS TO TRAUMA

It is curious that we do not appear to have a single term that is widely understood and accepted to identify the broad range of typical reactions to trauma. As noted earlier, *grief* is the term that designates reactions to loss, but there is no parallel term describing reactions to trauma. One reason for that may be because it is only in recent years that the distinctive features of trauma have been brought to the fore and delineated in detail. Another reason may be that different commentators may wish to categorize reactions to trauma in different ways. For example, many have linked the stress response syndromes that result from traumatic events to posttraumatic stress disorder (PTSD)—whose basic symptom categories include reexperiencing the traumatic event, avoiding stimuli associated with the traumatic event or numbing of general responsiveness, and increased physiological arousal. By contrast, some authors (Jacobs, Mazure, & Prigerson, 2000; Prigerson & Jacobs, 2001) have recently argued that reactions to trauma constitute a distinct form of complicated grief, one that needs to be understood in its own terms.

However that may be, Rando (1996) has described many of the features of common reactions to trauma in four ways. First, when the loss or death is sudden and unanticipated its shock effects tend to overwhelm a mourner's capacity to cope. There is no opportunity to say good-bye and finish unfinished business. Because the traumatic encounter does not seem to make sense, there is often an obsessive effort to reconstruct events so as to comprehend and prepare for them in a retrospective way. Also, traumatic events are frequently accompanied by intense emotional reactions (such as, fear, anxiety, terror, and a sense of vulnerability, helplessness, and loss of control) and increased physiological arousal. Further, trauma is often followed by major secondary losses, such as having no body to view to confirm the death, a need to rescue others or attend to the wounded, and the demands of legal inquiries.

Second, the violence, mutilation, and destruction in traumatic events may produce feelings of terror, fear, and anxiety. These feelings may be accompanied by a sense of vulnerability, victimization, and powerlessness. There may also be fantasies of grotesque dying and aggressive thoughts of revenge.

Third, when a traumatic event is perceived as preventable, those who are left alive tend to view it as something that could have been avoided. It appears to be both a willful or irresponsibly negligent event as well as an unprovoked violation. As a result, victims of trauma may become angry, outraged, and frustrated. Hence, they strive intensely to find the cause of the event, fix responsibility, and impose punishment. By contrast, when a traumatic event is perceived as random, its unpredictability and uncontrollability can be terrifying. To ward off such terror, victims often blame themselves for such events, choosing that alternative as a way to defend themselves against the perception that events in the world are truly random and unpredictable, that they cannot be protected against.

Fourth, as we have noted earlier, experiencing multiple deaths or losses in a traumatic encounter—especially when they occur simultaneously or in rapid succession as happened on 9/11—can produce a form of bereavement overload in which mourners find it difficult to sort out and work through their losses, grief reactions, and mourning processes for each individual tragedy.

Fifth, a mourner's personal encounter with death in a traumatic event can involve a significant threat to personal survival or can follow a massive or shocking confrontation with the death and mutilation of others. In the former instance, one is likely to experience fear, terror, heightened arousal, a sense of abandonment and helplessness, and increased vulnerability; in the latter instance, horrifying sensory stimuli (sights, sounds, smells) often produce reactive phenomena, such as nightmares, flashbacks, and intrusive images or memories.

Adapting to a New World

Corr and Doka (2001) observed that there are two main elements in ongoing responses to public tragedy: coping with loss, grief, and trauma and finding ways to adapt to a changed world. As Weisman (1984) noted, coping involves more than an automatic response or a defensive reaction. In fact, a posture of defense is largely a negative one; it channels energy into avoiding problems rather than achieving some kind of adaptive accommodation. By contrast, coping is, or at least can be, an active process—a positively oriented effort to resolve problems or adapt to challenges in living. It is a process in which one seeks to manage specific demands that are perceived as stressful and that are appraised as taxing or exceeding the resources of the person (Corr, Nabe, & Corr, 2003). Adaptation may include coping, but it often implies longer term processes that help one go forward with healthful living and loving. In light of this chapter's emphasis on reactions to trauma and loss, the remainder of this analysis will focus on coping.

Janoff-Bulman wrote about the relationship between coping and trust in the following way: "In the end," she argued, "it is a rebuilding of this trust—the reconstruction of a viable, nonthreatening assumptive world—that constitutes the core coping task of victims" (1992, p. 69). This is the path from being merely a victim of a traumatic event to becoming a survivor in the full sense of that word. It requires the mourner to cope with both the traumatic aspects of the encounter and the loss and grief found in all bereavement (Corr, 2002). Thus, Janoff-Bulman (1992) described survivors who have coped effectively with traumatic events and challenges to their fundamental convictions and assumptive worlds:

> [T]hese survivors recognize the possibility of tragedy, but do not allow it to pervade their self- and worldviews. . . [For such survivors] the world is benevolent, but not absolutely; events that happen make sense, but not always; the self can be counted on to be decent and competent, but helplessness is at times a reality. . . There is disillusionment, yet it is generally not the disillusionment of despair. Rather, it is disillusionment tempered by hope. . . [In the end, this view] involves an acknowledgment of real possibilities, both bad and good—of disaster in spite of human efforts, of triumph in spite of human limitations. (pp. 174-175)

These are the tasks that follow in the aftermath of many public tragedies.

TASKS IN COPING WITH PUBLIC TRAGEDY

A task-based approach to coping with death-related challenges (Corr, 1992) offers one way to understand coping with public tragedies. Tasks emphasize a proactive approach to coping, as contrasted with stage-based models or metaphors, which seem to emphasize an exclusively passive or reactive way of understanding such coping. Tasks foster empowerment in terms of how they will or will not be taken up and implemented and which among them will be selected or emphasized. Tasks are not merely needs, even if needs underlie the task work that one undertakes. The term task identifies what a person is trying to do in his or her coping, the specific effort that he or she is making to achieve what he or she requires or desires. In this way, a task-based approach can suggest to potential helpers the tasks that they might choose to support, assist, or (sometimes) redirect for the individual being helped. In general, helpers and advocates should try to enable individuals to help themselves. In some cases, it will be necessary to take direct action on behalf of or in place of the individual, and, rarely, redirect counterproductive behaviors.

There are four primary dimensions in the life of a human being: the physical, the psychological, the social, and the spiritual (Corr, 1992; Corr, Nabe, & Corr, 2003). These four dimensions suggest four corresponding areas of task work involving both the persons affected by public tragedy and those assisting them as these individuals learn to cope with loss, grief, trauma, and their responses to trauma.

Physical Tasks

In the aftermath of a public tragedy, physical tasks and the physical dimensions of human life are almost always key. Every effort must be made to save lives and rescue those in danger. In cases such as an assassination attempt on a prominent person by a single individual, efforts are focused on shielding the intended victim, providing prompt emergency care if that person or others have been wounded, protecting others on the scene who may be at risk, and capturing the perpetrator so that the individual cannot harm others or himself or herself.

In larger scale public tragedies, physical task work becomes more complicated. In cases of a natural disaster such as an earthquake or hurricane, in cases of a major accident such as the crash of an airliner, a train, or a series of motor vehicles, or in cases of a deliberately perpetrated disaster such as the explosion of a bomb or an assault involving firearms at a workplace or school, there may be many issues to consider almost simultaneously. A triage system may be needed to determine who most urgently needs immediate assistance, who can wait for help for some time, and who is already dead or beyond the reach of effective resuscitative efforts. In the midst of destruction and debris, it may be necessary to find or develop ways for emergency workers to reach the scene. In a wide variety of public tragedies, it will be immediately necessary to remove affected persons from dangerous or horrific scenes and deliver them to a safe location, where they can care for their immediate physical requirements.

Psychological Tasks

Psychological tasks are also vital in responding to public tragedies. Perhaps the most important of these is to diminish a sense of terror and the horrific, coupled with generating a renewed sense of security. For example, simply by removing persons from the immediate scene of a public tragedy, one may distance them in some degree from a context of death, destruction, and horror. Beyond that, by placing affected persons in the hands of skilled professionals or volunteer caregivers, it may be possible to suggest that some degree of normality does continue. Giving shelter, food, and comfort to affected persons is a way of addressing both their physical and their psychological needs in the immediate aftermath of a public tragedy. Effective programs of postvention can help affected persons in other ways with psychological tasks arising from a public tragedy.

Social Tasks

A third area of task work in public tragedy involves social tasks. An appropriate command structure—preferably one based on a comprehensive, pre-existing plan of response—must be implemented as quickly as possible. Professional helpers, volunteers, and other caregivers will want to know if their skills are required and where or how they can best be deployed. Affected persons and their family members or loved ones will have strong needs to communicate with each other and to share information about their status. The media and other interested parties will need to be provided with accurate information about what has happened and what is being done in order to inform the larger community and to forestall misinformation and distorted rumors. Intruders and other unwelcome bystanders, who can delay or disrupt legitimate response and rescue efforts, will need to be fended off.

Spiritual Tasks

Finally, spiritual tasks in response to public tragedy should not be neglected. Existential questions are always prominent in cases of significant loss and trauma: How could something terrible like this happen? How can this horror befall our community, my family, and myself? How can I make sense of these horrific events? To whom can I turn for succor and solace? Spiritual tasks typically focus on issues of meaningfulness, connectedness, and transcendence. These tasks reframe the psychological language of assumptive worlds in spiritual perspectives and link them to the key concept of hope. Religious and spiritual perspectives, including prayer, sacramental gestures, and simple presence, may provide comfort and aid in addressing spiritual issues and tasks of these types. Others may find that in the initial moments when spiritual tasks present themselves, one is only just beginning a long struggle to apply, animate, or even restructure his or her spiritual perspectives. Rituals and other forms of symbolic behaviors may be especially useful in carrying out spiritual tasks.

Note that tasks in responding to public tragedy will be taken up by individuals each in their own way. Different people will prioritize different ways, partly as a result of how they assess the situation and partly as a result of their preparation or their capacity to respond. Further, an emphasis on one versus another type of task is likely to change as time passes and the situation changes. This is a common feature of many tragic events, as those who intervene come to see their role as shifting from rescue to recovery. Responses to loss and trauma will be mediated by many variables, including

- The nature of the prior relationships that are affected by the tragic events, relationships whose values and roles may only be fully appreciated in hindsight

- The way in which the loss and trauma take place

- The concurrent circumstances of those affected by the tragic events

- The coping strategies that the bereaved person has learned to use in efforts to manage previous encounters with loss and trauma

- The developmental status of the bereaved person (whether that individual is a child, adolescent, adult, or elderly person will affect how he or she can cope with the situation and will determine which normative developmental tasks he or she is also already coping with)

- The support or assistance that the bereaved person receives from others after the loss, including the nature of the support or assistance, how it is offered or made available, and how the bereaved person perceives that support

SOME SUGGESTIONS FOR HELPING

Several suggestions from this analysis and other accounts of disaster (IWG, 2002) may be of use to those who seek to help persons coping with public tragedies:

- Prepare and periodically review a plan for responding to public tragedy in as comprehensive a way as possible; offer advance training to those whose services are most likely to be needed in any type of public tragedy.

- Assess the specific public tragedy you are facing. Who needs help and what type of help do they need?

- Appraise the specific features of the particular public tragedy that has occurred; each will have its own different forms.

- Evaluate the resources available to you. What can you contribute and what are your limitations? What can others who are nearby or otherwise available contribute and what are their limitations?

- Prioritize responses. What is most urgently needed? What tasks should be undertaken first, by whom, and how?

- Anticipate that needs and tasks will change over time; adjust your own responses and those of others accordingly as time passes and circumstances change.

- Although public tragedies can involve intensive and extensive loss, trauma, and disaster, there is much you and the community can do in their aftermath to mitigate exaggerated responses and problems.

- Even when you are acting with the best will in the world, do not take over what individuals can do for themselves in the aftermath of a public tragedy. Wherever possible and appropriate, seek to enhance for those individuals their sense of control and self-efficacy and to reinforce their decision-making capacity.

- Give special attention to persons with particular needs such as children and adolescents, those who are unaware that help is available and is likely to be beneficial, and those who are reluctant or unable to ask for help.

- Offer appropriate support and assistance to helpers themselves, both while they are intervening and as an ongoing resource. ▪

Charles A. Corr, Ph.D., is Professor Emeritus, Southern Illinois University Edwardsville, a member of the Executive Committee of the National Kidney Foundation's TransAction Council, a member of the Board of Directors of the Hospice Institute of the Florida Suncoast, and a member and former Chairperson of the International Work Group on Death, Dying, and Bereavement. Dr. Corr is the author of numerous books, articles, and chapters in the field of death, dying, and bereavement. His most recent publication is the fourth edition of Death and Dying, Life and Living *(Wadsworth, 2003), co-authored with Clyde M. Nabe and Donna M. Corr.*

REFERENCES

Corr, C.A. (1992). A task-based approach to coping with dying. *Omega, 24,* 81-94.

Corr, C.A. (2002). Coping with challenges to assumptive worlds. In J. Kauffman (Ed.), *Loss of the assumptive world: A theory of traumatic loss.* New York & London: Brunner-Routledge.

Corr, C.A., & Doka, K.J. (2001). Master concepts in the field of death, dying, and bereavement: Coping versus adaptive strategies. *Omega, 43,* 183-199.

Corr, C.A., Nabe, C.M., & Corr, D.M. (2003). *Death and dying, life and living* (4th ed.). Belmont, CA: Wadsworth.

Elias, N. (1991). On human beings and their emotions: A process-sociological essay. In M. Featherstone, M. Hepworth, & B.S. Turner (Eds.), *The body: Social process and cultural theory.* London: Sage.

International Work Group on Death, Dying, and Bereavement (IWG). (2002). Assumptions and principles about psychological aspects of disasters. *Death Studies, 26,* 449-462.

Jacobs, S., Mazure, C., & Prigerson, H. (2000). Diagnostic criteria for traumatic grief. *Death Studies, 24,* 185-199.

Janoff-Bulman, R. (1992). *Shattered assumptions: Towards a new psychology of trauma.* New York: The Free Press.

Kastenbaum, R. (1969). Death and bereavement in later life. In A.H. Kutscher (Ed.), *Death and bereavement.* Springfield, IL: Charles C. Thomas.

The Oxford English Dictionary (2nd ed., 20 vols.). (1989). Ed. J.A. Simpson & E.S.C. Weiner. Oxford: Clarendon Press.

Prigerson, H.G., & Jacobs, S.C. (2001). Traumatic grief as a distinct disorder: A rationale, consensus criteria, and a preliminary empirical test. In M.S. Stroebe, R.O. Hansson, W. Stroebe, & H. Schut (Eds.), *Handbook of bereavement research: Consequences, coping, and care.* Washington, DC: American Psychological Association.

Rando, T.A. (1993). *Treatment of complicated mourning.* Champaign, IL: Research Press.

Rando, T.A. (1996). Complications in mourning traumatic death. In K.J. Doka (Ed.), *Living with grief after sudden loss: Suicide, homicide, accident, heart attack, stroke.* Washington, DC: Hospice Foundation of America.

Weisman, A.D. (1984). *The coping capacity: On the nature of being mortal.* New York: Human Sciences Press.

Worden, J.W. (2002). *Grief counseling and grief therapy: A handbook for the mental health practitioner* (3rd ed.). New York: Springer.

■ CHAPTER 7 ■

Effects of Public Tragedy on First Responders

Dana G. Cable and Terry L. Martin

*There were people screaming. I saw people jumping
out of the building. Their arms were flailing.
I stopped taking pictures and started crying.*
—Michael Walters, freelance news photographer

INTRODUCTION

In addition to the sheer scope and magnitude of the 9/11 disaster, an
additional fact distinguishes it from the Oklahoma City bombing, the
shootings at Columbine High School, and other recent public tragedies—
the role, and the deaths, of significant numbers of rescuers. Rescue personnel,
who usually work behind the scenes, became instant celebrities. Entire agencies, such as the Fire Department of New York and the New York Police
Department, were elevated to the status of superheroes as their personnel
threw themselves into peril trying to save those caught in the towers. Of the
first responders, 343 firefighters, 37 Port Authority police, and 23 New York
City police officers died when the towers collapsed.

Who are first responders? For the purposes of this chapter, the term refers
to police, fire, and medical personnel who arrive at the scene of a public
tragedy well before additional resources have been put into place. These

personnel and others who are first on the scene are deeply affected not only by the immediate event but also by the saturation news coverage that gives millions witness to their efforts.

GRIEF: PRIVATE AND PUBLIC

All grief experiences have both a private and public side. When an individual dies, the private side of grief permits the bereaved loved ones to deal with their reactions privately, either alone or with family and close friends. The public face of grief after such an event generally is seen in the rituals that surround the funeral or memorial service and in public announcements of the death through obituaries and death notices. This aspect of personal grief is usually structured, as well as short lived, and the bereaved individual is allowed to grieve with his or her own support system.

Public tragedies are different; the entire nation mourns for an extended period. In addition, the unrestricted nature of these events reveals emotions—raw, untempered, and chaotic—that usually are expressed in private. In the immediate aftermath of 9/11, first responders suddenly found themselves protagonists on a vast national stage. Their initial reactions were viewed and reported by the news media. Virtually every time they left the scene of the tragedy, news cameras showed to the public the despair on their faces, the dejected slump of their shoulders, and their tears. Ironically, journalists experienced much the same thing. Reporters who normally are stoic, even chatty, cried openly on camera. Much of America witnessed CBS News anchor Dan Rather's tears as his voice broke on a late-night talk show.

RESCUE VERSUS RECOVERY

The potential of saving a human life propels first responders to action. The possibility of finding living victims enables exhausted and emotionally taxed individuals to perform at a heroic level. Yet even when there is real hope of rescue, the pressure of the search often conflicts with the necessity of securing a safe rescue environment. In lower Manhattan and in Oklahoma City, rescuers faced fragile and potentially deadly buildings, while the siege at Columbine High School in Littleton, Colorado, created an atmosphere of war.

One of the things that stands out about the tragedy of 9/11 was the relationship of the rescuers to many of those trapped—other first responders. Examples abound in the news media of the electric tension of those first moments after the collapse of the towers. One news report described the efforts of a 225-pound firefighter who had just identified his partner by his boots trying in vain to dig him out with his bare hands. A news photograph showed several firefighters emerging from the debris bearing the lifeless body of one of their own.

In most cases of disaster, responders continue to make active attempts to rescue the living during the first 72 hours. Then slowly, painfully, efforts to rescue the living merge with recovery of remains. For rescuers at the World Trade Center, the intensity of this transition was exacerbated by the knowledge that many of their own had in effect been pronounced dead.

Even the canine partners of first responders become frustrated by not finding survivors. One report from Oklahoma City said that volunteers had hidden in damaged buildings near the scene just so they could be "rescued" by the search dogs, prompting effusive praise for the dogs from their handlers.

COMPLICATIONS IN DISASTER DEATHS

Raphael has discussed issues that complicate mourning and that are associated with posttraumatic reactions (1986). Two of these issues apply to disasters. They are (1) confronting sudden, massive, and shocking exposure to the deaths and mutilation of victims; and (2) experiencing a significant risk to one's own life.

Many of the dead at the World Trade Center buildings and the Pentagon were so dismembered that it was difficult to reconstruct whole bodies. Body parts that were recovered were often small, charred, and unidentifiable. Especially in New York, body parts belonged to colleagues of the recovery workers. First responders could only imagine the horror of the suffering and death that occurred that day. Some studies have suggested that high rates of posttraumatic stress disorder (PTSD), as well as high risk for suicide and physical illness, will likely occur for workers dealing with "grotesque" deaths (Deahl, Gillham, Thomas, Searle, & Srinivasan, 1994).

In the terrorist attacks of 9/11, the Oklahoma City bombing, and the Columbine school shootings, first responders encountered significant personal risk. At Columbine, it was not known, initially, how many shooters were involved or how heavily they were armed. In both Oklahoma City and New York City, the heavily damaged structures themselves represented a grave threat to all who entered them. In addition, responders recognized that only the chance of timing and location may have prevented their own deaths.

At the World Trade Center, some first responders experienced survivor guilt, which was exacerbated by their elevation to hero status by the press and public.

Some first responders were injured early in the recovery efforts and could not continue. These responder-survivors were isolated from their colleagues and the immediate environment of the tragedy. They were not able to feel a part of what was going on; instead, they had to settle for watching the events unfold on television. In many cases, the responders' injuries were so severe that they could not play a part in any funeral or memorial activities following the tragedy. This was especially wrenching when a close personal friend or companion was among the dead.

Multiple deaths are another potentially complicating factor in reactions following disaster deaths. On 9/11, many first responders lost not one but several colleagues among the dead. Rando identified a variety of dilemmas facing mourners after multiple deaths (1993). In particular, survivors confront the decision of which loss to mourn first—in essence, which loved one was of greater value.

Perhaps the most difficult complicating factor for most first responders was the duality of the issues they confronted. First, they had their own reactions to these public tragedies. As first responders confronted the student-killers at Columbine or dug through the rubble in Oklahoma City and lower Manhattan hoping to save lives, they represented all Americans who would have chosen to be there and do the same things. Many first responders were keenly aware of their roles as surrogates for millions of Americans.

At the World Trade Center, where so many rescue workers were buried in the rubble, first responders had to deal with their own sense of personal disaster at the loss of colleagues and friends. They were torn between the macro and the micro impacts of the tragedy, between public and personal evaluations of their efforts. This conflict was especially powerful as rescue became recovery. In the eyes of the world, the 9/11 first responders performed magnificently. In their own eyes, however, they fell short, haunted by what they wanted to find and could not.

Another complicating factor in public tragedy arises when the violence is intentionally and maliciously inflicted. The 9/11 terrorist attacks, the bombing in Oklahoma City, and the shootings at Columbine High School all resulted from deliberate, premeditated attempts by some people to kill other people. All involved murder in one form or another. Homicide is recognized as a potentially complicating factor in bereavement (Rando, 1993).

Despite the traumatic experiences of those first on the scene at these tragedies, most of the public's sympathy went to families of the dead. For a long time, the public failed to recognize the tremendous losses that recovery workers themselves had experienced. This is a classic example of disenfranchised grief (Doka, 1989), in which either the relationship to the deceased or the loss itself is not recognized. In some cases, however, support and sympathy were showered upon first responders. Still, many of them were unable to publicly mourn. First, there was always pressure, both internal and external, to return to the site of the tragedy and continue efforts to rescue potential survivors. Second, the "code of the warrior" frowns upon open displays of grief. Finally, for some, the initial numbness and shock persisted well beyond the first weeks and even months of rescue-turned-recovery.

Some first responders expressed their grief in publicly (and privately) sanctioned ways: floods of tears, collapse, confusion, and a strong desire to share their experiences with others. Other first responders also grieved publicly—but their grief went unnoticed. Many of these first responders were likely more instrumental in their grief than intuitive (Martin & Doka, 2000). Instrumental grievers express their grief by mastering their feelings, solving problems, and using action as an outlet for their grief.

IMPLICATIONS AND CONCLUSION

The potential physical risks to first responders prompted a national working conference in New York City in December, 2001. Conference proceedings were published by the National Institute for Occupational Safety and Health and are available online at www.rand.org/publications/CF/CF176/. In brief, the conference identified the need for better protective equipment for individual responders, re-evaluation of emergency practices, and more and better training for both front-line responders and managers.

In addition to the physical risk confronted by first responders, there is the potential risk to their mental health. Multiple roles, multiple duties, and multiple losses mark the experiences of first responders. It has been widely held that efforts to identify and treat those responders most affected by their experiences would mitigate any negative long-term consequences to their psychological health.

The technique used most often for assisting high-risk occupational groups following public tragedies is Critical Incident Stress Debriefing (CISD)

(Mitchell, 1983). This technique was specifically designed to provide immediate crisis intervention or "preventive intervention" (Caplan, 1969). Additional modalities used to treat trauma include cognitive-behavioral therapy (CBT) (Beck, 1976) and pharmacological treatments. In all cases, it is critical to intervene as soon as possible after the tragedy (Solomon, 1999).

A recent Dutch study (Emmerik, Kamphuis, Hulsbosch, & Emmelkamp, 2002) questions the wisdom of using debriefing as the intervention of choice with trauma survivors. While there is little in the grief or trauma literature to challenge the acceptance of debriefing as a first line of defense, it should not be embraced as a one-size-fits-all treatment modality. Common sense and anecdotal evidence suggest that debriefing works; however, its widespread adoption has outpaced any convincing scientific evidence (Wortman & Silver, 1989). As Rando (1993) and Martin and Doka (2000) have emphasized, it is important to tailor any intervention to the individual's needs and to avoid generalizing grief reactions.

In an editorial in the same issue of *Lancet* as the Dutch study, Richard Gist and Grant Devilly chastise those who continue to promote CISD:

> The meta-analysis by Arnold van Emmerik and colleagues in today's Lancet [September 7, 2000] about the efficacy of post-trauma psychological debriefing stands among the more potent entries in an increasing litany of reports, reviews, and consensus statements… indicating that debriefing yielded no demonstrable effect on subsequent resolution of traumatic exposure and may inhibit or delay resolution for some participants. (p. 741)

Gist's statement resonates with a statement issued by the National Institute of Mental Health that resulted from a workshop held in October 2001:

> Early intervention in the form of a single one-on-one recital of events and expression of emotions evoked by a traumatic event… does not consistently reduce risks of later developing PTSD or related adjustment difficulties. Some survivors (e.g., those with high arousal) may be put at heightened risk for adverse outcomes as a result of such early interventions. (p. 8)

Thus, the most popular and arguably most effective form of post-traumatic intervention is being challenged not only for unproved efficacy, but also for potential risks to survivors.

One caveat to wide acceptance of the validity of these challenges is that CISD often is lumped together with other types of debriefings. Therefore, interested parties must first define what exactly is being disputed. Another caution is the failure to identify the competency, training, and experience of those applying the CISD model.

While there is little question that the experiences of first-responders are extremely stressful, even dangerous, most are still on the job, awaiting the next tragedy. In fact, out of the nearly 11,000 responders at the World Trade Center, only about 250 remain on leave with service-connected, stress-related problems (CDC, 2002). Perhaps the natural healing that evolves from support provided by loving families and supportive friends is enough to enable first-responders to do it all over again. ■

Dana G. Cable is a professor of Psychology and Thanatology at Hood College in Frederick, Maryland. He is a Licensed Psychologist, Certified Death Educator, and Certified Grief Counselor. Since 1973, he has maintained a private practice specializing in grief and death related issues. In 1995, he received the Clinical Practice Award from the Association for Death Education and Counseling. Dr. Cable is on the Editorial Board of the American Journal of Hospice and Palliative Care. *He is a frequent presenter of programs on grief for professionals throughout the United States.*

Terry L. Martin is an associate professor of Psychology and Thanatology at Hood College. He is a Licensed Clinical Professional Counselor, Certified Death Educator, and Certified Grief Therapist. Dr. Martin maintains a private counseling practice and also serves as consultant to hospices, nursing homes, and hospitals. His published work includes chapters in Kenneth J. Doka's Disenfranchised Grief *(1987, 2002) and chapters in earlier books in the* Living with Grief *series (1996, 1998, 2000). He co-authored (with Kenneth Doka)* Men Don't Cry...Women Do: Transcending Gender Stereotypes of Grief *(2000).*

REFERENCES

Beck, A.T. (1976). Cognitive therapy and emotional disorders. New York: International Universities Press.

Caplan, G. (1969). Opportunities for school psychologists in the primary prevention of mental disorders in children. In A. Bindman & A. Spiegel (Eds.), Perspectives in community mental health. Chicago: Aldine.

Centers for Disease Control and Prevention (CDC). (2002). Stress-related illnesses during the 11 months after the attacks (September 11, 2001-August 22, 2002). *Morbidity and Mortality Weekly Report, 51* (Special Issue), 5.

Deahl, M.P., Gillham, A.B., Thomas, J., Searle, M. M., & Srinivasan, M. (1994). Psychological sequelae following the Gulf War: Factors associated with subsequent morbidity and the effectiveness of psychological debriefing. *British Journal of Psychiatry, 165,* 60-65.

Doka, K.J. (1989). Disenfranchised grief: Recognizing hidden sorrow. Lexington, MA: Lexington Books.

Emmerik, Kamphuis, Hulsbosch, & Emmelkamp, (2002). Single-session debriefing after psychological trauma: a meta-analysis. *Lancet, 360,* 766-771.

Gist, R., & Devilly, G.J. (2002). Post-trauma debriefing: The road too frequently traveled. *The Lancet, 360,* commentary.

Martin, T.L., & Doka, K.J. (2000). Men don't cry…women do: Transcending gender stereotypes of grief. Philadelphia: Brunner/Mazel.

Mitchell, J.T. (1983). When disaster strikes: The critical incident stress debriefing process. *Journal of Emergency Medical Services, 8,* 36-39.

National Institute of Mental Health. (2002). Mental health and mass violence: Evidence-based early psychological intervention for victims/survivors of mass violence. A workshop to reach consensus on best practices. NIH Publication No. 02-5138. Washington, DC: U.S. Government Printing Office.

Rando, T. (1993). Treatment of complicated mourning. Champaign, IL: Research Press.

Raphael, B. (1986). When disaster strikes: How individuals and communities cope with catastrophe. New York: Basic Books.

Solomon, Z. (1999). Interventions for acute trauma response. *Current Opinion in Psychiatry, 12,* 175-180.

Van Emmerik, A.P., Kamphuis, J.H., Hulsbosch, A.M., & Emmelkamp, P.M. (2002). Single session debriefing after psychological trauma: a meta-analysis. *The Lancet, 360,* 766-71.

Wortman, C. B. & Silver, R. C. (1989). The myths of coping with loss. *Journal of Consulting and Clinical Psychology, 57,* 349-357.

■ CHAPTER 8 ■

Public Grief
and the News Media

Paul R. Dolan

We live in a high-speed information world. Every possible media source bombards us with news and noise, from unfiltered Internet material to live helicopter images on cable news channels to highly polished and edited newspaper articles.

Our world has changed greatly in terms of how we get information, but one thing has not changed: at a time of tragedy, information can play a positive or corrosive role in coping with the immediate and long-term impact of the tragedy. Unfortunately, we have too many case studies to learn from: the terrorist attacks on the World Trade Center and Washington, plane crashes, school shootings, suicide bombers, and war.

On a smaller scale, but equally important, we need to learn as journalists, grief counselors, teachers, parents, and public officials about how to cope in an information age with teen suicides, kidnapping, murder, and other tragedies.

At a time of tragedy and public and private grief, the role of the press and the conflicting needs of families and communities can create serious conflict. Families and victims may also have very conflicting feelings about wanting privacy and wanting to get the news media to focus on their loss.

ROLE OF THE PRESS

According to the Radio Television News Director Association (RTNDA) Code of Ethics and Professional Conduct, professional electronic journalists should recognize that their first obligation is to the public. They should operate as trustees of the public, seek the truth, report it fairly and with integrity and independence, and stand accountable for their actions. Specifically, they should

- Understand that any commitment other than service to the public undermines trust and credibility
- Reflect the diversity of the community and guard against oversimplification of issues and events
- Provide a full range of information to enable the public to make enlightened decisions
- Fight to ensure that the public's business is conducted in public

Like the U.S. news media, the British press also has a code. Ratified by the United Kingdom's Press Complaints Commission in 1997, the Code of Practice is the basis of self-regulation by the British news media. This code is excerpted below.

Privacy

Everyone is entitled to respect for his or her private and family life, home, health, and correspondence. A publication will be expected to justify intrusions into any individual's private life without consent. The use of long lens photography to take pictures of people in private places without their consent is unacceptable. (Note: Private places are public or private property where there is a reasonable expectation of privacy.)

Harassment

Journalists and photographers must neither obtain nor seek to obtain information or pictures through intimidation, harassment, or persistent pursuit. They must not photograph individuals in private places without their consent; must not persist in telephoning, questioning, pursuing, or photographing individuals after having been asked to desist; must not remain on their property after having been asked to leave, and must not follow them. Editors must ensure that those working for them comply with these requirements and must not publish material from other sources which does not meet these requirements.

Intrusion into Grief or Shock

In cases involving personal grief or shock, inquiries must be carried out and approaches made with sympathy and discretion. Publication must be handled sensitively at such times but this should not be interpreted as restricting the right to report judicial proceedings.

Children

Young people should be free to complete their time at school without unnecessary intrusion. Journalists must not interview or photograph a child under the age of 16 on subjects involving the welfare of the child or any other child in the absence of or without the consent of a parent or other adult who is responsible for the children. Pupils must not be approached or photographed while at school without the permission of the school authorities.

Unfortunately, both in the United Kingdom and the United States media codes are often disregarded. They are nevertheless important to review and understand, particularly as they pertain to coverage of a public tragedy.

THE REALITY OF CRISIS AND TRAGEDY

A code of conduct is rarely consulted in the race to cover a news event. Increasingly, the public is also receiving unfiltered, unedited news coverage via national and regional 24-hour news channels. These channels have instant access to satellite news trucks and helicopters with live coverage camera capabilities. This instant coverage is a fact of life—a painful fact of life for families who may learn of a tragedy from live coverage.

The terrorist attack on the World Trade Center was seen live on television by millions, including family members of those trapped and who were desperate for information. Horrific images of people falling or jumping to their death flashed across the television screens. Live television does not allow the caution and discretion necessary.

During the Trade Center tragedy there was an immediate effort in United States coverage to withhold the most horrific images. Most newspapers and television stations withheld footage and images of people leaping to their death. In Europe and other parts of the world, however, the coverage was far more graphic.

Needs of Families and Survivors

Those assisting families at times of tragedy should do everything possible to help the families deal with media coverage. Designating a family or community spokesperson to answer press questions is one approach. Publicly asking for privacy and criticizing any inappropriate press activity are also possible actions. Families will be torn between wanting to know every possible bit of news to being overwhelmed by the pain of the news.

The Public's Conflicting Needs

The public's response to tragedy is also very conflicting. People may have a genuine interest in reaching out to help families or they may be compelled to interject themselves out of morbid curiosity. The public wants extensive details and information about a crime or tragedy when often families and victims want privacy. The media is expected to answer all questions and provide extensive background. The public often indicates it does not like media prying or invasions of privacy, but in fact the public expects many details, including extensive personal details behind a tragedy.

The New York Times faced this dilemma with special sensitivity when, after the World Trade Center attack, it began to print a series of well-written, sensitive profiles of those who died. *The Times'* profiles quickly became a positive and healing contribution to families and also served to reflect the size and human face of the tragedy for the general public.

WHAT GRIEF COUNSELORS CAN DO

Along with their crucial role as mental health caregivers, counselors may be expected to serve as intermediaries between shocked and grieving survivors and families and a scrambling and invasive media. In any tragedy, grief counselors simply have to expect that media coverage will be an important part of the immediate aftershock. Following are a few steps counselors can take to ensure that media coverage does not exacerbate the grief and shock felt by survivors, families, and the larger community.

- Protect the privacy of survivors and families. Counselors should insist that members of the media respect families' need for privacy.

- Provide support for families being inundated by images and information. No matter how painful the story, many families will not want any filtering of the news they receive, but they will need emotional and spiritual support.

- Take a role in planning and publicizing healing ceremonies and responses to tragedy, which can be an effective way to help the larger community cope with a public tragedy.

- Write articles or letters for newspapers and be interviewed on such topics as coping strategies, depression, and short- and long-term grief.

- Help create special Internet sites with coping guidance created after a tragedy. The best approach may be to work with a local newspaper or TV station web site to get professional and accurate information on grief posted as soon as possible.

- Respond quickly and thoroughly to editors and journalists seeking recommendations on how best to respond to very difficult situations like teen suicides in a community. The press generally does not cover teen or youth suicide but may on occasion. Here journalists are often looking for opinions—do they cover multiple suicides or not cover? Does not covering a suicide help limit future suicides or contribute to an atmosphere of denial and ignorance?

The press is a force capable of making a contribution or of creating greater stress at a time of crisis or tragedy. Counselors must be vocal about press responsibility. Acknowledge good reporting and do not refrain from criticizing the media when that is deserved. In a free society you will never be able to "manage" the media or expect you will agree with all of its actions, but never give up on trying to make it more responsive to the needs of families and individuals coping with tragedy. ▪

Paul Dolan is Executive Director, International and Cable Business, ABC News. He has also served as a volunteer on the planning and funding of pediatric and family bereavement programs by Calvary Hospital and the New York City Fire Department at Sterling Forest, New York.

CHAPTER 9

Different Faiths, Different Perceptions of Public Tragedy

Janice Harris Lord, Melissa Hook, and Sharon English

INTRODUCTION

Among the forces converging after a public tragedy are the uncertainty of life and connection to the sacred. When our ability to control life and death fails, we tend to look to the spiritual aspects of suffering and death in an effort to make sense of a senseless act. In tumultuous places of uncertainty lie connections to mystery (Dwoskin, 2002).

Some people say, "It was God's will." For some, these words identify a God who literally controls the actions and events of unspeakable tragedy. More often, however, these words are meant to convey a belief that God's ways are more complex than we may understand.

Others wonder if God is trying to teach us something through tragedy. Some think God is testing or punishing. Others conclude that neither God nor any spiritual force had anything to do with unspeakable tragedy. They believe the law of karma, or cause and effect, is the factor that controls our destiny. Regardless of our personal beliefs, most of us struggle to incorporate traumatic and tragic death into our spiritual journey.

This chapter offers basic guidance in understanding the significance of the body and the spirit to bereaved persons of several faiths, including Hinduism, Judaism, Buddhism, Christianity, and Islam. These faiths are discussed throughout in chronological order based on their approximate dates of origin. The writers' intent is to foster greater respect, dignity, and sensitivity among caregivers. Since it is not possible to fairly summarize any faith in one limited chapter, we strongly encourage a continuing inquiry. We acknowledge the wide variance of beliefs and practices within a particular faith, and caution against stereotyping on the basis of this chapter or any other writings.

The issue becomes even more complex when caregivers consider the ethnic and cultural backgrounds of survivors and how they interact with their faith perspectives. For example, a first generation Cambodian Buddhist, a first generation Japanese Buddhist, and a third generation Chinese Buddhist likely will react in different ways to a traumatic event. Generally speaking, the longer immigrants are in this country and the farther they are from their homeland, both in terms of physical and generational distance, the less likely their reactions will be influenced by heritage. Individuals who speak their native language at home tend to react more in line with traditional responses (R. Lamb, personal communication, August 5, 2002).

Therefore, spiritually and ethnically sensitive caregivers must learn their community's spiritual and ethnic makeup. They should identify people in the community who represent each group and enlist their help in supervising or consulting on individual cases. A spiritual leader who has an established relationship with surviving family members usually is happy to work with a counselor or caregiver.

BELIEFS ABOUT JUSTICE

The dynamics of spiritual reaction to collective trauma differ from those of individual and family trauma. Spiritual reactions to natural disasters, such as earthquakes, tornadoes, and hurricanes, often referred to as "acts of God," differ from reactions to man-made trauma. When death, injury, and destruction are intentional, as in the Holocaust, Pearl Harbor, the Oklahoma City bombing, and the 9/11 tragedy, the sense of security of a large group of people is shattered (Clinebell, 2002). Survivors ponder the providence of God, justice, and evil. This terrifying awareness of human vulnerability triggers widespread anxiety, depression, and posttraumatic stress (North, Smith, & Spitznagel, 1997; North, Nixon, Shariat, Mallonee, McMillen, Spitznagel, & Smith, 1999; Galea, Ahern, Resnick, Kilpatrick, Bucuvalas, Gold, & Vlahov, 2002).

This chapter focuses on man-made public trauma. Although the question of where is the spiritual in the midst of evil human acts may be common to all faiths, basic understanding of evil and justice differ among the five faith groups addressed in this chapter. The beliefs described are mainstream and general. Some of the members of a particular faith may disagree with the positions offered. It is nevertheless useful to compare basic differences in faith when attempting to assist people in a sensitive and compassionate way.

Hinduism, which is thought to be the oldest of religions, differs from the other well-known faiths in that it acknowledges no precise beginning, founder, or geographical center. In Hinduism, deities like Brahma, Vishnu, and Shiva are considered manifestations of one Supreme Being who provides guidance and benevolent patronage to pilgrims as they journey toward enlightenment. Hindus draw their beliefs and practices from multiple sources. While most consider the Vedas, four ancient sacred books of stories that describe the interplay of the Gods, as formal authority, most Hindus' beliefs and practices are drawn from their regional culture, countless regional scriptures, and the individual teachings of their guru or spiritual guide.

Hindus traditionally believe that one's spirit (or consciousness) moves through cycles of life and death until it achieves true enlightenment. The moral law of karma ensures full accountability for every thought, word, and deed. Every action affects its perpetrator, sculpting individual destiny. The law of karma renders the cosmos just. A typical Hindu response to a public tragedy may be sadness and pain but not guilt, which is a Western concept. Hindus believe the actions of large groups of people, a city, or a country can influence their personal destiny. According to University of Hawaii Associate Professor of Religion and former monk Ramdas Lamb (personal correspondence, August 6, 2002), many families of Hindus who died in the terrorist attacks of September 11, 2001, believed the deaths were a consequence of living in America and sharing the nation's karma. It is important to note that this does not mean that Hindus absolve the perpetrators. It simply means that a Hindu will attempt to reconcile belief in an almighty divinity with belief in karmic balance.

Judaism includes four basic movements: Orthodox, Conservative, Reform, and Reconstructionist. There is much flexibility among the divisions, however, most followers agree that the revolutionary idea of Judaism is that there is one God with no separate manifestations. They believe God is not indifferent to human experience and participates in human history.

Jews believe that God spoke directly to Abraham, Isaac, and Jacob and revealed the Torah—the first five books of the Bible—to the patriarch, Moses. Jews view human beings as essentially good, having been created in the image of God. But good, like evil, is infinite, they contend, and the capacity for both is present within humankind.

Jews believe God is ultimately just and that God expects humankind to act justly and ethically. When individuals act contrary to goodness, they sin and are required to seek forgiveness. Jews seek forgiveness from God for sins against God, and from people for sins against people. A Jew does not forgive his enemy unless the enemy asks forgiveness (Weisel & De Saint-Cheron, 1990, p. 46). Jews believe that those who perpetrate terror must repent and change their ways or expect to be dealt with justly by both God and humankind. Jews face evil in the world with hope that good will prevail over evil as the faithful imitate God and enter partnership with Him. Justice tempered with mercy will result in overcoming evil, they believe.

In the *Buddhist* belief system, which evolved from the teachings of Gautama Buddha, humans are believed to be temporary incarnations of an eternal universe of absolute being. Notably absent in the Buddha's teachings is the existence of a creation God or a pantheon of Gods upon whom humans rely for salvation.

Like Hindus, Buddhists believe in karma as the law that conditions action. Human suffering is unavoidable. Death represents the "in-between" or transition stage when the consciousness has a series of experiences independent from the body before it settles upon a new incarnation. Practicing Buddhists prepare spiritually for their own deaths and feel a profound duty to assist and support their dying or deceased loved ones throughout the death process until rebirth. To escape the cycle of rebirth and suffering, humans must acquire wisdom, practice compassion, do good acts, achieve control over mind and body, and purify their negative karma.

Today, there are three main schools of thought regarding Buddhism, and all three are found in the United States. Theravadan Buddhism developed in Cambodia, Laos, Sri Lanka, and Burma. Zen Buddhism evolved in China, Korea, South Vietnam, and Japan. Tibetan Buddhism originated in Tibet but is practiced throughout Asia.

Schools of thought vary regarding the concept of collective karma. Ethnic Theravadan Buddhists tend to view karma as a uniquely individual condition and therefore assume the plight of a victim is a consequence of some previous negative action. Expression of blame, however, is not part of the culture. Theravadans understand a tragedy such as 9/11 in terms of the individual karma of each victim and hijacker (T. Bhikkhu, personal communication, August 4, 2000). Zen and Tibetan Buddhists view collective karma similarly to Hindus and strive to understand the karmic origins of a public tragedy. These groups address their collective responsibility as human beings to alter the conditions that led to tragic events (S. Sunim, personal communication, August 7, 2002). Similar to Hindus, they believe those who died in the 9/11 attacks were victims of a negative collective karma (G. Rinpoche, personal communication, August 5, 2002). Vietnamese monk and Nobel Peace Prize nominee Thich Nhat Hanh writes: "What happened in New York [Washington, D.C., and Pennsylvania] caused great suffering, but if we can learn from it, the suffering can become a bell of mindfulness in waking up the whole nation" (Hanh, 2001).

Christianity includes more than 900 different denominations. Understanding and opinions of justice and evil vary widely among them. While Christians agree with Jews that God created humankind as "good," they tend to place more emphasis on the fact that all people sin and fall short of God's expectations. Conservative Christians tend to focus more on the dark side of humanity, while liberal Christians may focus on positive potential. Evil intervenes in the form of sin, they believe, or rebellion against the will of God. Human beings are called by God to act in loving relationships with each other. God does not initiate evil events, most agree. People who choose to live outside of harmony with one another commit evil acts.

Christians believe Jesus Christ to be the central figure of their religion. Christ, they contend, is truly human and divine, and was the Son of God. Many Christians believe that Jesus' death paid for their sins and that they were forgiven of their sins when they accepted the gift and made a commitment to follow his teachings. A distinction of Christian belief is that God was willing to suffer the death of his son, Jesus, just as humans suffer. Most Christians, therefore, believe God understands human suffering and is present in the midst of it (Bonhoeffer, 1959). While human evil and God's ultimate judgment defy human understanding, Christians believe God walks through suffering with them, ultimately bringing them into His presence. In his book, *Spiritual Crisis: Surviving Trauma to the Soul* (1998), Christian pastoral counselor J. LeBron McBride writes, "The good news of Christianity is that in the midst of chaos, there is creation, in the midst of darkness a light appears, in the midst of death, there is a resurrection, in the midst of a world self-destructing, there is a new earth" (1998). Reflecting on his work in New York City after 9/11, Rev. Gary Hellman (2002) similarly states: "The amazing presence of God is so abundant and available, not in talking about the presence of God but in getting up and getting another cup of coffee for someone you don't know and finding out how he feels about being racked with pain, grief, and suffering and is still alive and available to you."

Islam, the youngest of the faiths described in this chapter, is based on total submission to the will and purpose of one God who is called Allah. Islam respects its roots in Judaism and Christianity, but claims that Allah's message to the world was not complete until it was dictated by the Angel Gabriel to the Prophet Muhammad in the seventh century. This message is recorded in the Qur'an, the Islamic scripture. In Islam, there is no separation between the religious, secular, or political spheres of life. All aspects of life fall under the providence of Allah. Allah creates human beings, determines their life span, and causes them to die. "Allah does what He wishes" (*Qur'an* Surah 3:35, 3:40). Allah determines what is just, and the faithful submit to Allah's will. Followers of the Prophet Muhammad are called Muslims.

A Hadith [sayings of the Prophet Muhammad (PHUB)] states, "One should live as though he or she is going to live forever, at the same time live as though he or she is going to die tomorrow." Reaching paradise is the ultimate goal of every Muslim. This is achieved by doing good deeds and practicing Islam's Five Pillars:

- Believe in one God (Allah), the Creator of heaven and earth.

- Pray five times a day.

- Give alms to the needy.

- Fast during the month of Ramadan, the ninth month of the Islamic calendar, with no food, drink, tobacco, alcohol, or sexual intercourse from sun-up to sunset to remind them of the suffering of those less fortunate.

- Make a pilgrimage to Mecca, Saudi Arabia, to the Kaa'ba, the first prayer house established on earth by the prophet Abraham and his son, Ishmael, for the sole worship of God. The pilgrimage is made at least once during a lifetime if physically, mentally, and financially able.

The Islamic community of believers is regarded as having a special mission from Allah to create a just society. The Qur'an condemns exploitation of the poor, widows, orphans, and slaves. It denounces economic abuse such as false contracts, bribery, hoarding of wealth, and usury.

DEATH NOTIFICATION

Families should be notified of the death of their loved one by a spiritual leader of their faith whenever possible. It is also important that the person providing notification speaks the same language and understands cultural distinctions within the family. While desirable, this requires significant understanding on the part of the notifying agency, such as law enforcement.

For example, since many Buddhist refugees from Southeast Asia experienced widespread genocide and lengthy internment in camps before they were admitted to the United States, they fear uniformed police. Therefore, the presence of a Buddhist priest is crucial when one of the notifiers is a police officer. Notifiers in second generation Asian communities must identify priests in the community who best understand the particular customs of that community. Most Southeast Asian Buddhist priests, however, have taken vows that include the strict separation of the sexes, rigorous dietary rules, renunciation of material possessions, and absolute celibacy. They cannot be alone with a female, cannot accept food or drink from a female, and cannot touch money. They may require considerable assistance to appear at the home or hospital to meet a grieving family.

Most public trauma deaths are violent. The bodies often are significantly damaged. This tragic violation of the sanctity of life has a profound and nega-tive effect on survivors, regardless of their faith. The death of a loved one that was avoidable and came at the hand of someone else, whether it is understood as human choice, individual karma, or collective karma, is deeply disturbing. In most cases, criminal law requires autopsies and investigations that can be extremely paradoxical to traditional beliefs and practices surrounding death. Persons involved in death notifications should be able to recognize these unique aspects of public trauma and incorporate this understanding during notification and in follow-up services.

When the surviving family's spiritual leader does not participate in the notification, notifiers should ask the survivors if they would like their pastor, imam, rabbi, or other spiritual leader to be called.

THE BODY

Whatever death takes away, it leaves a body. Rituals surrounding the body become a focus for grief and mourning. A defining factor of trauma deaths is that some bodies are never recovered and others are recovered only in part. Sometimes, there is no body to weep over.

All the faiths addressed in this chapter view the physical body as the case or shell in which the spirit dwells. The *Hindu* perception of reincarnation is described in the Bhagavad-Gita: "Worn out garments are shed by the body; worn out bodies are shed by the dweller." Traditional Hindus believe that the soul leaves the body within a short time after death. After the soul departs, the body is considered highly impure. Mourners wear white and gather at the home for a final viewing. They believe that until the body is consumed by flame, the soul may choose to re-enter it, rather than proceed on its journey to a future existence. During the mourning period, the relatives minister to and nourish the dead person's spirit. Without this care, the spirit could become a troublesome demon. Hindus have difficulty with required autopsy as possibly having a negative effect on the departing soul. Hindu funerals are conducted by priests who offer special prayers and rituals over the body before cremation, the choice of most Hindus, generally within 24 hours of the death. Ashes are then distributed in a sacred body of water. Some Hindus in America transport ashes of loved ones back to India and travel to the Ganges to release the ashes. Hindus feel a great deal of anguish when the body is not properly disposed of after death (Professor Lamb, personal communication, August 6, 2002).

Jewish treatment of the body emphasizes reality, simplicity, and respect for the body, which they believe was created in God's image. An autopsy is discouraged unless it is crucial from a legal perspective because it violates the Jewish mandate to bury the dead as soon as possible. When an autopsy is required, Jewish tradition requires that all body parts be placed back within the body. Traditional Judaism is opposed to cremation because it fails to honor natural decomposition of the body. The body is not to be embalmed, except when governmental regulations require or when it must be transported a long distance for burial.

Ideally, the body is not left alone from the time of death until it is buried. In traditional Judaism, it is taken to the funeral home where two or three persons of the same sex from the congregation cleanse and bathe the body (tahara). The face remains covered. All adornment, such as dentures and nail polish, are removed so that the body leaves the world as purely as it entered. The body is dressed in a white, unseamed, linen or muslin shroud including a shirt, pants, belt, and hood-like head covering, the front of which resembles a veil.

Most conservative and reform Jews are buried in ordinary clothing. Some wear their prayer shawls (talits) and head coverings (yarmulkes). Some reform Jews are prepared for viewing similarly to Christians (see below). The body is placed in a simple wooden coffin, which is then closed. Traditional Judaism does not support public viewing of the deceased, but liberal Judaism considers viewing an opportunity for the mourners to beg forgiveness for any wrongdoing left undone.

After the funeral, the body is taken to the cemetery where it is buried in the ground. Mourners shovel earth onto the grave as their last respectful act for the deceased. They often do so with the back of their shovels to indicate their reluctance to perform the ritual.

Any violation of the body that interferes with the performance of these rituals causes distress to Jewish people. When a body or its parts are not recovered, liberal Jews begin to plan the funeral after their loved one is declared legally dead. Traditional determinations are more complex. When a loved one is killed in a fire or a body is not recovered, Jewish people suffer significant emotional and spiritual pain. After 9/11, Orthodox Jewish students from Yeshiva University in New York kept a prayerful vigil beside three sealed trucks of body parts because they believed some of the parts were Jewish (Gross, 2001). Sitting with the dead is considered one of the purest Jewish rituals because there can never be reciprocity.

Buddhist families want the body to remain undisturbed for several hours after the individual has stopped breathing in order that a priest can administer immediate prayers and chants. In cases where the individual is badly hurt and expected to die, the family places an image of the Buddha within eyesight of the dying person. Theravadan Buddhists frequently perform a forgiveness ceremony before the body is moved, preferably in the presence of a priest. During the ceremony, the body is laid out with one hand extended out, open palm facing upwards. A bowl is placed under the hand. As friends and family members pour water into the open palm, they ask the deceased for forgiveness for harm they have caused. The ceremony is believed to improve the karma of those participating and invigorate the consciousness of the deceased as it embarks on its journey to rebirth.

After initial rites, Buddhists desire that the body be removed as quickly as possible and placed in a calm and peaceful environment until they perceive that consciousness has left the body, usually within 45 to 50 hours. The family washes the body and prepares it for visitation by relatives and friends.

Buddhists, like many other faiths, resist autopsy. Bodies are generally cremated three to six days after the death.

When the body is violently destroyed, it is assumed that the consciousness has been dispersed quickly and may be confused. The family performs dedications of merit on behalf of the deceased that are presented with an offering to the priest at the temple. A dedication of merit involves the performance of a meritorious act. It is dedicated to the consciousness of the deceased to enhance the preparation for rebirth.

Christians may vary considerably in their comfort with the remains of the body of a loved one. Many may choose to be with the person at the time of death, but they generally prefer that the body be removed shortly thereafter. In public tragedies, however, family members are rarely present at the time of death. Some family members choose to view the body at the scene of the death or at the medical examiner's office if they have not had time to say goodbye or psychologically prepare for the death. Other family members are uncomfortable at the thought of seeing an "unprepared" body. It is extremely important that the wishes of all the survivors be honored. Denying access to the body can be devastating to a family member. Family members who wish to see the body, however, should be told of its condition in detail before choosing to view it. This provides the opportunity for a loved one to reconsider the viewing if damage to the body is more than they believe they can face. On the other hand, no one should be forced to view a body, which can be emotionally devastating. Each survivor should be given a choice about viewing (Lord & Frogge, 1997).

Cremation is acceptable in many Christian traditions. For some Christians, cremation demonstrates stewardship of earth space and financial resources. Since Christians place significant emphasis on the continuance of the deceased's spirit or soul in heaven, many have no qualms about cremation.

Whether cremated or buried, the body generally is transported to a funeral home. There, body fluids are replaced with preservatives; this is called embalming. If the body is to be viewed, funeral professionals apply makeup to the face, arms, and hands. Hair is washed and styled and ordinary clothing is placed on the body. The body is prepared to look as if it is sleeping. While most funeral directors are willing to allow family members or their designees to participate in preparation of the body, most Christians decline. Once prepared, bodies are usually on display for viewing at the funeral home for several days before the funeral. Wakes or visitations offer family and friends time to view the body and stay as long as they wish. Those who attend are free to touch the deceased, if they desire, and share memories of the deceased. Many Christian families place photos of the deceased around or near the casket. Others play videotapes that celebrate the life of the deceased.

Muslims do not embalm and cremation is forbidden. As soon as possible after death, the feet, arms, and face of the deceased are washed with soap and camphor by same-sex members of the faith community (gushul). This act imitates washing that is required before the five daily prayers. Verses from the Qur'an often are recited during the washing. Cotton is placed in the body's orifices and the body is wrapped in an unstitched white shroud (kafan). The body is placed in a casket, which is closed, and taken to the Mosque. The casket and the mourners face east for the funeral (Janazah), which is held as soon as possible, usually within 24 to 48 hours. The funeral home takes the body to the cemetery where it is removed from the casket and placed on its right side, facing east (toward Mecca). Burial in the ground is mandatory. A stone may mark the burial site's location, but no writings on the stone are allowed. As with Jews, Hindus, and Buddhists, interruptions of this process, including an autopsy or loss of the body or any of its parts, is highly stressful on the surviving family members and friends who are denied the opportunity to perform these loving death rituals. A prayer service is held, even if there is no body after the family has been notified of the death. Caregivers who tend to encourage family members to view the body of a deceased loved one are reminded that such a suggestion is highly insensitive to the Muslim tradition.

THE SPIRIT

The spirit is eternal for the *Hindu*. The spirit has no beginning and no end and enjoys a long cycle of incarnations in the quest for perfection. Hindus believe that, in addition to the physical realm, there are three realms of disembodied existence. First is the "in between" realm before incarnation. Second is a multi-level "hell like" realm, similar to a purgatory where the spirit suffers the effects of bad karma. Third is the bliss/paradise/heaven realm, which is temporary. Here the spirit obtains more knowledge to move toward greater spiritual progress in the next life.

In *Judaism*, God uses the afterlife to provide ultimate justice, either directly in the traditional sense ("Man is reminded that he must give an account to the Eternal Judge. None will escape His punishment, and no virtue will be unrewarded." *Mishna, Aboth,* 4:16-17) or in the more liberal sense that the spirit is eternal through remembrance of the good or evil done by those who went before them.

Traditional Judaism believes that in time, the bodies of the dead will rise to be reunited with their souls. Liberal Judaism holds that human beings transcend death in a more naturalistic fashion. They are immortal in body through their children, in thought through memories, in influence as a force among descendants, and in the presence of the loved ones that survivors continue to feel. Some Jews believe in resurrection and immortality, but generally more figuratively or poetically than literally. More emphasis is placed on the integrity and ethical behavior of the deceased that will influence future generations.

Buddhists from all traditions believe that the consciousness, or spirit, remains in the body for at least a few days after the individual ceases to breathe and before it embarks on its journey. Once separation occurs, the consciousness assumes its own form and passes into an "in-between" state before the next rebirth. How the consciousness leaves the body after death and its path to rebirth is described in greatest detail in a 9th century text known as *The Tibetan Book of the Dead.* During the bardo, which is the 49 days before rebirth, Tibetan Buddhist families read from this text to help guide their deceased loved one through the transition to a new life. Most traditional Buddhist families perform memorial services in their home or at their temple on behalf of the deceased. These services take place every seventh day after death until the 49th day. The 49-day period may be extended if the death is not settled, such as when a person has died from violence or when an investigation regarding an unexpected death is incomplete. In these cases, survivors say, "My 49 days are not over" (Klass & Goss, 1998).

Most *Christians* believe that Jesus was raised from the dead three days after He was crucified. Protestant Christians believe the spirits or souls of their loved one transcends to heaven at the moment of death. Catholic Christians believe that souls with unconfessed minor sins reside in purgatory for a period of time to achieve purification before entering heaven. Time in purgatory can be decreased by the intercessory prayers of the living. Most Christians believe that claiming Jesus Christ as lord and obeying His command to be baptized are assurances that the soul will enter heaven. Little emphasis is placed on good deeds or "earning your way" into heaven. Assured of a place with God after death, Christians are expected to be able to love God and love their neighbors. Thus, good deeds are a consequence of salvation rather than a requirement for it. Christians see the resurrection of Jesus as proof that the spirit of the deceased will rise and dwell in the presence of God for eternity.

Muslims believe all human souls come from Allah through Adam, the first prophet, and enter bodies designed by biological parents. The mind is the basic essence of one's environment, they believe. When the dead body is placed in the ground, the Angel of Death (malak al-mawt) arrives, sits at the head of the deceased, and addresses the soul. Muslims believe in angels who serve Allah and come to human beings as messengers. The soul or spirit of the deceased then returns to the mercy of Allah (paradise) or to the wrath of Allah (hell) based on deeds performed during life.

RELATING TO FAMILIES AND THEIR RITUALS

In *Hindu* and *Buddhist* families, the elements of karma and rebirth greatly influence how they deal with a violent death. They contemplate karma in an effort to determine why the event occurred. "For one whose belief in the law of karma is strong, the individual will be less likely to feel obsessed with blame and retribution. Instead, he or she will try to figure out what past actions may have brought on the negative experience," says Ramdas Lamb. "Because violent deaths are generally seen to be the results of bad karma, it is important for Hindus to identify positive aspects of the death such as attempting to help or defend someone" (R. Lamb, personal communication, August 5, 2002).

Equally important is coming to terms with the anger and bitterness they feel in losing their loved one to an untimely, violent death. One Buddhist practice intended to address "the problematic feelings of grief among the living" is a guided meditation that evokes the Buddha and calls upon the family "to open their heart to the pain, grief and tears they are experiencing" (Goss & Klass, 1997).

Based on their understanding of karma, Hindus and Buddhists may not want to be involved in the justice process and should not be pressured to participate. Submission of a victim impact statement to the court or parole board, for example, might generate bad karma, especially if the statements are interpreted as being vengeful. Revenge inevitably leads to bad karma, irrespective of the outcome. On the other hand, some Buddhists and Hindus reason that bringing the offender to justice is an act of compassion because it prevents the offender from committing more crime and accruing more bad karma.

Families appreciate an awareness and respect of their habits. For example, Hindus remove their shoes before entering the home or temple. Their homes may have small shrines to their patron God where they worship three times a day. Shrines may be adorned with flower petals, oil, milk, and honey. Hindus pray before sunrise, facing east, and often apply ashes to their foreheads, arms, ribs, and knees. Respecting rather than questioning these rituals is appreciated.

In *Judaism*, the family should not be disturbed during the brief period between death and burial, which is usually accomplished within a day or two, unless one is an especially close friend. After massive public trauma, however, in which it may not be known for some time if a person is dead or alive, emotional support from the faith community and others is appropriate as soon as it is determined that a loved one is missing.

Shiva is the seven-day mourning period following a Jewish burial where community support is crucial. Flowers are generally not part of Jewish funerals or mourning periods, and many Jews consider a donation to a worthwhile charity more appropriate. For Jews, *Sheloshi* is the remaining 23 days of the month when mourners return to their normal routine but avoid celebrations, and *Avelut* is the year following the death. After a year passes and a headstone is unveiled, mourning generally is concluded and focus returns to living. Visitors often lay small stones on the headstone to show they have visited the grave. The names of the deceased are recorded on a memorial board in the synagogue and are remembered every year on the anniversary of their death. While allowing for a year of mourning may be emotionally healing, Jews acknowledge that massive trauma survivors often require additional support. Rabbi Ned Soltz points out that no one can bring people out of grief or mourning by demand (personal communication, August 12, 2002). Emergence is, by nature, gradual. Caregivers should inquire about contradictions between the actual experience of the mourners and unrealistic expectations they may have placed on themselves based on tradition.

Many *Buddhist* refugees from Southeast Asia will distrust service providers and caregivers based on their own victimization experiences in refugee camps. Extra kindness and care are required when assisting these families after a tragic death. Service providers living in a city with an ethnic Buddhist community should get to know the respected leaders of the community, including the priest at the temple and the civic leader.

A number of rituals, dedications, and memorial services are performed after a Buddhist dies, especially when the death is violent. Buddhist families feel a great sense of responsibility toward putting their loved ones to proper rest. They may need financial assistance to pay for these activities. While state Crime Victim Compensation programs pay for some funeral and burial expenses of crime victims, service providers should inquire if their state program will pay for nontraditional death rituals.

Christians may be the most likely to be treated sensitively by caregivers because their death and burial rituals have generally formed societal standards. Caregivers should be sensitive to the significant variance of beliefs and practices among Christians. When a survivor identifies as "Christian," even a Christian caregiver must not assume that he or she practices the same type of Christianity or has the same theology. Caregivers who deal with Christian survivors in the immediate aftermath of death may need to advocate with hospitals, medical examiners, or funeral homes to allow survivors access to the bodies of the deceased, if that is their wish. Spending time with the body is often discouraged, especially when it was significantly damaged. Caregivers sometimes take a protective position and attempt to deny access.

Bereaved Christians generally welcome a caregiver's inquiry about whether they wish to incorporate their spirituality into ongoing services. The death notification, damage to the body, and how the body was handled after public tragedies weigh significantly on survivors. Most survivors welcome the opportunity to discuss these issues with a caregiver who does not prod them beyond their comfort level. Christians also may wish to discuss how they felt supported or let down by their faith communities. A common complaint following a tragic death is that the faith community failed to recognize the unique characteristics of the trauma surrounding the death and had unrealistic expectations that they should return to "normal" within a few months. Well-meaning caregivers do a disservice to survivors by suggesting they focus on their loved one's presence with God. Total recovery is never complete following a sudden, violent death. Christian pastors, as well as spiritual leaders of other faiths, must recognize the unique characteristics of trauma death and support survivors accordingly.

Muslims reject physical touching between males and females. Therefore, restraint in this area is required not only at the funeral and burial but in all care-giving relationships. Muslims prefer caregivers of the same sex. In most cases, Muslims consider a three-day mourning period as generally adequate, except for widows who are allowed up to three months after the death of a husband because of Iiddah, the waiting period before remarriage. Prolonged mourning may cause a Muslim to doubt his or her submission to the will of Allah, but "excessive" mourners are treated with compassion by their faith community.

Since there is no separation between religious and secular spheres of life in Islam, caregivers should *not* ask Muslims if they wish to incorporate their faith or spirituality into ongoing services. The community orientation of Muslims basically means that any good caregiver is a good Muslim. The helping process itself is understood as a spiritually significant relationship.

All the faiths addressed in this chapter welcome practitioners of others faiths to funerals as long as they remain respectful and unobtrusive. ■

ACKNOWLEDGMENT

The authors express gratitude to the following who graciously agreed to interviews for this chapter: Ramdas Lamb, Professor of Religion and Hindu Monk; Dr. Richard Lord, Christian Pastor; Muhsin Shaheed, Muslim Chaplain; Rabbi Ned Soltz; Samu Sunim, Zen Master; Thanissaro Bhikkhu. Monastery Abbot, and Kyabje Gelek Rinpoche.

Janice Harris Lord is a national consultant on crime victim issues and the author of No Time for Goodbyes: Coping with Sorrow, Anger, and Injustice after a Tragic Death. *She was awarded the U.S. Presidential award for excellence in crime victim services in 1993.*

Melissa Hook has been a writer and journalist for 20 years. She conceived of, and was story consultant for, a one-hour documentary on victim/offender dialogue that was nominated for a 2002 Emmy Award.

Sharon English is a crime victim advocate whose mother was murdered by a parolee she tried to help through her church's prison ministry work. Sharon was awarded the U.S. Presidential Award for excellence in crime victim services in 1994.

REFERENCES

Bonhoeffer, D. (1959). *Prisoner for God: Letters and papers from prison.* New York: The Macmillan Co.

Clinebell, H (2002, Summer/Fall) 9-11: Exploring the shadowed mystery of collective trauma and grief. *Journeys, 4,* 2, p. 11.

Dwoskin, J. (2002, Spring). Continuing the conversation: Reflections on 9/11. *The Spirituality and Social Work Forum, 9,* 2, p. 13.

Galea, S., Ahern, J., Rsnick, H., Kilpatrick, D., Bucuvalas, M., Gold, J., & Vlahov, D. (2002). Psychological sequelae of the September 11 terrorist attacks in New York City. *New England Journal of Medicine, 346,* 982-987.

Goss, R., & Klass, D. (1997).Tibetan Buddhism and the resolution of grief: the bardo-thodol for the dying and the grieving. *Death Studies, 21,* 377-395.

Gross, J. (2001, November 6). A nation challenged: Vigil; Stretching a Jewish vigil for the September 11 dead. *The New York Times.*

Hanh, T.N. (2001). Waking up the nation. *Tricycle: The Buddhist Review, XI,* 2, 23.

Hellman, G. (2002). God is present when the sky rains fire: Reflections of pastoral counselors at ground zero. Symposium at the annual conference of American Association of Pastoral Counselors, Snowbird, Utah.

Klass, D. & Goss, R. (1998). Asian ways of grief. In K. Doka & J. Avidson (Eds.), *Living with grief: Who we are and how we grieve* (pp. 13-26). Washington, D.C.: Hospice Foundation of America.

Lord. J.H. & Frogge, S. (1997). *Trauma death and death notification: Clergy and funeral directors* (Rev. ed.). Washington, D.C.: U.S. Department of Justice, Office for Victims of Crime.

McBride, J.L. (1998). *Spiritual crisis: Surviving trauma to the soul.* New York: The Haworth Press.

North, C.S., Smith, E.M., & Spitznagel, E.L. (1997). One-year follow-up of survivors of a mass shooting. *American Journal of Psychiatry, 154,* 1696-1702.

North, C.S., Nixon, S.J., Shariat, S., Mallonee, S., McMillen, J.C., Spitznagel, E.L., & Smith, E.M. (1999). Psychiatric disorders among survivors of the Oklahoma City bombing. *Journal of the American Medical Association, 282,* 755-762.

Weisel, E. & De Saint-Cheron, P. (1990). Evil and exile. Notre Dame: University of Notre Dame Press.

CHAPTER 10

Funeral Directors and Public Tragedy

Elizabeth M. Bradley and LaVone V. Hazell

*Show me the manner in which a nation or a community cares for its dead
and I will measure with mathematical exactness the tender mercies of its people,
their respect for the law of the land, and their loyalty to high ideals.*
—William Gladstone

INTRODUCTION AND OVERVIEW

There always have been individuals willing and able to assume the responsibilities that mortality creates. Today they are called funeral directors, but they also have been known as undertakers, morticians, or embalmers. No matter what the title, the vocation is as old as human experience, and these individuals play an important part in the life of every community.

The funeral is not only a rite of ending, but also a part of grieving and healing. Rich in history and symbolism, the funeral ceremony helps us acknowledge the reality of death. It honors the life of the deceased and encourages the expression of grief consistent with personal, religious and cultural values. The funeral provides support to the mourners, allows for the embracing of faith and beliefs about life and death, and offers continuity and hope for the living.

Although most people will die in old age, many deaths occur under tragic circumstances. At the scene of a tragedy, emergency personnel, search and rescue workers, and police officers aid the injured, rescue the trapped or stranded, and search for survivors. Then, the focus shifts to the recovery effort of human remains. Pathologists, anthropologists, dentists, forensic specialists, and funeral directors are engaged to identify the dead and prepare them for interment. When there are mass fatalities, there will be mass funerals and civic memorials. Funeral directors perform a valuable public service by planning and orchestrating the complex details of these events. For many funeral directors, their work is a ministry and a calling.

This chapter has two goals: to highlight the funeral service community's tradition of volunteerism in times of public tragedy, and to describe the individual funeral director's roles and responsibilities at the disaster site and in the community.

A Tradition of Volunteer Disaster Aid

When tragedy strikes and mass fatalities occur, funeral directors often provide immediate volunteer assistance at the disaster site. They may volunteer as individuals on behalf of their own funeral homes, or through their local, state, and national trade and professional associations.

At the scene of a disaster, funeral director volunteers assume two major functions. The first is to work with grieving families, a sensitive and essential task to which they bring broad experience. Funeral directors interview the family members and close friends of disaster victims to collect useful information that can be used in identifying remains.

The second major responsibility is dealing directly with human remains—assisting in their preparation for eventual release to the families. After the crash of TWA Flight 800, for example, funeral directors were on hand to prepare the recovered bodies for return to their home communities. At the site of the Oklahoma City bombing, funeral directors staffed the Notification Center, helping families find information about other family members in the building.

In addition to volunteering through their trade associations, there is another avenue of response for funeral directors who wish to aid at the sites of natural disasters and other tragedies. They may apply for membership in an elite corps of mortuary officers who serve as members of Disaster Mortuary Operational Response Teams (DMORT). Although this program now is part of the federal government's national disaster response capability, it originated 20 years ago in the efforts of a volunteer committee of funeral directors. Today, funeral directors remain the backbone of this program, which is described in greater detail elsewhere in this chapter.

Case Example: The Funeral Service Community Responds to 9/11

Shortly after the terrorist attacks of September 11, 2001, the National Funeral Directors Association, based in Wisconsin, called the New York City Medical Examiner's Office and offered assistance in the form of volunteers, supplies, equipment and money. The offer was gratefully accepted. The trade association then called upon its membership, and within 48 hours, more than 1,500 funeral directors across the country volunteered to work at Ground Zero— far more, it turned out, than would be needed. The association also collected $56,000 in member donations to pay for housing, transportation and meals for the 50 funeral director volunteers who ultimately went to New York and served two-week rotations in the medical examiner's office from the fall of 2001 through the summer of 2002. They assisted hundreds of grieving families (NFDA, 2001).

At Ground Zero, as in other disasters, funeral directors assisted in a number of ways. In makeshift morgues, they worked alongside anthropologists, pathologists, photographers, medical examiner's staff and police to identify recovered remains. Volunteer funeral directors also manned computers, entering data that would help in the identification of the dead and return of the remains.

Outside of New York and across the country, funeral directors volunteered their time and skills to help individuals and communities mourn and grieve. They organized candlelight vigils, collaborated with members of the clergy to organize special services, distributed grief literature, and offered access to staff grief counselors (NFDA, 2001). One chain of funeral homes donated over $60,000 worth of bereavement materials, including teachers' guides, to schools and community organizations in the New York City and Washington, DC, metropolitan areas, and in Pennsylvania.

DMORT: Public Service in Times of Public Tragedy

In the early 1980s, several members of the National Funeral Directors Association formed a study committee to evaluate the nation's ability to handle disasters involving mass fatalities. Committee members soon discovered that no standards existed for a proper disaster response. They decided to work toward the creation of consensus standards, a national response protocol, and a national organization open to all forensic practitioners, not just funeral directors. They acquired the country's first portable morgue and took it to disaster sites in Michigan, Illinois and Indiana, and even to Guam (DMORT, 2002a).

The all-volunteer efforts of the early years gained momentum and visibility. In addition, airline tragedies of the 1980s and 1990s created a demand for action by the federal government. In 1996, the Clinton Administration established the National Disaster Medical System (NDMS) of which the Disaster Mortuary Operational Response Teams (DMORT) are a part. The purpose of these teams is to help localities in the event of a "mass fatality incident," defined as any situation in which the number of deaths overwhelms local resources. DMORT members respond only when officially asked to do so by local authorities (DMORT, 2002b).

At the site of a disaster, DMORT members provide facilities (e.g., mobile morgues), equipment (e.g., communications gear), and personnel, including funeral directors and other forensic specialists. DMORT members handle forensic examinations, DNA acquisition, embalming and casketing, data collection, and record-keeping. They process victims' personal effects, coordinate the release of human remains, staff family assistance centers, and document the disaster scene. They also serve as liaisons to the U.S. Public Health Service (DMORT, 2002c).

Today there are 1,200 trained mortuary officers who respond to requests for help from communities in need (DMORT, 2002a). One of them is Cliff Oldfield, a funeral director and the DMORT Commander for Region II (New York, New Jersey, Puerto Rico, Virgin Islands). He has responded to nine mass fatalities including 9/11. How does he cope? "By completely immersing myself in the job and avoiding television and newspapers and reporters. Attending one-year anniversary services allows me to clear my mind. Each incident takes on a life of its own. Having an open mind and listening attentively make me a valuable member of the team" (Personal communication, August, 2002).

Challenges at the Disaster Scene

Funeral directors assisting at disaster sites must learn the chain of command, work cooperatively and productively with emergency response teams from all over the country, and assist willingly whenever and wherever a need arises.

They must be available for 12-hour shifts and be accountable for that time during the entire tour. At the end of each shift, the funeral director should attend a debriefing session before resuming the next 12-hour shift.

When deployed to the scene of a tragedy, disaster workers often must leave their homes and find temporary housing close to the site. They should maintain contact with family members, who can be a source of ongoing support throughout the tour of duty. At the scene of a public tragedy, funeral directors are no less vulnerable to traumatic stress than other disaster professionals. Following 9/11, funeral directors and support staff at funeral homes in the New York City area needed crisis debriefings, as did many other first responders working at Ground Zero. DMORT policy requires daily debriefing sessions.

Organizational support and self-care are essential for funeral directors working at the scene of a disaster. Because of the physical and emotional demands of the job, funeral directors and other disaster workers should limit tours of duty to two to three weeks, and they should take at least one week off before returning for another tour of duty.

Self-care remains an important issue in other, smaller-scale disasters as well. After a community tragedy such as a tornado or other disaster, for example, funeral directors are at risk for secondary trauma. Like community clergy, they may share responsibility for handling and preparing the remains of neighbors, close friends and associates. They may be required to organize many funerals over a short period of time. Unfortunately, their own needs often are submerged or ignored altogether as they rise to the challenges of the moment. This can be exacerbated in smaller funeral homes, where there may be limited support or contact with other funeral directors.

The challenge for the funeral service community is to create mechanisms of self-care such as support groups for funeral directors who assist in community tragedies, or large-scale national disasters, or both. These mechanisms should supplement crisis-based debriefings. One way to develop models of support and to encourage self-care would be for the National Funeral Directors Association to add such a standard to its criteria for excellence. This program facilitates industry-wide recognition of individual funeral homes for exemplary service to their communities. Perhaps the association could add this question to the program's award application: "In what ways does the funeral home encourage and support self-care for its staff?"

ORGANIZING MASS FUNERALS AND MEMORIAL SERVICES

In the context of public tragedy, funeral directors' responsibilities are not limited to the support of families at the scene and the identification and preparation of human remains for burial or other disposition. An additional responsibility is to plan, organize and direct very large funerals and public memorial services. When the New York City Medical Examiner released the final count of those who died as a result of 9/11, the toll was 2,819. This translated into three to five funerals and memorial services each and every day for three months. These services were organized and conducted by funeral directors. Many of them were attended by more than 500 individuals. Coordination of such large, high-profile funerals required much preparation and meticulous attention to detail.

Long before 9/11, the funeral directors at Frank E. Campbell Funeral Home in upper Manhattan offered to assume responsibility for conducting services for law enforcement officers and firefighters. The services for these uniformed officers have been provided as a courtesy to the families through the Dignity Memorial Public Servants Program (Dignity Memorial, 2002). This program provides honorable tributes, at no cost, to public servants who fall in the line of duty. It has been in effect for 20 years.

Marty Kasdan, a funeral director at Schwartz Brothers—Jeffer Memorial Chapels in New York, described his involvement in some of the services following 9/11: "The emotional capital, the frayed nerves, and the pressures did not seem evident as we did our work. But it did hit me at the end of the service, when the drained feeling of having given everything we had to the service and the family, finally set in. Recharging our batteries and doing it all over again the next day was the only option we had" (Personal communication, October, 2002).

Making certain that large services proceed smoothly and to the satisfaction of families and other mourners is a challenge under any circumstances. Against the backdrop of a horrific tragedy, in the glare of publicity and with the involvement of public officials, managing these rituals can be especially difficult.

Beyond handling rituals and conducting memorials, funeral directors are able to provide other kinds of assistance in the aftermath of public tragedy.

These include:

Practical help. Funeral directors are trained to secure information for death certificates and to help survivors complete necessary legal paperwork, including paid death notices, obituaries, and claim forms for insurance and for benefits available through the Social Security Administration, Department of Veterans Affairs, and trade unions.

Crisis counseling. Funeral directors can fulfill a useful counseling role, especially in the days soon after a death. They are trained to answer questions about coping with death, to recognize when a person is having difficulty accepting the loss, and to recommend sources of professional help to those who want and need it (Rando, 1991).

After a death, there may be a need for someone to listen to the pent-up feelings people are reluctant to share because they fear they may be mentally ill, or because they think they did not love the lost family member enough (Manning, 1992). The funeral director often becomes a sounding board, helping survivors begin to come to terms with their loss.

A Safe Place to Grieve. Most experts believe it is essential to work through the pain of grief. Parkes affirms this when he says, "If it is necessary for the bereaved person to go through the pain of grief in order to get the grief work done, then anything that continually allows the person to avoid or suppress this pain can be expected to prolong the course of mourning" (Parkes, 1972, p. 173). The funeral director is an individual with whom people can feel comfortable. Funeral homes and cemeteries, like churches, chapels, and temples, offer peace, solace and comfort to those who grieve.

Accessibility. Funeral directors are accessible. Generally speaking, they are in a community for the long term. In a community tragedy, funeral directors are probably the most accessible of people, for unlike many other professionals, funeral directors still make house calls in the middle of the night.

SUMMARY AND CONCLUSION

Although their efforts in response to public tragedy may go unacknowledged, funeral directors are the behind-the-scenes professionals who are entrusted with the obligation to remove and prepare human remains and to coordinate and direct final services for the victims. Whether a tragic event is small-scale and private, or large-scale and public, the funeral director is an essential resource in the community. Funeral professionals and their trade associations have a noteworthy history of volunteerism and public service in times of tragedy. ▪

ACKNOWLEDGMENT

The authors thank Todd Van Beck, Marty Kasdan, Kevin Mack, Cliff Oldfield, and Vincent O'Neill for their assistance.

Elizabeth M. Bradley, MA, is a licensed funeral director in Florida. As Director of Community Development for Service Corporation International, she is responsible for overseeing the community outreach efforts of more than 2000 Dignity Memorial providers across North America. Ms. Bradley is an adjunct professor at St. Petersburg College, where she teaches thanatology in the college's mortuary science program. Ms. Bradley is a member of the Region 5 Critical Incident Stress Management Team in Florida. She has been a member of the Association for Death Education and Counseling (ADEC) since 1992.

LaVone V. Hazell, MS, is a certified family therapist and a New York State-licensed funeral director. She is certified by ADEC as both as a death educator and grief therapist, and she is a member of the ADEC Board of Directors. Ms. Hazell teaches psychology, thanatology, and bereavement counseling at the American Academy McAllister Institute of Funeral Service in New York City. She also directs the Palliative Care Training and Education Program (PTEP) for minority communities, a project sponsored by North General Hospital and Memorial Sloane-Kettering Hospital. Ms. Hazell is an active member of DMORT Region II.

REFERENCES

Dignity Memorial Funeral, Cremation and Cemetery Providers. (2002). Available from Dignity Memorial Web site, http://dignitymemorial.com

Disaster Mortuary Operational Response Team (DMORT). (2002a). *How it all started...* Retrieved October 26, 2002, from http://www.dmort.org/DNPages/DMORTHistory.htm

Disaster Mortuary Operational Response Team (DMORT). (2002b). *Families we serve.* Retrieved October 26, 2002, from http://www.dmort.org/DNPages/DMORTWhy.htm

Disaster Mortuary Operational Response Team (DMORT). (2002c). *What can DMORT do to help?* Retrieved October 26, 2002, from http://www.dmort.org/DNPages/DMORTHelp.htm

Manning, Doug (1992). *The Gift of Significance.* Hereford: Insight Books, Inc.

National Funeral Directors Association. (2001). *NFDA wins top national honor for September 11 community service.* Retrieved on December 16, 2002, from http://www.nfda.org/pressRelease.php?eID=95

Parkes, C.M. (1992). *Bereavement Studies of Grief in Adult Life.* New York: International University Press.

Rando, Therese A. (1991). *How To Go On Living When Someone You Love Dies.* New York: Bantam Books.

Van Beck, Todd. (1999). *Winning Ways: The Funeral Profession's Guide to Human Relations.* Stamford, CT: Appleton & Lange.

PART III

Coping with Public Tragedy

Often, crisis counselors can become comfortable with a few selected approaches to helping individuals and communities cope with tragedy. One theme emerges in these chapters: Effective approaches are most likely to be eclectic—selecting the best interventions based on appraisal of the individual or community in the context of the event. There is no single best approach, no magic bullet.

In his chapter, Louis Gamino develops this theme. He discusses several counseling approaches for trauma and assesses their underlying assumptions and supporting data. He emphasizes the need to select approaches based on the circumstances and groups that frame the intervention.

As both Linda Goldman and Barbara Bouton point out, children can be deeply upset by both the tragic event itself and the reactions to it of the adults around them. Yet children, especially when not directly affected, may be ignored during times of crisis. Ms. Goldman offers advice to parents about talking with children about tragedy and terrorism; Ms. Bouton addresses school-based personnel. Both emphasize the importance of offering honest reassurance, open dialogue, and opportunities for children and adolescents to participate in meaningful action and ritual.

In some cases, philosophical stances or faith systems allow one to make sense of a tragic event. In other cases, spiritual assumptions are shattered. David Thompson and Edward Holland remind faith communities that one of their roles is to assist individuals struggling with these spiritual questions, helping them focus less on the unanswerable "why" and more on the "what now?"

The power of ritual is emphasized in the next two chapters. Kenneth Doka offers an overview of ritual and memorials. He describes the roles that ritual and memorials play in the context of public tragedy. He then articulates practical guidelines for counselors, policy makers, and ritual leaders so they can harness the power of ritual and memorials.

David Benke illustrates that power in his thoughtful examination of the interfaith event at New York City's Yankee Stadium in the aftermath of 9/11. That event, which brought together civic, religious and cultural leaders, as well as bereaved families and friends of those lost in the attacks, was a powerful display of unity and courage in a traumatized city.

Sandra Bertman reminds us that the arts can facilitate healing in the face of tragedy. She explores the roles that the arts can play—through consoling or raising the voice of protest. She reminds us that the arts are tools available to persons of all cultures and age groups.

Advocacy and action can also be therapeutic. Marlene Young reaffirms that victim advocacy and legal action can play critical roles as survivors cope with tragedy. More than seeking revenge, such actions can facilitate meaning making by allowing the story to be told yet again, thereby mitigating feelings of powerlessness. Through these actions, individuals can feel that something of value, some benefit, may yet emerge from their loss and pain.

Virtually every chapter in this book discusses or at least mentions post-traumatic stress disorder, or PTSD. In his chapter, Alfonso Batres reminds us that most of what we know about this complex condition has been learned from combat veterans, primarily veterans of the Vietnam War. He also describes the innovative program developed by the U.S. Department of Veterans Affairs to help veterans deal with PTSD and other issues confronting many of them as they readjust to civilian life.

Rachel Kaul examines the importance of the workplace as a focal point for intervention. When tragedy directly strikes the workplace, employees are likely to experience not only grief but personal vulnerability as well. In discussing services provided to the Pentagon following 9/11, Kaul reinforces again that a range of services can and should be offered.

Finally, Therese Rando describes aspects of public tragedy that can complicate the mourning process. She emphasizes that the effects of public tragedy can be long-lasting. For some bereaved individuals, extensive treatment may be recommended.

Together these chapters describe a variety of methods and approaches that can be used to assist individuals as they cope with public tragedy. They affirm the need for careful assessment, intentional and skilled interventions, and continuing evaluation. ■

CHAPTER 11

Critical Incident Stress Management and Other Crisis Counseling Approaches

Louis A. Gamino

INTRODUCTION

A decade ago, Therese Rando (1992-3) warned, "the onslaught is just beginning" in reference to an increased prevalence in complicated mourning based in part on sociocultural trends in how death happens. Specifically, she cited increases in violent crime, terrorism, assassination, political torture, and genocide as factors that affect mourning. Leviton (1991) argued that horrendous death (i.e., when the motivation exists to kill others in large numbers) constitutes one of the greatest threats to public health and well-being in our time. These predictions were verified in a massive and macabre way with the terrorist attacks of September 11, in which more than 3,000 people were killed. This public disaster underscored the sad truth that the manner in which death occurs (e.g., suddenly, deliberately, maliciously, violently, needlessly) can affect dramatically the mourning response and course of adaptation for survivors (Rynearson, 2001).

Victims and Survivors

The attacks of September 11 created several categories of victims and also blurred traditional distinctions between victims of a disaster and helpers (Raphael, 1986). Besides civilians and military personnel killed or injured in the attacks, hundreds of "first responding" police officers and firefighters in New York City were killed. Thus, would-be helpers became victims. Grieving families and relatives mourned both the innocent who were killed and the heroes who tried to come to their aid.

In addition, there were the thousands of individuals who assisted with rescue, fire containment and extinguishing, public safety, first aid, medical care, site demolition and clean-up, memorial and burial services, physical and emotional support to the workers, or media coverage. They experienced varying degrees of exposure to the attack sites themselves and to the tragic misery of the bereaved. These legions of helpers were also victimized.

Meanwhile, millions of others in this country and around the world were traumatized vicariously by witnessing the attacks and their aftermath in numerous television replays and extensive media coverage. Despite being more geographically remote and not directly harmed, these viewers also were emotionally wounded. The impact on the general public was illustrated in this poem by M. Kelley of San Diego, one of countless mementos left at Ground Zero in New York City.

> I don't know you, we've never met
> Yet you are my brothers, my sisters,
> my sons and daughters.
> You're my lost lovers, my neighbors
> and friends.
> My heart cries and whole of my
> spirit mourns your passing.
> You are everyone I've ever known
> and your death leaves me lost,
> alone and hurting for the life that
> was yours, now gone…

Roles for Mental Health Providers

Given the staggering dimension of the public tragedy of September 11, mental health providers have a variety of roles in helping those victimized, traumatized, and bereaved. The most immediate roles involve crisis intervention. In this chapter, an important contemporary model of crisis intervention, Critical Incident Stress Management (CISM; Everly & Mitchell, 1999), is reviewed. In addition, some alternative crisis intervention models are described.

While most people seem to endure the trauma and losses of a public tragedy without lasting psychological problems or a need for professional or paraprofessional intervention, some do develop complicated bereavement reactions or post-traumatic stress disorders. In these cases, mental health professionals may perform longer-term roles involving bereavement counseling or treatment of post-traumatic stress disorder. Special considerations in the treatment of those with post-disaster bereavement reactions and stress disorders are reviewed also in this chapter.

CRITICAL INCIDENT STRESS MANAGEMENT

Critical Incident Stress Management (CISM; Everly & Mitchell, 1999) is considered by many to be the contemporary standard of care in the field of crisis intervention. Conceptualized as providing emotional "first aid" to those traumatized by crisis events involving death and destruction, it has its origins in efforts to assist emergency service providers such as firefighters, police officers, and paramedics. As the nature of CISM programs have become more formalized, its principles have been applied to the care of victims' families, hospital and support personnel, and even whole communities affected by public tragedies.

Rationale

The goal of CISM, especially Critical Incident Stress Debriefings (CISD) often referred to as the Mitchell model (Mitchell, 1983; Mitchell & Everly, 1996), is to limit development of potential post-traumatic stress disorders and to facilitate return to "normal" functioning among those individuals exposed to a "critical incident." A critical incident is defined as a traumatic event that can exert such a stressful impact as to overwhelm an individual's usual coping mechanisms, resulting in psychological distress and a disruption in adaptive functioning. Fires, car wrecks, accidents, storms, and floods involving loss of life and/or extensive destruction of property are understood to be critical incidents. Transportation disasters such as airplanes crashing, trains colliding, and boats sinking also constitute critical incidents.

A key element of CISM is to deliver crisis intervention in the field by going on-site when a traumatic event occurs and providing help to individuals who otherwise are not likely to seek mental health treatment. Much of its focus is on assisting workers to disengage from the traumatic scene, to decompress negative emotions generated by the event, and to activate basic stress management principles before attempting re-entry to everyday work and home life. For those who require it, referral for follow up with a mental health provider is arranged.

Description of CISM

Seen as a comprehensive program of stress management strategies, CISM consists of seven core components: pre-crisis preparation; individual crisis intervention; large group demobilizations or information briefings; critical incident stress debriefing (CISD); defusing; family/organizational consultation; and follow-up referral. Each of these core components of CISM is described below.

Pre-crisis preparation. Just as firefighters and police officers prepare for hazardous duty through simulations and mock training, Everly and Mitchell (1999) argue that "psychological preparedness" education should occur as well. This includes helping workers anticipate the nature of possible traumatic events and recognize signs and symptoms of psychological distress. In crises of longer duration, Raphael (1986) has pointed out that it may be possible to prepare rescue workers for the particular trauma to be encountered, such as body retrieval.

Individual crisis intervention. This is a one-on-one form of crisis intervention that focuses on diverting a distressed individual from the immediate stresses of the crisis situation. Once some "psychological distance" has been established, the individual is given an opportunity for cathartic ventilation, reassured that his or her reactions are "normal" responses to an abnormal situation, and guided toward an active plan for coping with the situation. This aspect of crisis intervention will be most familiar to mental health professionals who have had some training in treating acutely distressed individuals.

Large group demobilizations or informational briefings. Demobilizations are for emergency response and rescue personnel who are finishing a shift or leaving the disaster site. Once behind the "operational lines," workers are provided with food and rest as well as information, often as a written handout, to aid psychological and psychophysio-logical decompression upon their departure. Group informational briefings are intended for school or business groups wherein large numbers have been affected by the disaster. The facts surrounding the incident are reviewed, common psychological dynamics are presented, and the opportunity is made available to access professional resources.

Critical Incident Stress Debriefing (CISD). Mitchell's CISD model is designed for use with a homogenous group of individuals who have experienced a traumatic event, generally conducted one to 10 days after a critical incident or as long as three to four weeks after a mass disaster at a venue away from the disaster site. CISD is interactive and is generally conducted by a knowledgeable mental health professional together with a non-involved peer facilitator (such as a fellow firefighter from a different unit). A specific seven-step format is used in order to help workers put the crisis event in perspective and to minimize adverse psychological aftereffects:

1. Introduce the facilitator team, explain the process and establish ground rules (i.e., it is not psychotherapy or an operational critique).

2. Allow participants to describe what happened and what their respective roles were in responding to the incident.

3. Facilitate cognitive processing of the events by exploring "what your first thoughts were."

4. Promote affective ventilation by probing for "what the worst part of the incident was."

5. Help participants identify symptoms of emotional distress or psychological discord generated by the experience.

6. Normalize the crisis reactions of the participants and teach basic stress management and coping techniques.

7. Summarize the process, seek "closure," and facilitate follow-up referral for those who may require it.

Defusing. This is a small group discussion of a traumatic event that is less formal than a debriefing and is held more immediately after an incident. It is similarly designed to reduce psychological tension and facilitate re-entry. Participants are asked about the facts of the crisis and their reactions to the experience. Stress reduction principles are taught. Strategic use of defusing may eliminate the need for debriefings or make the debriefing experience more effective.

Family/organizational consultation. Essentially, this is a debriefing for families, organizational units or community groups who have been contagiously affected by the traumatic event. It follows the CISD format.

Follow-up referral. Individuals may be referred for additional help that is psychologic/psychiatric, medical, spiritual, financial, or legal in nature.

Evaluation of the CISM Model

Crisis interventionists who have been trained in and use the Mitchell model of CISD tend to be fiercely loyal and believe ardently in its value, often based on firsthand observation of benefits during debriefings. Those outside the model tend to view it more skeptically and often see its practitioners as unquestioning devotees. For these reasons, a brief review of the CISM model's advantages and disadvantages follows.

Structure. A key benefit of CISM is that it provides those doing crisis intervention work a specific, structured way of approaching individuals who are potentially traumatized by a disaster. Because most trauma events have an inherent aspect of chaos and disorganization, the ability to bring a cool head and a rational perspective into that domain is enormously helpful. Crisis interventionists who have a plan of action and know how to implement it (while respecting the specific circumstances of a given disaster) can more readily gain access to affected individuals and are more likely to be effective in reducing their psychological distress.

On the other hand, in this very structure lies a potential downfall of the CISM model. There is a danger that the model may be applied too mechanically or too inflexibly across a variety of trauma situations as if one size fits all. Practitioners need to be sensitive enough to decipher context cues and adroit enough in their clinical skills to adapt the model to the specific demands of a particular disaster scenario.

Conceptual economy. CISM is a model that, once mastered, has an elegance of economy in its conceptual framework. In other words, it is a relatively simple concept applied in a straightforward fashion that makes sense. Especially when properly introduced and explained, this down-to-earth quality makes CISM interventions much more palatable to the intended recipients who may otherwise forgo any contact with mental health providers.

Unfortunately, sometimes the terminology used in CISM programs contributes to a confusion of concepts. For example, how a "demobilization" differs from a "defusing" and how a defusing differs from a "debriefing" may not be entirely clear, especially as each of these interventions share some common elements. The acronym CISD is sometimes used to refer to different aspects of the overall program even though, strictly speaking, it is a designation for the debriefing procedure. This confusion may account, in part, for why crisis intervention debriefings are often carried out in nonsystematic ways.

Practice-driven. A distinct advantage to CISM is that the model is derived from the field experiences of those responding to traumas and emergencies. Based on the premise that the role of theory is to provide a roadmap for those "in the field" facing the front line, CISM gives the crisis worker an authentic, grounded approach evolved from the experience of many.

At the same time, a major criticism of CISM is that it lacks empirical support for its efficacy and that claims of its success remain unproven. The scholarly debate on this point is ongoing. Despite vocal defense of the model by its originators (Everly & Boyle, 1999; Everly & Mitchell, 1999; Mitchell & Everly, 1997) and support from others (Chemtob, Tomas, Law, & Cremniter, 1997; Nurmi, 1999), some researchers remain unconvinced (Deahl, Gillhan, Thomas, Searle, & Srinivasan, 1994; Kaplan, Iancu, & Bodner, 2001; Kenardy, Webster, Lewin, Carr, Hazell, & Carter, 1996; Raphael, Meldrum, & McFarlane, 1995). This skepticism is due in part to the fact that some evidence supporting the efficacy of CISM consists of satisfaction ratings and perceptions of helpfulness by those who have been debriefed using the Mitchell model (Burns & Harm, 1993; Nurmi, 1999), which is analogous to providers' convictions that it is helpful. Demonstration of treatment effects on psychometric outcome measures of psychopathology, however, has been less uniform (Kaplan et al. 2001; Raphael et al. 1995).

Homogenous groups. CISM was originally intended for homogenous groups of emergency service personnel in the aftermath of a discrete "critical incident." Beyond the goal of limiting psychological morbidity after a traumatic event, CISM also has the potential to help public servants such as firefighters and police officers develop greater unit cohesion and camaraderie as a result of facing a stressful event together. The idea that persons can become stronger after exposure to a traumatic event, i.e., post-traumatic growth, is a notion gaining wider acceptance in the trauma literature (Tedeschi & Calhoun, 1995).

While the CISM model has seen success in the past, when applied to heterogeneous groups of survivors, as well as emergency service personnel, in the wake of a large-scale national disaster, its applicability weakens (Hiley-Young & Gerrity, 1994). Particularly in community-wide meetings, the diversity of the participants along dimensions such as social support networks, history of mental health problems, or previous traumatic experiences may work against attaining a collective sense of relief and closure. Caution is advisable when extrapolating the CISM model beyond the traditional groups and settings in which it was developed.

ALTERNATIVE CRISIS INTERVENTION MODELS

Reviewing alternatives for crisis intervention and debriefing following disasters such as 9/11 gives additional clues for how mental health providers can assist victims and survivors of public tragedies.

Raphael's Model for Psychosocial Care

In her 1986 book, *When Disaster Strikes,* Beverly Raphael drew on her extensive field experience and research to propose an umbrella of psychosocial care for those struck by disaster. Mental health consultants were exhorted to work closely with victims, workers and the community in a variety of ways:

- Provide triage and psychological first aid to victims (e.g., comfort, consolation, and protection), reestablish some sense of security, try to reconnect victims with separated loved ones, and promote networks of support.

- Directly counsel victims through empathic listening, exploration of feelings, acknowledgement of suffering, facilitation of "working through" the trauma (e.g., shock, death, loss, and grief), and encouragement of adaptive coping.

- Assess and manage individuals and groups at risk.

- Conduct psychological debriefings of workers and helpers. Debriefing is a group process promoting integration and mastery of the experience by exploring several dimensions: roles in the disaster, perceptions and emotions, negative and positive aspects, relationships with others, empathy with victims, disengagement from the disaster, and transition back to everyday life.

- Treat specific problems such as post-traumatic stress disorder, survivor syndrome (e.g., guilt or conflict about living when others have died, or feeling in some way responsible for the disaster), or complicated bereavement.

- Provide long-term follow-up care.

Raphael's model is a conceptual one and represents a distillation of what was known at that time about dealing with disaster. As a scholarly work, it is considered a classic contribution to the literature of how to respond to catastrophe in the human condition.

Multiple Stressor Debriefing Model (MSDM)

Armstrong, O'Callahan, and Marmar (1991) adapted Mitchell's model for CISD to address the needs of Red Cross and other emergency personnel who faced multiple stressors over an extended period of relief operations following the 1989 San Francisco earthquake. Stressors faced by workers included multiple contacts with trauma victims, long hours, poor work environment, fear of aftershocks or belief that a subsequent larger quake would strike, demands of an urban disaster (such as lack of space to house those who lost their domiciles), being away from home (e.g., from out-of-state), Red Cross policy changes, hostile political environment, and negative publicity.

In response to these stressors, the four-phase Multiple Stressor Debriefing Model (MSDM) was developed:

1. Disclosure of events is the initial phase, wherein workers share distressing incidents that occurred during their disaster work, a process intended to build group cohesion.

2. The feelings and reactions phase is an opportunity to ventilate strong feelings generated by troubling events. Facilitators strive to normalize workers' chronic stress experiences and encourage talking about them.

3. The purpose of the coping strategies phase is to educate workers about normal and pathological responses to stress. Healthy self-care through exercise, good nutrition, breaks from work, relaxing diversions, sharing feelings, participating in staff meetings, staying in touch with family and friends, and use of other coping methods that have helped in the past are encouraged.

4. The termination phase concludes the process. As workers prepare to leave the disaster site, they acknowledge their accomplishments, say goodbye to co-workers, anticipate the return home, and are referred for additional counseling if needed.

The MSDM has been utilized subsequently elsewhere (Armstrong, Lund, McWright, & Tichenor, 1995) and additional recommendations have been made to improve its effectiveness. To date, there appears to have been no empirical tests of its efficacy beyond that of workers' perceptions (Armstrong, Zatzick, Metzler, Weiss, Marmar, Garma, Ronfeldt, & Roepke, 1998).

National Organization of Victim Assistance (NOVA)

Evolved from the field of criminal victimization, NOVA's program for crisis intervention (Young, 1993) initially involved training advocates to help victims of criminal attacks both immediately after the adverse event and later during criminal justice proceedings. Increasingly, NOVA's crisis response teams help not only crime victims but also victims traumatized by natural or man-made disasters. Their mission is to provide crisis intervention, supportive counseling, and advocacy.

NOVA's crisis intervention model is seen as a humanitarian effort to reduce the severity of a victim's crisis, to assist the victim in winning as much mastery as possible over the crisis experience, and to restore to the victim a sense of control over his or her life. Beginning with on-scene crisis intervention, NOVA trains victim advocates in three basic principles: safety and security; ventilation and validation; and prediction and preparation (Young, 1993).

Safety and security. The first priority is to ensure not only that the victim is physically safe but also that the victim feels safe. Providing as much information as possible about the disaster in progress, efforts to locate loved ones, or the extent of additional threat helps increase a sense of security. Advocates are encouraged to shield victims and survivors from media scrutiny or to help them respond to media inquiries. Advocates traditionally assist victims in communicating with law enforcement or civil defense authorities.

Ventilation and validation. Allowing victims and survivors to tell their story helps with emotional ventilation and promotes emotional re-equilibrium. Advocates may help victims find the words to express their reactions and understand their experience. Validation comes from listening, from honestly acknowledging what has been described and from reassuring the person that his or her reactions are "not uncommon" (rather than "normal reactions to an abnormal situation").

Prediction and preparation. Victims can best regain control when they know what has happened and what will happen. Advocates convey information about immediate concerns (e.g., physical needs, obligations of a bereaved survivor for the dead) as well as what can be expected regarding physical and emotional reactions, legal events, and rebuilding property and lives.

OTHER CRISIS COUNSELING APPROACHES

Psychological counseling for complicated bereavement reactions or for post-traumatic stress disorders (PTSD) requires specialized knowledge and clinical skills built on a basic foundation of training in mental health intervention (Rando, 1992-93). Whole volumes have been written on complicated mourning (Rando, 1993) and on the treatment of PTSD (Meichenbaum, 1997). Rather than attempting to summarize these comprehensive reviews, special considerations in the treatment of these disorders among victims and survivors of public tragedies will be highlighted.

Nature of the Disaster

When disasters are "man-made" and deliberate, tremendous psychic horror and rage are engendered among the victims. This is different from the anxiety and grief brought on by natural disasters such as earthquakes, hurricanes, or diseases. Raphael (1986) described how modern weaponry brings cruel mutilating injuries and sudden, untimely, violent deaths. When civilian centers become the targets of war, the incineration of great buildings and cities has frightening and devastating effects.

Phases of Response to a Disaster

Raphael (1986) proposed a phase model for how communities respond to disasters: impact, post-impact, disillusionment, and recovery. Each phase is characterized by a primary emotion that is key to understanding victims and survivors as members of affected communities.

The impact phase is when the disaster strikes bringing with it death, injury, and destruction. Victims and survivors take stock of their immediate losses. Fear is the dominant emotion, arousal is high, and there are often heroic activities of rescue and recovery.

The post-impact or "honeymoon" phase begins after initial recovery and may last several weeks following a major disaster. Altruistic responses as well as convergence of attention and assistance may create a temporary therapeutic community with a kinship bond among those who endured the experience together. Some "super volunteers" who are not ready to deal with their own losses may work continuously for very long hours. There may be unrealistic expectations of help from government agencies.

The disillusionment phase begins when the disaster is off the front pages and organized support starts to be withdrawn. Realities of losses, bureaucratic constraints, breakdown of informal support networks, financial insecurity, and the permanent changes brought by the disaster must now be faced. Anger and frustration increase rapidly. Questions arise about whether the disaster could have been avoided. Disillusionment may result in depression, social withdrawal, estrangement from family, domestic violence, and alcohol or drug misuse. When these problems become severe and chronic, they are often thought of as a "second disaster." Disillusionment may persist for several months or last one or two years following a major disaster.

The recovery phase is a prolonged period of return to community and individual adjustment or equilibrium and may take years. The rate of emotional recovery is linked to whether rebuilding is delayed. Survivors come to realize that rebuilding their property, restoring order to their lives, and getting back to normal are primarily their responsibility.

Vulnerability of Victims and Survivors

Many factors influence the psychological vulnerability of individual victims and survivors of public disasters (Meichenbaum, 1997). Some of the key elements are the person's proximity to the epicenter of the disaster, the emotional intensity of his or her experience, and the duration of exposure to the events. Particularly if the person suffered significant physical injury, or witnessed the violent, sudden death or injury of a loved one, the psychological trauma is compounded. When an individual is exposed to grotesque sights, sounds, and smells (such as mutilated or disfigured bodies) in scenes of mass destruction, there is a greater risk of psychological harm. Dislocation and displacement are additional destabilizing factors.

Personal characteristics also can affect the individual's psychological vulnerability. Prior traumatic events such as childhood abuse, criminal victimization, bereavement, or other "personal disasters" (Raphael, 1986) may be reactivated by the events of a public tragedy. A history of adjustment problems, mental health disorders, or addictive behaviors can reduce a person's resiliency when disaster strikes. Individuals who are socially isolated and lack a network of interpersonal support or whose relationships are marred by conflict and discord may not have the benefit of the basic human responses of consolation and comfort. Any of these "liabilities" (Rando, 1993) put an individual at greater risk for developing emotional difficulties following a disaster.

Trauma and Loss

Rynearson (2001) has outlined a dual set of distress responses to violent death: trauma distress and separation distress. Trauma distress is a response to the manner in which the person died. Separation distress is a response to the irreversible loss of the loved one. Intense trauma distress, with its numbness, fear, avoidance, and intrusive reenactment fantasies takes precedence initially and may be rather prolonged. Only when trauma distress has subsided does separation distress, with its longing, searching, and reunion fantasies, become predominant. Rynearson asserts that "our central nervous system is programmed to process the trauma of violent dying before the more complex reprocessing of the emotional connection with the deceased."

A similar viewpoint was espoused by Rando (1996). She argued that sudden, unanticipated death, such as occurs in disasters and public tragedies, is personally traumatizing for the mourning survivor. In addition to grief and loss, there will be trauma responses such as shock, intense acute anxiety, a sense of being overwhelmed, an inability to cope, and a catastrophic loss of security and confidence in the world. Rando proposed that counseling those who have suffered sudden, unanticipated loss proceed according to a basic clinical caveat—there must be a joint focus on working through the trauma as well as the loss. In pursuing these twin goals of trauma mastery and loss accommodation, very often the trauma mastery must be addressed first in order to create a psychological space in which the mourner can experience a subjective sense of control and safety. Only then can the mourner deal with the loss-related emotions and issues.

CONCLUSION

Public tragedies such as the terrorist attacks of September 11 pose enormous challenges to mental health providers seeking to assist the many victims and survivors struggling to cope with devastation and death. Several models exist for crisis intervention, or "emotional first aid," the most visible of which is Critical Incident Stress Management. CISM has many salutary aspects, although practitioners must be able to adapt the model to the specific demands of a particular disaster scenario and recognize its limitations when extrapolated beyond the model's traditional groups and settings. Crisis intervention and psychological debriefing constitute only the first steps in helping victims recover from disaster. Follow-up counseling for post-traumatic stress disorder, survivor syndromes, or bereavement reactions complicated by sudden, unanticipated, violent death should take into account factors such as the nature of the disaster, phasic responses to disasters, the vulnerability of individual victims, and the interrelationship between trauma and loss. ▪

Louis A. Gamino, Ph.D., ABPP, is a Diplomate in Clinical Psychology on staff with the Scott & White Clinic and Memorial Hospital in Temple, Texas. He is an Associate Professor of Psychiatry and Behavioral Sciences at the Texas A&M University Health Science Center College of Medicine. He holds a doctorate in Clinical Psychology from the University of Kansas, Lawrence, Kansas, and also trained at the Baylor College of Medicine in Houston, Texas. Currently, he is Editor of The Forum, *the newsletter for the Association for Death Education and Counseling (ADEC). In addition to maintaining a clinical practice specializing in treatment of bereavement-related problems, Dr. Gamino is the principal investigator of the Scott & White Grief Study and is developing a model of adaptive grieving.*

REFERENCES

Armstrong, K.R., Lund, P.E., McWright, L.T., & Tichenor, V. (1995). Multiple stressor debriefing and the American Red Cross: The East Bay Hills fire experience[electronic version]. *Social Work, 40,* 83-90.

Armstrong, K.R., O'Callahan, W., & Marmar, C.R. (1991). Debriefing Red Cross disaster personnel: The Multiple Stressor Debriefing Model. *Journal of Traumatic Stress, 4,* 581-593.

Armstrong, K.R, Zatzick, D., Metzler, T., Weiss, D.S., Marmar, C.R. Garma, S. Ronfeldt, H., & Roepke, L. (1998). Debriefing of American Red Cross personnel: Pilot study on participants' evaluations and case examples from the 1994 Los Angeles Earthquake relief operation. *Social Work in Health Care, 27,* 33-50.

Burns, C., & Harm, N.J. (1993). Emergency nurses' perceptions of critical incidents and stress debriefing. *Journal of Emergency Nursing, 19,* 431-436.

Chemtob, C.M., Tomas, S., Law, W., & Cremniter, D. (1997). Postdisaster psychosocial intervention: A field study of the impact of debriefing on psychological distress. *American Journal of Psychiatry, 154,* 415-417.

Deahl, M.P., Gillhan, A.B., Thomas, J., Searle, M.M., & Srinivasan, M. (1994). Psychological sequelae following the Gulf War: Factors associated with subsequent morbidity and the effectiveness of psychological debriefing. *British Journal of Psychiatry, 165,* 60-65.

Everly, G.S., & Boyle, S.H. (1999). Critical Incident Stress Debriefing (CISD): A meta-analysis. *International Journal of Emergency Mental Health, 1,* 165-168.

Everly, G.S., & Mitchell, J.T. (1999). *Critical Incident Stress Management (CISM): A new era and standard of care in crisis intervention* (2nd ed.). Elliott City, MD: Chevron.

Hiley-Young, B., & Gerrity, E.T. (1994). Critical Incident Stress Debriefing (CISD): Value and limitations in disaster response [Electronic version]. *NCP Clinical Quarterly, 4,* 17-19.

Kaplan, Z., Iancu, I., & Bodner, E. (2001). A review of psychological debriefing after extreme distress. *Psychiatric Services, 52,* 824-827.

Kenardy, J.A., Webster, R.A., Lewin, T.J., Carr, V.J., Hazell, P.L., & Carter, G.L. (1996). Stress debriefing and patterns of recovery following a natural disaster. *Journal of Traumatic Stress, 9,* 37-49.

Leviton, D. (Ed.). (1991). *Horrendous death, health and well-being.* New York: Hemisphere.

Meichenbaum, D. (1997). *Treating post-traumatic stress disorder: A handbook and practice manual for therapy.* Chichester, West Sussex, England: John Wiley & Sons.

Mitchell, J.T. (1983). When disaster strikes...The critical incident stress debriefing process. *Journal of Emergency Medical Services, 8,* 36-39.

Mitchell, J.T., & Everly, G.S. (1996). *Critical Incident Stress Debriefing: An operations manual for the prevention of traumatic stress among emergency services and disaster workers.* Ellicott City, MD: Chevron.

Mitchell, J.T. & Everly, G.S. (1997). Scientific evidence for Critical Incident Stress Management. *Journal of Emergency Medical Services, 22,* 87-93.

Nurmi, L.A. (1999). The sinking of the Estonia: The effects of Critical Incident Stress Debriefing (CISD) on rescuers. *International Journal of Emergency Mental Health, 1,* 23-31.

Rando, T.A. (1992-93). The increasing prevalence of complicated mourning: The onslaught is just beginning. *Omega, 26,* 43-59.

Rando, T.A. (1993). *Treatment of complicated mourning.* Champaign, IL: Research Press.

Rando, T.A. (1996). On treating those bereaved by sudden, unanticipated death. In Session: *Psychotherapy in Practice, 2,* 59-71.

Raphael, B. (1986). *When disaster strikes: How individuals and communities cope with catastrophe.* New York: Basic.

Raphael, B., Meldrum, L., & McFarlane, A.C. (1995). Does debriefing after psychological trauma work? *British Medical Journal, 310,* 1479-1480.

Rynearson, E.K. (2001). *Retelling violent death.* Philadelphia: Brunner-Routledge.

Tedeschi, R.G., & Calhoun, L.G. (1995). *Trauma and transformation: Growing in the aftermath of suffering.* Thousand Oaks, CA: Sage.

Young, M.A. (1993). *Victim assistance: Frontiers and fundamentals.* Washington, DC: National Organization for Victim Assistance.

CHAPTER 12

Talking to Children about Terrorism

Linda Goldman

Adults may wonder, after time has passed, if the vivid images of 9/11 disappear or remain for children to revisit. They may question if children can forget this horrific event and move forward. Informed by continuing talk of war, our children are now living in a world that did not exist for them before. This world brings new fears, new worries, new questions, and few resolutions.

Childhood fears are a normal part of development, and children create internal and external mechanisms to cope. The assault upon America, however, has for some children, transformed ordinary fear into survival fear as a natural reaction to a dangerous real life event.

RELIVING PAST EVENTS

Long after 9/11, a child may carry the memory, reacting to triggers of this event without realizing the underlying cause. Watching the news may retrigger previously experienced trauma.

Darian, a first grader living near Washington, DC, began having headaches, nightmares, and difficulty concentrating after the terrorist attack. The sounds and sights of helicopters and fighter jets invaded his world. "If I see an airplane, or hear one go by," he said, "I think, will it be us, are we next? I feel jittery all the time." Darian drew a picture about it. With young children, drawing is an age-appropriate grief resolution technique.

This is a plane that hurt nice people.

Darian. N

CHILDREN'S UNDERSTANDING OF DEATH

A child's understanding of death changes as he or she develops, as explained by Piaget's cognitive stages of development (Piaget, 1998; Ginsberg & Opper, 1969). Gaining insight into children's developmental stages allows predictability and knowledge of age-appropriate responses. Customarily, children between the ages of two and seven are part of what Piaget calls the preoperational stage. Magical thinking, egocentricity, reversibility, and causality characterize it.

Developmentally, young children live in an egocentric world. For example, after five-year-old Sam screamed at his older brother, "I hate you and I wish you were dead!" he was haunted with the idea that his words actually caused his brother's murder the following day.

Angela, a six-year-old first grader, was very sad after her father died in a plane crash, but she perceived death as reversible, and told her friends and family that her father was coming back. She even wrote him a letter and waited for the mailman to bring a response. In talking with her daughter, Angela's mother used this definition of death for young children: Death is when a person's body stops working. Usually, people die when they are very old, or very sick, or their bodies are so injured that the doctors and nurses cannot make their bodies work again (Goldman, 2000).

Piaget's next stage of development, concrete operations, generally includes ages 7 through 12. During this stage, a child is very curious and realistic about death and seeks information. Ten-year old Mary wanted to know everything about her mother's death. She said she had heard so many stories about her mother's fatal car crash that she wanted to look up the newspaper story to find out the facts. Eleven-year-old Julia wondered about her friend, one of the children who died in the Pentagon plane crash. "What was she thinking before the crash, was she scared, and did she suffer?"

Tom, at age 12, wondered if there was an afterlife and exactly where his father was. At this stage of development, children commonly express logical thoughts and fears about death. They struggle with their spirituality. They understand that all body functions stop, and they begin to internalize the universality and permanence of death. They may ponder the facts about how the terrorists got the plane to crash, wanting to know every detail. When working with children in this age group, it is important to ask, "What facts would you like to know?"

The response of children who are 13 and older often is characterized by the adolescent's concept of death as described by Piaget's formal operational stage. Many are self-absorbed at this age; they see death as a natural process but one that is very remote from their day-to-day life and something they can't control. Teenagers are preoccupied with shaping their own life and denying the possibility of their own death.

For adolescents, peer support and discussion groups are an excellent technique for resolving grief because, at this age, they are much more comfortable talking about death with peers than with adults. Many teenage survivors of the terrorist attacks felt comforted and free to share only in support groups for young people like themselves.

SIGNS OF TRAUMATIZED CHILDREN

The most common signs that children are re-experiencing a traumatic event are play re-enactment, nightmares, reoccurring waking memories, and disturbing thoughts and feelings. After the death of his Aunt Joan in the World Trade Center, five-year-old Tommy repeatedly created the twin towers with blocks, then knocked them down.

Ten-year-old Alice's mother died in the Pentagon crash. She blames herself. Her mother had felt sick that morning. "If only I made her stay home, she would still be alive." Children may believe they are capable of recognizing the warning signs of a future catastrophe. Jane imagines that if only she can stay very alert, listening through the night for airplanes in the sky, she can prevent terrorists from attacking her house.

Traumatized children may feel "powerless to change what happened to them, hopeless to see a future, and helpless to stop their bad feelings" (Sheppard, 1998). They feel unable to change the event, unable to stop their fear and sadness, and unable to see that life can be different. Sometimes children avoid reminders of the traumatic event and show little conscious interest. Many withdraw and isolate themselves or become anxious and fearful. Traumatized boys and girls may exhibit hyperarousal by increased sleep problems, irritability, inability to concentrate, startle reactions, and regressive behaviors.

CHILDREN'S LOSSES

Children processing their grief may not progress in a linear way through predetermined grief phases or stages. Newer models of the grief process tend to examine common issues, processes, or "tasks" that individuals must confront as they adapt to loss (Worden, 1991). For example, in one model, the four tasks of grief are understanding, grieving, commemorating, and going on (Goldman, 2000; Fox, 1988). These may surface and resurface in varying order, intensity, and duration. Children may be overcome with grief while sitting in the car listening to a song; or a siren, a soldier, a postal letter, or a balloon bursting may trigger intense feelings without warning and often without any conscious connection to the trauma and loss.

Tom, a middle-school student, told his teacher, "I can't do my homework, I just want to feel safe. I keep thinking it doesn't matter anyway." Amy, an eighth grader, also had difficulty with homework. "I can't concentrate anymore. I just keep seeing the airplane hitting the World Trade Center." A caring teacher might have Tom and Amy write about their feelings as a classroom or homework activity. A guidance counselor could begin a support group for students affected by the terrorist attack because children this age respond well to sharing with peers.

Some children may have an overlay of trauma as well as pre-existing grief issues. One little girl had experienced multiple losses before 9/11. Since her parents' divorce, she had lived with her mother. She had experienced the loss of her family unit, her family home, and her daily routine. Then her mother was killed while at work at the World Trade Center. The sudden traumatic death of her mother, together with her move to New Jersey to live with her father, compounded her pre-existing grief.

COMMON SIGNS OF GRIEVING CHILDREN

Learning to recognize the signs of grieving and traumatized children is essential to normalizing their experience of grief and trauma. In an earlier work (Goldman, 2000), I described many of the physical, emotional, cognitive, and behavioral symptoms commonly exhibited by children in grief. Grieving children may retell events about their loved ones and their deaths. They may feel their loved ones are present in some way and speak of them in the present tense. They may also dream about their lost loved ones and long to be with them or idealize them and assume their mannerisms.

Children may experience nightmares and sleeplessness. They may be unable to concentrate on schoolwork, complain of headaches and stomachaches, worry excessively about health issues, and appear to be preoccupied with death. In addition, they may fear being left alone, cry at unexpected times, wet the bed, or lose their appetite. They may become bullies or class clowns, or reject old friends, withdraw, or act out.

VULNERABILITY OF CHILDREN

When predicting a child's reactions to a terrorist attack, three key considerations are physical proximity to the disaster, psychological proximity to the disaster, and the child's age (Rosenfeld, 2001). Eight-year-old Joseph's father died in the Pentagon crash. He doesn't sleep well and he has nightmares. Joseph sleeps on the floor because, he says, that way he will be ready if the terrorists come. Dwayne, who attends school in lower Manhattan, drew a picture about 9/11. It included the warning, "Run for your life."

Young children may regress and become clingy. Teenagers may withdraw, or bully others, or resort to drugs and violence. Five-year-old Susie was terrified by the events of 9/11. She knew "bad people had killed lots of Americans." She cried whenever she was separated from her mother, and she wanted to sleep in her mother's bed at night. Months later, her kindergarten play showed that she was still frightened. She pretended that terrorists were coming and she hid under her rest mat. In contrast, 15-year-old Carlos said he didn't care about the terrorist attack. He said he wasn't afraid, yet he got a gun for protection and carries it wherever he goes.

Another predictor of children's vulnerability may be their experience of previous traumas. An event such as 9/11 is likely to cause a child to re-experience stress-related feelings and thoughts. Suzanne's mother was killed in a car crash. Watching images of the demolished plane and wrecked buildings brought screams of horror from her as she realized again, "That's what my Mom went through!"

CHILDREN'S RESPONSES TO TERRORISM

While there are several reactions common to traumatized children, they vary widely. Some children will listen to a parent's explanation and then go out to play. Others will want to stay nearby and talk at length or ask to be driven to school instead of taking the bus. Still others may be angry that adults can't immediately fix the problem.

Children normally assume they live in a friendly, safe, and caring world. The terrorist attacks of September 11 amplified any pre-existing fears that their world may be unprotected and scary with an uncertain future. One teenager created a photograph of blackness. He explained his loss of his assumptive world of safety and his projected future destruction: "This is a picture of nothing because the President said we might have nuclear war and the world would look like this" (Stepp, 2001). This deepened loss of the assumptive world of safety creates a new set of voices that parents, educators, and health professionals must acknowledge.

Andrew, age 16, was angry when he watched television replays of the destruction of the twin towers. Living in Washington, DC, he knew people affected by the assault on the Pentagon. He told friends and family that he wanted to go to the National Mall in downtown Washington to show terrorists that he wasn't afraid. He didn't want to talk about any other feelings.

A year later, Andrew still said he would not be intimidated. His admiration for emergency personnel led him at 17 to pursue certification to become an emergency medical technician. He wrote this poem:

> When terrorists provoke fear they win
> Their victims aren't the deceased
> Their victims are those who change their lives due to
> The fear stemming from the terrorist
> To be scared is to lose
> To lose is to die

TALKING TO CHILDREN ABOUT TERRORISM

Finding methods to create dialogue can be challenging for parents and professionals. We must deal with the difficult question of how to talk to our children about war, terrorism, prejudice, biochemical attack, and nuclear destruction. Children know and sense the world events that are happening all around them and we need to create language to allow them to speak about it. Children have questions that seem unanswerable. "Will we go to war?" "Will terrorists attack again?" Many children who usually like to draw and write may seem reluctant to do so. They may say it is too difficult or they are not ready. Young children may not process information accurately. They may misinterpret the facts. We can ask, "What do you think happened with the terrorists attack?"

One four-year-old thought the terrorists had destroyed hundreds of buildings because of the repeated airing of news footage of the planes crashing into the twin towers. Jose, a five-year-old living in Panama, began to cry to his grandmother as they talked on the telephone. After watching the plane crash on TV, he said, "Grandma you live in New York. Now that the plane crashed I'll never be able to come and visit America!" He thought the plane he had seen blow up was the only plane to take people to the United States.

Initiating Discussion

Sometimes it may help to ask children if they have been "thinking about world events." If they say they have, then it may be possible to open a dialogue. Some children don't want to talk. Some live in fear they will be killed; others say there is nothing to worry about. Some may want to know the facts, and so we need to provide appropriate language and meanings.

We can open up a dialogue with children in many ways. Most important, we can be ready to talk and listen to them, and make sure their understanding is accurate. We can emphasize that they are survivors of an incredibly difficult experience. We can learn what continues to trouble them, and we can help develop the mental ability and emotional stamina to work with what life has given them. We can ask, "In what ways are you now wiser, stronger, and better prepared?" and "How could you now help family, friends, and strangers?"

Memory Work

Memory work can be a helpful tool to safely process the events of a traumatic event. Memory books allow children to express their thoughts and feelings about 9/11. We can ask children questions that might help them to share thoughts and feelings about this national tragedy, for example: "Where were you when it happened?" "What was your first thought?" "What scares you the most?" "What makes you feel peaceful?" "What can you do to feel better?"

Memory books are one way children attempt to make sense of their altered world. One page of a memory book can be a child's drawings of the catastrophe. Shainna, age 8, drew a picture of the events of 9/11. She decided to title it "Trouble." Eight-year-old Julia's best friend Zoe and her family died in the terrorist attack. She created this poem as a tribute to her friend in her memory book.

Julia

Active, funny, kind

Good Friend of Zoe

Loss, anger, grief

Who misses her funny, caring and silly ways

Who worries about war and our President

Stomachaches, headaches, muscles get tense

Who heals by reading, laying down, talking

Remembers by memories and hearing her name

Who wishes for peace and unity

Strong

Writing letters in memory books helps children regain control, formulate ideas, voice opinions, and make themselves heard. Six-year-old Kyle decided he wanted to help. He suggested that he and his classmates could get "Gatorade and energy bars for the firemen, and new work gloves, and coats and warm clothes to keep them warm." Kyle was given an opportunity to offer suggestions, make choices, and feel empowered as part of the national recovery.

One page in fourth-grader Alex's memory book asked, "What is your biggest fear?" He responded, "My biggest fear is that someone might bomb us." Jasmine, a teenager in Washington, DC, created a memory page about her "over and over" feelings after 9/11. "My over and over thoughts were that something would happen to my Mom's building where she works after the Pentagon was hit. I feel anxious as though I have no control over it."

HELPING CHILDREN FEEL SAFE IN TODAY'S WORLD

In the wake of public tragedy, normalizing children's feelings is important. We can do this by explaining that what they are feeling is very common and reminding them that everyone shows their feelings differently and that is okay. Reassuring children that problems are being handled, people who were hurt are being cared for, buildings are being cleared, and things are getting a little better each day helps to restore their confidence.

Tony was asked about his continuing reactions after 9/11. He explained, "What sticks with me after a year is that I'm scared of another attack." Reminding him of increased safety measures, absence of further terrorism in America, the philosophy of living with risk in day-to-day life, and the historical perspective of experiencing and surviving threatening events may increase his feelings of safety.

Parents and other adults can encourage children to remember that they are a part of a nation and a world that has survived a terrible experience and we are all working together to stop terrorism. They can remind children that many bad things have happened in the past to our country and our world, and that good people were strong and survived.

It is sometimes useful to talk to children about strategies. The adults in their lives might ask them if they have been thinking about the world situation and if they would like to help change things. Children feel more empowered to create change in themselves and their world if they are given a forum for discussion and action.

Children of all ages can help themselves in a variety of ways. Parents, teachers, and other adults might suggest making a list of worries and talking about them in order of importance. Children can learn relaxation techniques such as deep breathing and visualizing happy experiences. They can tell or write stories about times in their lives they will never forget. They can draw pictures of safe places to go.

Children might create a "peace box" with objects and pictures that are comforting, or make a collage of family photographs, or draw a "circle of trust" with names of people and phone numbers to remind them of who is available to help them when needed. Older children can brainstorm ways to reduce prejudice and ethnic stereotypes in schools and communities, and they can develop contingency plans with contact numbers, strategies, and emergency kits. They might write about community spirit, activism, support systems, and personal empowerment.

Parents can monitor the television news their children view in order to limit their exposure to repetition of traumatic events. Parents can help children process and interpret their observations. These teachable moments allow children to express, with adult guidance, their thoughts and feelings about what they see and hear.

Organizing family activities help to reassure children and help re-establish their sense of order. Keeping to a daily routine renews a sense of security. Preparing meals together, eating dinner as a family, reading stories aloud, walking the dog, and playing games maintain continuity and normalcy in children's lives. By simply being with their children without outside distractions, parents can produce a comfortable climate in which to begin a dialogue at home, in the car, or on a peaceful walk. Children often choose to talk about their worries at bedtime. An increase in transition time, storytelling and book-reading creates a peaceful and reassuring nighttime ritual.

Adults can demonstrate responsible roles for children during traumatic times. Children look to adults' reactions as a barometer of their own safety. After 9/11, adults reacted in many different ways. One mother slept in her clothes with a packed suitcase next to her bed; another, with her child, collected clothing and food to help the firefighters, police, and victims. It is important to remind children that we can all help each other, just as people always have done in difficult times.

Adults can help children by respecting their spiritual belief system. Some children may feel comforted by thinking about their feelings about God and may choose to express these feelings. They can light a candle or say a prayer. Second-grader Shainna created her own prayer as reassurance: "Lord, Thank you for giving us strength to go on after such a tragedy. Bless everyone. Amen."

School systems can help by organizing assemblies about prejudice, with participation by culturally diverse members of the community. Communities can involve children in organizing and participating in fund-raisers for the survivors or for special groups such as firefighters and police.

It can be helpful to remind children that our nation has the support of many people around the world. Karen, a sophomore in high school, was amazed that Great Britain virtually came to a standstill the day after 9/11 to commemorate the loss of life in the United States. Schoolchildren, motorists, government workers, and others respectfully observed moments of silence.

CONCLUSION

Living with the possibility of more terrorist attacks creates both fear and hope. We ask ourselves what we can do for our children. The response might well be to allow them to grieve their losses, help reduce their fears, instill in them a sense of safety and protection, and empower them to imagine a future of peaceful coexistence for all human beings. ■

Linda Goldman is a certified grief therapist and certified death educator. She worked as a teacher and counselor for 20 years. She now maintains a private practice in grief therapy and teaches at Johns Hopkins University and the University of Maryland School of Social Work. Her workshops and courses on children and grief also are taught at many other universities. Ms. Goldman was twice named by Washingtonian Magazine *(1988, 2001) as one of the top therapists in the Washington, DC, area. She has served on the board of ADEC, the Association for Death Education and Counseling, and SPEAK, Suicide Prevention Education Awareness for Kids. She is the author of* Life and Loss: A Guide to Help Grieving Children *and* Breaking the Silence: A Guide to Help Children with Complicated Grief.

REFERENCES

Fox, S. (1988). *Good grief: Helping groups of children when a friend dies.* Boston, MA: The New England Association for the Education of Young Children.

Ginsberg, H., & Opper, S. (1969). *Piaget's theory of intellectual development.* Englewood, NJ: Prentice Hall.

Goldman, L. (2000). *Life and loss: A guide to help grieving children.* New York: Taylor & Francis.

Goldman, L. (2001). *Breaking the silence: A guide to help children with complicated grief.* New York: Taylor & Francis

Piaget, J. (1998). *The equilibrium of cognitive structure: The central problem of intellectual development.* Trans. T. Brown & K. Thampy. Chicago: University of Chicago Press.

Rosenfeld, L. (2001). Children's responses to terrorism, *NASW Online,* 1-9. Retrieved December 17, 2001, from http://www.naswdc.org/terror/rosenfeld.htm

Sheppard, C. (1998). *Brave Bart.* Grosse Pointe Woods, MI: TLC.

Stepp, L.S. (2001, November 2). Children's worries take new shape. *The Washington Post,* C1.

Worden, J.W. (1991). *Grief counseling & grief therapy: A handbook for the mental health practitioner.* New York: Springer, 35.

■ CHAPTER 13 ■

Schools, Children and Public Tragedy

Barbara L. Bouton

INTRODUCTION

Each of us can immediately call to mind an example of how schools, children, and public tragedy intersect. The images—of school children fleeing downtown Manhattan after planes hit the World Trade Center, of hands-linked preschoolers led by police after a shooting rampage at their California daycare, of the Columbine High School massacre and its aftermath—are all too clear. Without a doubt, there are multiple examples of public tragedy in our country that have profoundly traumatized our children.

When children's lives are disrupted by these traumatic experiences, they need education, intervention, and support that can ameliorate common posttraumatic stress reactions and help them return to pretrauma levels of function. Schools play an important role in this process, as well as in identifying at-risk children who may need additional intervention. Depending upon how well educators respond to children's needs at these critical times, schools can have a significant and lasting effect upon children traumatized by public tragedies.

In many ways, the school setting is an ideal environment for identifying traumatized children, as educators can readily observe and assess children's reactions and responses to tragedy. In addition, because schools provide access to children in a "developmentally appropriate environment that encourages normalcy and minimizes stigma" (Pfefferbaum, 1997), schools are excellent settings for the delivery of support and intervention services following a tragedy. In fact, a study conducted in Manhattan shortly after 9/11 found that for the 22 percent of children in the area who sought counseling services following the attacks, 58 percent of those services were provided in the schools (Stuber, Fairbrother, Galea, Pfefferbaum, Wilson-Genderson, & Vlahov, 2002).

This chapter begins with a brief overview of the impact of traumatic experiences on children and the posttraumatic stress reactions, both normal and abnormal, that can result—reactions that can affect children's abilities to cope. In this overview, specific implications for schools and educators are noted. Following this discussion, specific roles and responsibilities for schools—on district, school, and individual child levels—are detailed.

FACTORS INFLUENCING CHILDREN'S REACTIONS TO TRAGEDY

Children's reactions to tragic events are influenced by several factors. The most significant influence is the child's level of direct exposure and proximity—physical and emotional—to the tragedy. Exposure and proximity are directly linked to the emergence of posttraumatic stress reactions in children—i.e., the more direct exposure children have to the traumatic event, the greater the likelihood of psychological stress and harm (NIMH, 2002).

Exposure and proximity include not only direct witness of the tragedy (the experience of child survivors of school shootings, for example) but also the child's perception of the threat to his/her life and disruptions in school, family, and community life that may result. In addition to physical proximity to the tragedy, emotional proximity (i.e., the more directly the child is affected by the injury or death of a loved one) is also a strong influence upon posttraumatic stress reactions the child experiences (Hamblen, 2002; LaGreca, Silverman, & Wasserstein, 1998; NASP, 2002; NIMH, 2002; Pfefferbaum, 1997; Pynoos, Frederick, Nader, Arroyo, Steinberg, Eth, Nunez, & Fairbanks, 1987; Zinner & Williams, 1999).

The age and developmental level of a child also significantly influence reactions to tragedy. The ability to accurately perceive and understand tragic events and place them in a meaningful context are important developmental factors in children's reactions to tragedy. For young children with limited verbal skills, levels of posttraumatic stress can be difficult to assess but generally can be surmised through behaviors, for example, clinging, regressive behaviors, somatic complaints, or fears (Deering, 2000; Koplewicz & Goodman, 1999; NIMH, 2002; NASP, 2002; Zinner & Williams, 1999).

The nature and cause of tragedy also affect children's ability to cope. Generally, tragedies that are of deliberate, intentional human design where significant loss of life is intended (such as 9/11 or the Oklahoma City bombings) are more difficult to cope with than natural disasters, such as hurricanes or tornadoes (Ursano, McCaughey, & Fullerton, 1994; Zinner & Williams, 1999).

The reactions of significant adults, particularly parents and parental figures, are another important influence on children's reactions to tragedy. Children take many of their cues about how threatening, dangerous and out of control a situation is from the adults who surround them. This has enormous implications for both parents and educators, who may be in a state of crisis response similar to that of the children for whom they are responsible (Deering, 2000; Pfefferbaum, 1997; NASP, 2002; NIMH, 2002).

Other important factors influencing children's reactions and the likelihood they will experience significant posttraumatic stress reactions are the post-trauma environment and how well that environment supports care and attention to children (LaGreca et al., 1998). The more disrupted, abnormal, out of control, and unsafe a child perceives the surrounding environment to be, the more posttraumatic stress reactions he or she is likely to exhibit. Conversely, the more attentive, supportive, calming, nurturing, safe, and controlled the environment is, the fewer posttraumatic stress reactions children will experience (NIMH, 2002). The ability of a particular school to provide the kind of posttrauma environment that children need depends directly upon the nature of the tragedy. A school that has been the site of a school shooting will not be as capable of immediately providing such an environment as a school that witnessed the 9/11 events during a news broadcast, for example.

CHILDREN'S REACTIONS TO TRAGEDY

Children experiencing trauma exhibit responses and reactions on a continuum that ranges from short term (four weeks or fewer) posttraumatic stress reactions to the long-term, debilitating effects of posttraumatic stress disorder (PTSD) (Goodman & Gurian, 2002; NASP, 2002; NIMH, 2002). In the school setting, children's reactions to tragedy are readily apparent, as they significantly affect a child's ability to attend, learn, engage in learning and social activities, and demonstrate appropriate behavior and academic performance. It is common for children to exhibit a variety of posttraumatic stress reactions following public tragedy: increased fear and anxiety, decreased academic performance, poor concentration, increased aggression and oppositional behavior, decreased frustration tolerance, increased irritability, emotional instability, symptoms of depression, regression in behavior, and/or the loss of a previously mastered developmental skill (AAETS, 1999; Deering, 2000; Hamblen, 2002; Koplewicz & Goodman, 1999; NCPTSD, 2002).

It is important to note that these reactions are not limited to children exposed to public tragedies; they are equally common in children exposed to community/family violence, physical, and sexual abuse (Goodman & Gurian, 2002; Koplewicz & Goodman, 1999; NIMH, 2002).

In addition, studies have shown that the biological fight-or-flight response often called into action by adults at times of fear and perceived threat is less adaptive in children (Pfefferbaum, 1997). Children initially may become hyperaroused in line with adults' experience of the fight-or-flight response, but if the traumatic event or experience continues without intervention and assistance, they are likely to become immobile and begin to dissociate, that is, psychologically separate themselves from their thoughts or feelings (Pfefferbaum, 1997).

CHILDREN AT RISK

Several studies have identified children at particular risk for significant posttraumatic stress reactions as well as those most likely to develop PTSD (Goodman & Gurian, 2002; NASP, 2002; NIMH, 2002; Norris, Byrne, & Diaz, 2002). While children who exhibit pretrauma problems with anxiety, attention, and academic achievement are likely to experience significant post-traumatic stress reactions for as long as three months, children most at risk for PTSD are previous victims or direct witnesses of traumatic experiences (physical and sexual abuse, family and/or community violence) and children who have high levels of pretrauma anxiety (LaGreca et al., 1998; Zinner & Williams, 1999). In fact, although the majority of children with posttraumatic stress reactions return to normal functioning within three months following tragedy, LaGreca et. al (1998) found that children with pretrauma anxiety are likely to experience significant distress for as long as seven months. Hamblen (2002) notes a study that found children with high levels of fear and arousal (i.e., fight-or-flight reactions) at seven weeks posttrauma to be at high risk for PTSD. Other studies suggest that girls generally have more significant and longer lasting posttraumatic stress reactions in response to traumatic events than boys, and that girls are at greater risk for developing PTSD (Hamblen, 2002; Pfefferbaum, 1997; NASP, 2002). LaGreca et al. (1998) also found that continuing high levels of posttraumatic stress reactions three months posttrauma are highly predictive of children who will have persistent trauma reactions and likely PTSD diagnoses.

From these and other studies, we can surmise that three factors characterize children at the highest risk for negative outcomes following public tragedy and other traumatic experiences:

- History of traumatic experiences such as abuse, family or community violence;

- Significant anxiety prior to the tragedy;

- Experience of significant posttraumatic stress reactions that do not return to pretrauma levels within three months following the traumatic event, particularly among girls.

POSTTRAUMATIC STRESS DISORDER (PTSD)

The diagnosis of posttraumatic stress disorder (PTSD) in children may be made when children exhibit specific, significant, and debilitating trauma reactions for at least one month. While the diagnosis of PTSD requires clinical assessment by a mental health professional, teachers and other school personnel are key observers of children's reactions and can help parents/guardians identify children at risk and recommend appropriate referral for assessment and intervention. Three key variables may lead to a diagnosis of PTSD: reliving the trauma, avoiding reminders of the tragedy or any strong emotional subject, and acute persistent arousal symptoms.

Re-experiencing or Reliving the Trauma

In the school setting, this may be observed in children's play or self-directed activities and assignments. As opposed to play that provides an outlet for expression and aids adaptation, posttraumatic play involves "compulsively repeating some aspect of the trauma" (Hamblen, 2002) without relief from posttraumatic stress reactions, especially anxiety. Adults with PTSD often experience flashbacks, but these are less common in children. Instead,

Hamblen (2002) notes that children are more likely to experience "time skew" (inaccurate memories of the sequence of events related to the tragedy). Re-experiencing or reliving the traumatic experience may also be evident in the child who experiences invasive thoughts, i.e., thoughts and images that seem to "invade" the child's mind and distract him or her from other activities.

Avoidance

The child may avoid all reminders of the tragedy and, in general, resist all emotionally laden topics or discussions, regardless of whether they relate to the traumatic event. In the school setting, this may be observed in children who are inattentive or distracted or who engage in distracting behaviors; children who are resistant to class activities related to the tragedy itself and to activities that tend to generate emotion in general; and children who withdraw or become noncommunicative at times when peers experience significant emotion.

Arousal Symptoms

The child may exhibit acute, persistent arousal symptoms. In the school setting, this may be observed in children who are extremely and uncharacteristically tired, as their arousal prevents adequate sleep; children who exhibit uncharacteristic anger, agitation, or irritability; children who have difficulty concentrating or attending to class activities and assignments, and children who show significant startle reactions. Sometimes, severely traumatized children experience "omen formation," a belief that there were signs in the environment—"omens"—that forecast the tragedy. Children so affected may believe they can avoid future trauma by staying alert and attentive to these perceived warning signs (Brock, Lazarus, & Jimerson, 2001; Hamblen, 2002; NCPTSD, 2002; NIMH, 2002).

Incidence and Effects of PTSD

The incidence of PTSD in children in our country is alarming. Each year, an estimated three million children show signs of PTSD (Koplewicz & Goodman, 1999; NIMH, 2002; Schwarz & Perry, 1994). Studies suggest that up to 43 percent of children have experienced at least one traumatic event, and the incidence of PTSD that can result from these experiences ranges from one to six percent in boys and three to 15 percent in girls. It is estimated that virtually all children who witness a parental homicide or sexual assault develop PTSD. Ninety percent of children who have been sexually abused, 77 percent of children exposed to a school shooting, and 35 percent of urban youth who have been exposed to community violence are likely to develop PTSD (Hamblen, 2002).

In addition to the debilitating effects of this disorder on children's mental health, recent studies suggest that several fundamental brain functions are altered in people with PTSD. Abnormal levels of chemicals that affect coping, behavior, learning, and memory have been detected in the brains of people with PTSD (NIMH, 2002).

PTSD has the potential to disrupt normal development, interfere with children's healthy adaptation, and prevent or delay development of cognition, attention, social skills, personality, self-concept, self-esteem, and impulse control (Pfefferbaum, 1997). A study by LaGreca (1998) indicates that 40 percent of children with high levels of posttraumatic stress reactions one year posttrauma continue to have substantial reactions and clinical impairment four years posttrauma (LaGreca, 1998). Finally, a diagnosis of PTSD prior to age 18 has been found to significantly increase the risk of other major mental health disorders, such as depression, anxiety, and alcohol and drug dependence (Pfefferbaum, 1997; NCPTSD, 2002).

Clearly, these findings and statistics mandate critical attention to the needs of children who experience ongoing posttraumatic stress reactions by the adults responsible for them.

ROLE OF SCHOOLS IN HELPING CHILDREN COPE

School District Roles and Responsibilities

The incidence of public tragedies and other traumas that affect today's children demand that school systems develop specific strategies to prepare for and respond to children's needs. Given the frequency of tragic events that affect our nation's schools and the children that attend them, it is surprising that most educators do not receive specific training in trauma response (AAETS, 1999).

An organized, prepared, and practiced school crisis response team is a critical element for providing efficient and effective intervention at the time of tragedy. These teams are developed by specific school districts and comprise school system employees (administrators, counseling professionals, medical staff, and related others) and community mental health professionals. Generally, such teams perform the following tasks: gather facts about the tragedy; assemble the crisis response team; ensure appropriate notification about the tragic event; provide on-site education, support, and intervention as needed for children and school personnel; respond to the news media as needed; participate in debriefing sessions; and assist with memorial or other appropriate ritual observances (AAETS, 1999).

In addition to the critical and immediate responsibilities fulfilled by school crisis response teams, school districts need to provide ongoing education of teachers and other school personnel about potential school and public tragedies, posttraumatic stress reactions, characteristics of at-risk children, PTSD, and recommended school and classroom intervention strategies. Educational efforts will help ensure that school personnel can adequately gauge the posttraumatic stress reactions of children for whom they are responsible and can alert parents and guardians to ongoing and maladaptive reactions. In fact, given our ability to identify at-risk children prior to tragic events, focused efforts to prepare, educate, and help them prior to tragic events will facilitate their posttrauma coping.

Likewise, school systems can help by taking responsibility for educating parents and guardians about children's normal and abnormal reactions to traumatic experiences and providing guidance to them as they strive to help their children. Pretrauma education efforts and ongoing communication with parents and guardians are essential to fostering a collaborative partnership between schools and families. Although these efforts may tax school systems with limited resources, they will benefit the entire school community when tragedy occurs and help ensure appropriate attention to the needs of affected children (NASP, 2002; NIMH, 2002).

School districts also can ensure that teachers, school personnel, parents and guardians, and other key people have resource materials to assist them in responding to the needs of children at the time of tragedy. Teaching sheets for adults can be created and distributed in advance of need that identify posttraumatic stress reactions, warning signs of maladaptive reactions, and other important information related to coping with tragedies. Schools can develop handouts for children that both provide tips for healthy coping and identify people available for support and assistance. They can compile resource lists that identify appropriate community agencies and practitioners available to assist with school interventions, discussions, or activities at the time of tragedy.

Individual School and Classroom Roles and Responsibilities

First and foremost, helping children cope with posttraumatic stress following tragedy involves assuring them that they are safe (assuming that they are), that adults are in charge and working to help the situation, and that everything possible is being done to prevent a recurrence of the tragedy (Gallagher, 2002). In fact, children's beloved Fred Rogers (of PBS's Mr. Rogers' Neighborhood) encourages adults to use the strategy his mother used to help him cope as a child when he experienced fear in response to tragic events. "Look for the helpers," she would tell him. "You will always find people who are helping" (Rogers & Bluestone Sharapan, 2001).

Ensuring that children have accurate information about the tragedy facilitates healthy coping. When children understand the "who, what, when, where, and why" circumstances of the tragedy, they regain a sense of control and stability. As noted earlier, however, repeated exposure to the tragedy does adversely affect children's coping, so exposure to the event, such as through news reports, should be limited. Throughout the nation, children of all ages were repeatedly exposed to television reports of the events of 9/11 as routine activities at school (and even many daycares) were suspended to watch news broadcasts; very likely this focus continued at home as well. Indeed, it is possible—and advisable—to provide children with information and ensure they have answers to their questions without exposing them repeatedly to images of tragic events (Koplewicz & Goodman, 1999; NIMH, 2002, Waddell & Thomas, 2002).

Providing opportunities for children to express the full range of feelings they have about the tragedy also facilitates coping and helps alleviate posttraumatic stress reactions. Combining opportunities for expression with learning activities that teach them about posttraumatic stress can be especially helpful. Assuring children that they are having normal reactions to abnormal events (using developmentally appropriate terminology) can help them better understand their reactions. Small group discussions and expressive or projective experiences—play, art, movement, storytelling, creative writing—are natural and familiar to children and provide a means through which they can express their thoughts and feelings. In addition to providing a forum for children's thoughts and feelings, such classroom activities also provide the opportunity to identify and correct misconceptions about the tragedy and its cause (Pfefferbaum, 1997; Waddell & Thomas, 2002).

If teachers lack the confidence to provide these opportunities for students, the school system, crisis response team, or local community may be able to provide mental health professionals to help guide and facilitate activities.

Helping children identify ways they can make a difference for those directly affected by the tragedy allows them to take an active role in responding, bolsters their self-esteem, and teaches them interdependence and responsibility for fellow human beings. These activities foster the idea that it is possible—given attention, help and care—for people to recover from tragedy and find hope and healing. These are lessons that serve children well as they mature and inevitably confront future losses and tragedies. After 9/11, schoolchildren spent many classroom hours creating cards, making drawings and posters, collecting money for needed supplies, and taking part in other supportive activities designed to help children feel a part of the nation's recovery efforts and to learn firsthand that they can make an important and positive contribution.

Healthy coping is also aided when children have the opportunity to create and participate in memorial events or appropriate related rituals. Encouraging children to create their own memorial events and rituals can help establish feelings of control and mastery, both of which facilitate healthy coping in children. These rituals can take a number of forms, such as creating a memory box or display board, planting a tree in memory of those who have died, or taking part in activities based on the children's own ideas (Waddell, 2002).

Following classroom discussion or projects tied to a tragic event, it is important for teachers or facilitators to assure children that they are safe. Such reassurance helps alleviate the posttraumatic stress reactions of heightened arousal or fear children may experience in response to the discussion or project. A classroom activity that has a calming, quieting effect upon children (such as reading a story or poetry, listening to quiet music, providing relaxation exercises) provides children with a sense of connection, comfort and security (NASP, 2002).

It is important to balance children's needs for supportive education, expression, and intervention with normal and routine school activities and assignments. In addition to providing opportunities for children to understand and express their feelings, schools should strive for a return to "normalcy" in order to help children cope with tragic events. At the same time, education and mental health professionals strongly recommend postponing

tests or completion dates for large projects, as children are likely to have difficulty working up to their full potential immediately following a public tragedy.
In general, however, returning to normal routines reestablishes stability and
safety for children as they learn that there are some things, regardless of the
tragedy, that they can count on to remain the same. Learning activities that
have a high degree of success—those that can help children experience mastery
and control over their environment—are especially helpful to traumatized
children and can be added into established curricula (Gallagher, 2002; NASP,
2002; Pfefferbaum, Call, Guy, & Sconzo, 1999; Waddell, 2002).

Responsibilities to Individual Children

Teachers and other school personnel have a responsibility to identify and
monitor how the children in their charge are coping, and to ensure appropriate follow-up for those who do not return to pretrauma functioning within a
reasonable amount of time (generally within one to three months, taking into
consideration the factors discussed earlier that influence children's reactions).
Children who continue to relive the experience through intrusive thoughts
or posttraumatic play, who avoid or withdraw from emotional expression
(even beyond the traumatic event) and who display persistent reactions of
hyperarousal will benefit from professional intervention.

Other warning signs for children who are having difficulty coping with
tragedy and for whom referral and professional intervention are indicated
include the following:

- Inability to return to pretrauma levels of participation in
  school tasks and activities;

- Significantly altered academic progress;

- Highly emotional and reactive state;

- Withdrawal, apathy, and lack of interest and communication;

- Expression of homicidal or suicidal thoughts or feelings, including
  incidents of intentional self-harm;

- Indications of alcohol or drug abuse;

- Significant change in physical health or appearance (e.g., weight gain
  or loss or lack of attendance to personal grooming); and

- Significant behavioral changes (AAETS, 1999).

Sometimes schools are fortunate to have on-site resources for counseling, to which teachers can refer students exhibiting maladaptive reactions. Community mental health agencies or well-developed hospice bereavement programs may also be able to provide on-site counseling services or support groups for children who are significantly traumatized.

Schools have a responsibility to keep parents and guardians informed about all programs, activities, and projects developed to help children cope following tragic events and, where possible, to enlist the help and participation of parents and guardians in the school's trauma response efforts. School personnel need frequent and ongoing communication with parents of children identified as exhibiting maladaptive posttraumatic stress reactions, and parents need to be involved early in the assessment and referral process. Helping parents understand their children's reactions, the school's concerns, and recommendation for intervention fosters a collaborative partnership that will facilitate appropriate attention to children's needs.

SUMMARY

Public tragedies have a profound effect upon children. A child's ability to cope with traumatic experiences can be positively influenced by well-planned, coordinated, and integrated support and intervention services. Schools are in a unique position to prepare and help community members—children and their families, teachers and school personnel, and the community at large—understand and respond to tragic experiences that affect children's lives. Schools not only can play a vital role in the identification of children who are at risk for negative outcomes following traumatic experiences, they can be a catalyst for ensuring that children receive the attention and intervention they need following public tragedies. ■

Barbara L. Bouton, MA, is Director of Bridges Center, a hospice bereavement and community grief and loss program of the Alliance of Community Hospices in Louisville, Kentucky. Ms. Bouton serves on the Board of Directors of the National Hospice and Palliative Care Organization, is the Chair of the National Council of Hospice and Palliative Professionals and served six years as its Bereavement Professional Section Leader. She has more than 20 years of experience in hospice care, grief counseling and education, and the development of hospice bereavement care programs and services. She serves as a consultant to developing hospice bereavement programs across the country.

REFERENCES

American Academy of Experts in Traumatic Stress (AAETS). (1999). *Practical guide for crisis response in our schools,* (4th ed.). Commack, NY: American Academy of Experts in Traumatic Stress.

Brock, S.E., Lazarus, P.J., & Jimerson, S.J. (Eds.). (2001). B*est practices in school crisis and intervention.* Bethesda, MD: National Association of School Psychologists.

Deering, C.G. (2000). A cognitive developmental approach to understanding how children cope with disasters. *Journal of Child and Adolescent Psychiatric Nursing, 13,* 7-16.

Gallagher, R. *Attack on the U.S.: Guidelines for teachers in the classroom.* Retrieved August 10, 2002, from http://www.aboutourkids.org/articles/ crisis_teachers.html

Goodman, R.F., & Gurian, A. *About posttraumatic stress disorder (PTSD).* Retrieved August 10, 2002, from http://www.aboutourkids.org/articles/ about_ptsd.html

Hamblen, J., *PTSD in children and adolescents.* National Center for PTSD. Retrieved August 10, 2002, from http://www.ncptsd.org/facts/specific/ fs_children.html

Koplewicz, H.S., & Goodman, R.F. (Eds.). (1999). *Childhood revealed: Art expressing pain, discovery and hope.* New York: Harry Abrams.

LaGreca, M., Silverman, W.K., & Wasserstein, S.B. (1998). Children's predisaster functioning as a predictor of posttraumatic stress following hurricane Andrew, *Journal of Consulting and Clinical Psychology, 66,* 883-92.

National Association of School Psychologists (NASP). *Memorials/ activities/rituals following traumatic events.* Retrieved August 10, 2002, from http://www.nasponline.org/NEAT/memorials_general.html

National Institute of Mental Health (NIMH). *Helping children and adolescents cope with violence and disasters,* NIH Publication No. 01-3518. Retrieved August 10, 2002, from http://www.nimh.nih.gov/publicat/ violence.cfm

Norris, F.H., Byrne, C.M., & Diaz, E. T*he range, magnitude, and duration of effects of natural and human-caused disasters: a review of the empirical literature.* Retrieved August 10, 2002, from http://www.ncptsd.org/facts/ disasters/fs_range.html

Pfefferbaum, B., Call, J.A., Guy, J.D., & Sconzo, M. (1999). Mental health services for children in the first two years after the 1995 Oklahoma City terrorist bombing. *Psychiatric Services, 50,* 956-8.

Pfefferbaum, B. (1997). Posttraumatic stress disorder in children: A review of the past ten years. *Journal of the American Academy of Child and Adolescent Psychiatry, 36,* 1503-11.

Pynoos, R.S., Frederick, C., Nader, K., Arroyo, W., Steinberg, A., Eth, S., Nunez, F., & Fairbanks, L. (1987). Life threat and posttraumatic stress in school-age children. *Archives of General Psychiatry, 44,* 1057-63.

Rogers, F., & Bluestone Sharapan, H. *Helping parents, teachers and caregivers deal with children's concerns about violence in the news.* Retrieved September 18, 2001, from http://pbskids.org/rogers/parents/sept11.htm

Schwarz, E.D., & Perry, B.D. (1994). The post-traumatic response in children and adolescents. *Psychiatric Clinics of North America, 17,* 311-26.

Stuber, J., Fairbrother, G., Galea, S., Pfefferbaum, B., Wilson-Genderson, M., & Vlahov, D. (2002). Determinants of counseling for children in Manhattan after the September 11 attacks. *Psychiatric Services, 53,* 815-22.

Ursano, R.J., McCaughey, B.G.F., & Fullerton, C.S. (1994). *Individual and community responses to trauma and disaster: The structure of human chaos.* New York: Cambridge.

Waddell, D., & Thomas, A. *Disaster: Helping children cope.* National Health and Education Center. Retrieved August 10, 2002, from http://www.naspcenter.org/safe_schools/safeschools_disteach.html

Zinner, Ellen S., & Williams, M.B. (Eds.). (1999). *When a community weeps: Case studies in group survivorship.* Philadelphia: Brunner/Mazel.

CHAPTER 14

Meaning Making in the Wake of Public Tragedy

David A. Thompson and Edward J. Holland

The meaning of life is the most urgent of questions.
—Albert Camus

In the immediate aftermath of the terrorist attacks on airline passengers and people in the World Trade Center in New York and the Pentagon in Washington, D.C., we gasped in horror and tried to comprehend the magnitude of the events that surrounded this public tragedy. The surprise attack on our nation left most of us riding a roller coaster of emotions as we tried to comprehend the losses in the largest human-caused public disaster in this country since the attack on Pearl Harbor in World War II.

Recently, almost a year after this tragedy, a hospice colleague posed a profound question to us: "How do we make meaning, make sense, out of what seems to be such a meaningless and senseless tragedy?" Initially we were silenced by such a question. Now we are ready to grapple with it, not to give pat answers to the age-old question of evil in the world, but to understand how humans make meaning in the wake of public tragedy.

Having spent years struggling with the "Why?" questions as we ministered to individuals and families dealing with grief and loss, we see meaning making as primarily a spiritual process that has psychological and developmental components. An essential part of meaning making involves an introspective and retrospective spiritual journey as we examine our assumptive world and find ways to nurture our faith in the wake of human-caused tragedy. Doka (1993) writes that for many people, there is a deep need to rebuild faith and philosophical systems that are challenged by loss.

THE INADEQUACY OF MEANING MAKING IN PUBLIC MOURNING

One of the difficulties in helping those affected by public tragedies in making sense and meaning out of sudden human-caused losses is that we are not well prepared to provide long-term interventions in people's lives. Instead, we tend to be geared to respond with quick fixes promoting the illusion that life can get back to normal quickly. We race to disaster scenes, deploying medical and mental health professionals to provide first aid and critical incident stress debriefings to survivors. The news media and some health care professionals talk about closure as if there really is such a thing. We organize public memorial events and hold private funeral services to mourn the lost and comfort the survivors.

Then, almost as quickly as they came, most of the first responders pack up and go home. First responders do provide invaluable services; however, after the initial interventions, survivors are often left to ponder the deeper questions on their own, with limited long-term support for this task. Culturally and institutionally, we are not prepared to engage in serious long-term meaning making discussions and interventions after disasters.

Memorial events in public tragedy are often the earliest attempts to verbalize our feelings and begin the process of meaning making. When well done, they can highlight the therapeutic value of ritual as a way of marking important transitions, expressing our grief, remembering, and building community. Often, however, especially if the disaster is the result of violence intentionally perpetrated against innocent people, mixed messages can be sent that confuse those who mourn. This is a particular problem if there is a political desire to frame events in ways that serve larger parochial or nationalistic agendas.

On Sunday September 16, 2001, the Governor of the State of Minnesota invited the citizens of Minnesota to gather on the lawn of the State Capitol

Building in St. Paul for a memorial service for those who had suffered loss in the events of 9/11. The crowd was subdued as a light rain fell and bands from the University of Minnesota and the Salvation Army played hymns and music befitting a memorial remembrance. Thousands carried American flags of all sizes, and veterans sported American Legion caps. Many showed up wearing well-worn military caps or ill-fitting uniforms retrieved from attic storage of many years.

In the midst of the speeches by politicians and prayers of interfaith spiritual leaders, the solemn crowd began to hear the haunting sound of helicopter rotors beating the air as a formation of National Guard combat helicopters approached and flew over the crowd. Suddenly the mood of the crowd changed, with cheering and shouting and flag waving, as this demonstration of military power passed over their heads. For some this was terrifying; for others, it helped to ignite a festering rage. In the midst of all the noise, angry voices yelled at the soldiers in the helicopters, *"Give 'em hell,"* seeking revenge on an unseen enemy. This was followed quickly by the roar of four F-16 fighter jets doing a fly-over/missing man formation over the capitol, as the crowd cheered.

Somehow, this demonstration of military might spoke to the impotence many people felt that day. Yet, when all the important people had spoken and the bands had played their final patriotic anthem, questions about meaning were still there. Questions of "Why?" and "What now?" had not been answered in all of the well-intentioned memorial efforts and displays of military muscle.

MEANING MAKING

Alfred Adler said, "Human beings live in the realm of meanings. We experience reality always through the meaning we give it; not in itself, but as something interpreted" (Nadeau, 1997, p. 3). Naylor, Willimon, and Naylor (1994, p. 11) expand upon Adler, writing that the search for meaning "involves coming to grips with what it is to be a human being who lives, loves, works, plays, suffers, and dies. A strong sense of meaning is what motivates us to get out of bed each morning and confront yet another day of life and all its uncertainty, to transform our fate into our destiny, to make life more an adventure than a bore."

What, then, is "meaning"? Taylor defined meaning as, "an effort to understand the event: why it happened and what impact it had. The search for meaning attempts to answer the question, what is the significance of the event? Meaning is also reflected in the answer to the question, what does my life mean now?" (Nadeau, 1997, p. 14).

Because the process of finding and making meaning is primarily a retrospective exercise, it naturally follows that insights about meaning gradually emerge over time. Even then, meaning changes as time passes and our perspectives change. How do we support and facilitate this process in the wake of human-caused tragedies? Perhaps even more importantly, can we can better prepare ourselves for the prospect of more tragedies of this sort through the process of finding and making meanings that are more durable and resilient in an increasingly dangerous world?

On the relationship between meaning and grief, Nadaeu (1997, p. 3) contends that

> It could be argued that a search for meaning comes out of the perturbation caused by death. The status quo is upset. Existential questions are raised. The struggle to find answers to these existential questions, which is the search of meaning, is central to the grieving process. Death and the threat of death drive the process of meaning making by their power to upset our sense of order and security of everyday life. Making meaning of the experience of death reduces the terror by allowing a return to everyday reality.

The very act of questioning is a mark of spiritual and psychological health. Without questions, even when they are only partially answered or finally categorized as mystery, we do not grow as persons following tragic events. Naylor, Willimon, and Naylor (1994, p. 13) address this issue by saying, "There can be no escape from spiritual emptiness, unless one learns to ask the right questions: Why am I here? Where am I going? What is the purpose of life? Is there a God? What will happen when I die? Is there life after death? These questions have in common a longing for a sense of grounding, purpose, or meaning in life."

It is the very knowledge of impending death that sharpens one's focus on living life fully.

Although many of us spend our lives denying that we are going to die, some like Albert Camus have discovered that death is an important source of meaning. The fact that life is finite makes every remaining moment precious and beautiful. In a very real sense, l ife without death would not be worthwhile. Death liberates us from the present, and grants us the wisdom to sort out our priorities as to how best to use our remaining time on earth. By earnestly contemplating our own death, we may begin to learn how to live in such a way that we avoid the pitfalls of a life based entirely on either self-love or withdrawal. (Naylor et al, 1994, pp. 67-70)

Naylor et al. (1994, p. 14) capture the essence of this meaning-making task. The quest for meaning gets to the essence of what life is all about— *the care and nurture of our soul.* We will never find meaning if we pretend there is no problem and that the questions will just fade away. The search is no bed of roses. It may be painful, stressful, and very difficult. Although we do not promise 'meaning kits' for those who stay the course, many find the journey to be a source of great joy and boundless energy. Life itself compels us to join the quest. Welcome to the search.

EXISTENTIAL AND PSYCHOLOGICAL PERSPECTIVES ON MEANING MAKING

Victor Frankl, author of *Man's Search for Meaning* (1959), and founder of logotherapy, focuses the search for meaning in the present moment by asking "What do I do now?" questions. His existential philosophy and therapeutic techniques, which placed a strong emphasis on taking action in the present to make meaning in life, was developed on the anvil of painful experiences as a Nazi concentration camp inmate in World War II.

From these experiences, "He (Frankl) took one overriding lesson: that persons who have a purpose or meaning for what they are experiencing can endure and grow even in the most devastating of circumstances, while those without meaning will wither and languish, and in a prison camp setting, might actually die because of their apathy and despair. From this, Frankl came to believe that there is a fundamental drive to have a meaning or meanings to live by, what is called the will to live" (Jones & Butman, 1991, pp. 281-282).

Frankl's response to the horror of the Holocaust was to take action in the present and choose reasons to live that would give meaning to his life. "Frankl felt that human beings were both capable and responsible to make choices about why they should live and thus assert themselves to pursue things that give value to their lives. Frankl argued that purely psychological interventions which ignored the spiritual side were inappropriate for problems of meaning" (Jones & Butman, 1991, p. 282). Frankl's approach to meaning making took the focus off understanding why something happened, and placed the focus on what are you now going to do about what has happened?

In more recent years, meaning reconstruction has emerged as a promising psychotherapeutic approach to helping people deal with significant loss in life. Thomas Attig is representative of the constructionist approach to meaning making. He says, "In grieving we must relearn our very selves, including our characters, histories and roles, and identities that we find in them. We must also relearn our self-confidence and self-esteem" (Neimeyer, 2001, p. 40).

According to the constructionist view, much of the structure that held life together is radically altered and much of the content of our lives is changed. Much of what reconstructionists do is listen to the narratives of people's lives and help them reconstruct the narrative in the light of new realities following tragedy. As Attig states, the focus of attention is in helping people to

> Learn again how to be and act in a world without those we love by our sides. We relearn in all dimensions of our lives: Emotionally, we temper the pain of suffering…Psychologically we renew self-confidence, self-esteem, and self-identity…Behaviorally we transform our habits, motivations, dispositions, and ways of doing things…Physically and biologically we expend great energy meeting challenges bereavement presents…Socially we reconfigure our interactions with others…Intellectually we question and seek answers and meanings and change understandings and interpretations… Spiritually we seek peace and consolation, modifying our hopes and deepening or modifying our faiths. We return to aspects of our lives that are still viable. We revive what works! We also transform ourselves as we reshape and redirect our individual, family, and community lives. (Neimeyer, 2001, pp. 41-43)

FAITH DEVELOPMENT PERSPECTIVES IN THE MEANING-MAKING PROCESS

Recognizing the central role spirituality plays in the meaning-making process, caregivers want to be able to assess where people are in their spiritual development and understanding to intervene effectively in the wake of public tragedy.

Fowler (1981), a leading proponent of faith development concepts, provides us a framework for entering into the faith structures of people's lives to assist them in meaning making. He identifies the following stages of faith:

- Intuitive-Projective Faith (Infancy & Early Childhood), which is fantasy-filled and imitative, easily influenced by examples, moods, actions, and stories of visible faith…strongly subject to reinforcement of taboos, moral, or doctrinal expectations,

- Mythic-Literal Faith (Early Childhood), identifies strongly with stories, beliefs, and observances of one's faith community…strong literal interpretations and excessively relies on reciprocity and justice as a principle,

- Synthetic-Conventional Faith (Adolescence), characterized by influences beyond the family circle, where one synthesizes values and information for oneself, but highly influenced by expectations of peers,

- Individuative-Reflective Faith (Young Adulthood), characterized by critical reflection on self-identity and outlook/ideology…strong dependence on mind and critical thought…easily disillusioned with one's compromises and the realization that life is more complex than first thought,

- Conjunctive Faith (Mid-Life and Beyond), characterized by a strong social consciousness…has known defeats and the impact of commitments and acts…alive to paradox and contradictions… retains vulnerability to truths of those who are "other,"

- Universalizing Faith (Late Adulthood), characterized by an enlarged vision of universal community and brotherhood…willing to spend and be spent in transforming present reality" (Fowler, 1981, pp. 113-213).

Fowler observes that an individual's predominant faith orientation can be found in one of these six categories of faith, what he calls "stages of faith." Within each of these faith categories, there are three characteristics of faith that emerge: "(1) It involves a patterned knowing, which we sometimes call belief, (2) it involves a patterned valuing, which we sometimes call commitment or devotion, and (3) it involves patterned constructions of meaning, usually in the form of underlying narrative or story" (Fowler, 1987, p. 56). It is our contention that the meanings one finds and makes in the wake of tragedy is dependent, in part, on one's stage of faith.

In addition to natural psychosocial developmental transitions throughout the life cycle and expanded life experiences, traumatic life events can challenge one's assumptive world and trigger movement in one's faith journey, especially as one moves out of adolescent and into more adult forms of faith. In order to maintain one's intellectual and spiritual integrity and allow faith to grow, one must move to a stage of faith that helps to interpret life and meaning in a more congruent and satisfactory manner.

Patterns of homeostasis and disequilibration take place in each stage of faith development. The individual swings dialectically from feeling at home in a certain pattern of knowing, valuing, and meaning making, to growing distressed with that pattern of faith due to a developmental transition or a life crisis that disequilibrates the homeostasis. The individual seeks new ways of knowing, valuing, and meaning making that fit the experience of new realities, pushing the person to another level of faith development.

An example of this transition can be seen when a person does not find satisfying answers to one's questions within the context of their faith community in the wake of public disaster. The individual begins a journey of critical reflection in hopes of finding better answers. This action may actually isolate and alienate the person from the faith community. This can be a painful journey, resulting in still another loss that needs to be grieved.

In a conversation overheard following 9/11, a person commented, "It is not satisfying just to say 'Such evil will be punished in the afterlife, so I should just relax, knowing terrorists will get their just desserts in the great by and by.' Justice in the afterlife does not do it for me anymore!" The incarnation of evil rocks one's assumptive world and triggers growth or regression. In the wake of a traumatic human caused public disaster, maintaining a spiritual status quo is not adequate.

Faith communities can play an important role in the wake of public tragedy. Fowler goes a step beyond the individual and existential psychology of Frankl, stressing the importance of families and the faith community in shaping the way we individually know, value, and make meaning: "The context in which we become selves and form stances and styles of faith is community. There is no faith that is not awakened and formed in the matrix of relationship, language, ritual, and symbol. In the practical theological effort to account for the dynamics of selfhood and faith, by which we become subjects in relation to God, no individualistic psychologies or theologies can be much help" (Fowler, 1987, p. 55).

Families and faith communities reinforce the individual's ways of knowing, valuing, and meaning making. It is critically important that spiritual leaders use great care in framing ultimate questions and in providing responses that satisfactorily speak to the human condition. Especially in the aftermath of public tragedy, it is imperative that we not dispense boilerplate answers to profound questions. These pat answers will only serve to alienate many and undermine faith.

What should be avoided at all costs is shunning or marginalizing those who are struggling for better understanding and meaning in their life of faith following a disaster. We do not want to add to their injury by abandoning or shaming them as faithless because they challenge the way a community responds to deep questions. The healthy, vibrant, and mature faith community will allow and encourage questions. It will encourage members to feel and express the pain of grief, to be critical of and challenge past ways of knowing, valuing, and meaning making. It will give people room to grow in faith, to feel understood, supported, and loved in a time when they are searching for a faith that can withstand the storms of life. In so doing, the faith community will save itself, for it will be forced to dig deeper to answer questions of meaning in the life of the greater community.

Providers of spiritual care want to be sensitive to the stage of faith of people who have suffered from public tragedy. Most spiritual care professionals have some training and some experience shepherding people through troubling situations. They are often skilled at brief intervention techniques but may find it difficult to walk with survivors of tragedy over months and even years of "the dark night of the soul." In our experience, this is an area of needed growth for spiritual caregivers. Hospice programs, with expertise in long-term bereavement aftercare, can serve as valuable resources and models of care for clergy and their faith communities.

As people probe deeply into the mystery of suffering, trying to integrate that experience with the life of faith, spiritual care professionals will be challenged to help people realign their faith to adapt to new realities. This will involve deeper engagement of time and attention to people's lives than brief therapy models of spiritual care currently provide. Because the essential component of meaning making is distinctly spiritual in nature, a referral to the psychological community, while important, is not enough. It will call for a partnering relationship between therapist and spiritual care provider to address both psychological and spiritual aspects of care following a tragedy.

Fowler's stages of faith can help care providers assess where people are in their faith development. If the meaning someone finds and makes in the wake of public tragedy is dependent, in part, on that person's stage of faith development, the spiritual care provider must learn to talk about faith issues in a language people can understand. The goal is to help clients explore meanings within their own stage of faith and, at the same time, to help them explore new spiritual vistas. This spiritual reconstruction and discovery process is a challenge for all involved, including the spiritual caregivers, who must also deal with their own faith issues in the wake of public tragedy.

Fowler (1987, p. 103) addresses the difficulties in making reconstructive change: "Few of us ever make fundamental changes in the shape of our character or in the deep patterns of our personalities by elective choice alone. The need or imperative for deep-going change in our lives usually comes in response to some experience of shipwreck, of failure in love or work, or of spiritual struggle or illumination."

Spiritual care in the wake of tragedy involves more than the exercise of good listening skills and life experience and more than crisis intervention. It requires an ongoing presence that comforts, confronts, guides, and sustains individuals and communities in the years following a traumatic event. This type of spiritual caregiving calls for holistic expertise in the area of psychosocial and faith development issues. Additionally, it demands the use of sound theological thinking and spiritual direction skills to shepherd people through the aftermath of public tragedy to a safe place where they can grow as persons of faith who are engaged in life and the ongoing quest for meaning. Since few clergy and congregations have this extensive expertise, they will want to partner with other community resources in order to provide the holistic care required so that they can serve their people well.

HOPE FOR THE BEST AND PREPARE FOR THE WORST

Ship captains spend a lot of time training junior officers on ship-handling skills in all kinds of circumstances. The captain shares his or her experience of what to do in various critical situations, teaching what to watch for in the way of threatening weather or dangerous currents. One day, after such a training session, a captain was overheard saying, "I never teach navigation in the midst of a storm. I do it on sunny days and following seas. If you can learn good ship-handling skills before the storms come, almost anyone can handle rough waters. Good ship-driving habits, learned on calmer days and better conditions, become instinctive in the midst of storms. These good habits will hold you in good stead in 80-knot winds and 40-foot seas when you are scared and not thinking clearly. The things you learn today in calm waters will save you and your shipmates when things get rough. My job is to teach you, to model for you, what was shown me many years ago so that you'll be able to handle the big storms that certainly will come your way someday."

It is this teaching approach to spiritual care that can be utilized to better prepare faith communities for the storms of personal and public tragedy that surely will come. Clergy, in addressing meaning making in the wake of public tragedy, need to equip congregations in mind and spirit to navigate through the storms of life. This involves taking a critical look at our teaching ministry—whether sermons, workshops, training events, or religious education classes—to determine if we are adequately preparing our people for the storms of life. On sunny days and following seas, is the content of sermons or education classes telling the truth about life, its ups and downs, good and bad moments, triumphs as well as tragedies? Is what is shared from the pulpit and in private conversation helping people frame healthy assumptions about the Divine, about good and evil, and truthfully telling about the way the world works?

An essential aspect of spiritual care involves patiently teaching and preaching in ways that help people grow out of childish and egocentric stages of faith to a more mature faith that can handle paradox, ambiguity, and mystery. The late comedian Gilda Radner, dying of cancer, spoke of this in the conclusion of her book *It's Always Something* (Radner, 1989, p. 268): "I wanted a perfect ending. Now I've learned the hard way, that some poems don't rhyme and some stories don't have a clear beginning, middle and end. Like my life, this book is about not knowing, having to change, taking the moment and making the best of it, without knowing what's going to happen next. Delicious ambiguity!" We look for teachable moments, especially in crisis, to help people stretch and grow in faith, to be able to survive and even thrive when greater challenges come their way.

Faith does not always have to be presented as bold courage in the face of impossible odds. It also can be understood as journeying through life with questions and doubts, yet continuing the search for meaning and clarity. Faith in storms may look different from what is seen on sunny days. Nevertheless, people need to see in these times that they are living by faith. It is helpful to portray faith in different shapes and forms in times of loss and transition following a personal or public tragedy.

A resilient and vibrant faith can be forged in the wake of a major trauma. In early stages of this process, in the immediate aftermath of a tragedy, faith has to do with holding fast to those aspects of our spirituality that have deep roots in order to keep us from being blown away. Later, in the midst of transition, when a person may be doing a lot of questioning and rethinking, faith has to do with trying new things, taking calculated risks, and exploring new options. Still later in this process, faith may involve letting go of those beliefs and behaviors that lack roots or will not support the person in the storm. Eventually, as things become more clear, we can, with courage in the face of the unknown, choose to commit ourselves to life again. For many, this means choosing a new course or direction in life and committing themselves to altruistic and just causes. In the process, new meanings are found and made as we learn that the journey itself is as important as the destination.

We cannot disaster-proof our lives. Even so, faith communities have the responsibility and opportunity to help their constituents to "hope for the best and prepare for the worst." Fowler (1987, p. 106) writes

> There are marker events that blast the landscape of our lives and
> shred the veil of our temples beyond all recognition. These devastat-
> ing events, against which none of us has protection or guarantees,
> can be prepared for, in limited ways, only by shaping a life ground-
> ed in faith and a community of faith that can form and support us
> in spiritual communication with a Ground of Being beyond our
> finite bonds of love and our webs of woven meanings.

Finally, and more practically, we can encourage and train people to diversify their lives; that is, to nurture a wide range of interests and connections in their lives. An important part of teaching people life skills is to help them learn damage control principles that will help to prevent any one event from completely sinking their lives.

When visitors view the Titanic exhibit at the Museum of Science & Industry in Chicago, they will see how this ship sank because it had no watertight compartments. When the Titanic hit an iceberg and tore a hole in one compartment, it had no capability to seal off that area. Instead water flooded the entire ship. Today, modern ships have watertight walls and doors between compartments. Especially if several compartments are damaged, they can be sealed off so that the ship will stay afloat and be able to reach port and make needed repairs.

This is not to take lightly the severity of the gash in our lives public tragedies can make, nor discount the severe pain associated with sudden and traumatic loss. If disaster does strike, however, and one has developed diverse interests, built significant support networks, and nurtured deep yet flexible spiritual resources, then these compartments can remain intact and provide buoyancy long enough to reach a safe place where repairs can be made.

CONCLUSION

Naylor et al. state that in facing death, "We must prepare ourselves for this final accounting through the never-ending search, always pushing our knowledge of life and death to the limit, always wrestling meaning out of meaninglessness" (Naylor et al., 1994, p. 27). Meaning making is also a critical part of the healing process in the wake of public tragedy. It is primarily a spiritual journey, involving an ongoing process of introspection, learning, and action in order to exercise the will to live again. Even so, we must also recognize and acknowledge our limited perspective on life and ultimate issues. We are nearsighted, yet we are called to remain faithful in spite of our many answerless questions. This means that, at some point during our healing journey, we will need to stop driving in the circle of "Why?" questions that only make us dizzy. Instead, we will be challenged to re-enter the freeway of daily living asking: "What now?" "What's next?" "How then, shall I live?" Our response to these questions will make all the difference in the world. ■

David A. Thompson, M.Div., MSE, Ed.D (Candidate) maintains a private counseling practice in Bloomington, Minnesota. He is an Adjunct Professor of Pastoral Care at Bethel Seminary, Saint Paul; an ordained minister in the Free Methodist Church of North America, and a retired U.S. Navy Chaplain (Commander). He has served in civilian ministries as a parish pastor, hospital chaplain, college professor, nursing home chaplain, congregational care minister, and denominational conference superintendent. He was a Grief Counselor for Methodist Hospital Hospice in Minneapolis from 1996-99. Rev. Thompson is the author of four books and numerous magazine articles. He is a national certified counselor (NCC) with NBCC and certified grief counselor (CGC) with ADEC.

Edward J. Holland, M.Div., LMFT, is Coordinator of Spiritual Care and Grief Support at Methodist Hospital Hospice, Park Nicollet Health Services, Minneapolis. He is a United Methodist Minister, board-certified chaplain (APC), certified Gestalt therapist and licensed marriage and family therapist. Chaplain Holland is a past president of Minnesota Hospice Organization (1993-94), and he has served on its Ethics Committee and chaired its Clergy Education Task Force. He also served on the National Council of Hospice Professionals committee that wrote the NHPCO Guidelines for Spiritual Care in Hospice.

REFERENCES

Doka, K.J (1993). *Death and spirituality.* Amityville, NY: Baywood Publishing.

Fowler, J.W. (1987). *Faith development and pastoral care.* Philadelphia: Fortress Press.

Fowler, J.W. (1981). *Stages of Faith.* San Francisco: Harper & Row Publishers.

Frankl, V. (1959). *Man's Search for Meaning.* New York: Pocket Books.

Jones, S.L., & Butman, R.E. (1991). *Modern Psychotherapies.* Downers Grove, IL: Inter-Varsity Press.

Nadeau, J.W (1997). *Families making sense of death.* Newbury Park, CA: Sage.

Naylor, T.H., Willimon, W.H., Naylor, M.R. (1994). *The search for meaning.* Nashville: Abingdon Press.

Neimeyer, R.A. (2001). *Meaning reconstruction & the experience of loss.* Washington, DC: American Psychological Association.

Radner, G. (1989). *It's always something.* New York: Simon & Schuster.

CHAPTER 15

Memorialization, Ritual, and Public Tragedy

Kenneth J. Doka

INTRODUCTION

In the aftermath of 9/11 there was ritual. People gathered in village squares, in public places, and in houses of worship. They sang, prayed, and stood in silent vigil. There also were memorials. In New York City, firehouses became shrines, as people brought pictures, flowers, and candles. It had been the same in other public tragedies. In Oklahoma City, people left flowers and teddy bears in tribute to the dead children. When Princess Diana died, British embassies throughout the world became spontaneous memorials.

Ritual and memorials are ancient ways we cope with tragedy—both private and public. Evidence from Neolithic humans suggests the presence of elaborate ritual and careful memorialization. Ritual and memorialization precede written history. One of the first written accounts, *The Egyptian Book of the Dead*, describes in detail the rituals that should accompany a death. The very antiquity of ritual and memorialization is testament to their power.

This chapter explores the power and role of ritual and memorialization in public tragedy. It asks two central questions: Why do we turn to ritual and memorialization in times of public tragedy, and how can clinicians and counselors effectively utilize that power as they assist individuals and communities in coping with private and public tragedy?

RITUALS IN PUBLIC TRAGEDY

Rituals may be defined as acts invested with meaning. For example, in many religious and spiritual traditions, water is used as a symbol of purification. The water that is used may be no different than water used for drinking or washing, but the meaning of that ritual makes it different. The individual is cleaned not only of dirt but also of something deeper—perhaps, depending on the religious tradition—wrongful acts, original sin, or spiritual impurity. The very simple act of washing with water is infused with new understandings. That is the power of ritual—it invests the commonplace with uncommon meaning.

Gennep (1960) uses the term *liminal* to describe the significance of ritual. To Gennep, liminal refers to the role that ritual has in crossing a threshold, or making a transition or a passage. Yet Gennep's use of that term suggests an even deeper meaning. At its root, liminal may be defined as the threshold between the conscious and the unconscious. In short, ritual works because it simultaneously engages both the conscious and unconscious.

Roles of Ritual in Public Tragedy

The roles of ritual in public tragedy are many. First, ritual permits meaningful action at a disorganized time; it allows people to "do something." By doing something, even engaging in ritual, we feel that we have symbolic mastery over events. Ritual allows a reorganization of community and continuity in a chaotic time. Collectively, it offers a reassurance that while we cannot control the tragedy itself, we have reasserted control in its aftermath.

Second, ritual reaffirms community. It offers an opportunity for the different strands of a community, potentially fragmented by a crisis, to stand together and publicly demonstrate their fundamental unity. During rituals after both Oklahoma City and 9/11, it was reassuring to see civic and political leaders, celebrities, and religious leaders of all faiths and traditions sharing solidarity. It was a visible symbol that even in crisis we were one. It not only reaffirmed unity, it promised that we would face this crisis and persevere together.

Third, ritual shows solidarity with the victims. Individuals personally affected by tragedy may have need for their own rituals. For those who have experienced the death of a friend or family member, funerals and memorial rituals will provide their own social, psychological and spiritual benefits (Rando, 1984). Public ritual, though, offers a context for these individual rituals. It provides social validation, a public recognition of the loss that was experienced, and a collective reassurance of societal recognition and social support.

Fourth, public rituals structure public grief. In addition to an invitation to grieve, public rituals offer cues on what we are supposed to feel and models how we are to mourn. The funerals of Prince Albert in England and John F. Kennedy in the United States influenced mourning customs and behaviors in both countries. Both offered contemporary perspectives on appropriate ways to grieve and mourn. The role of mass media is critical here since it allows a level of collective participation. Aron and Livingston (1999) note that the funeral of Princess Diana was not only an event for the monarchy; the constant images of grieving citizens added a level of participation that allowed the nation, even the world, opportunity to grieve.

Finally, public ritual reconstructs the narrative—interpreting the death in a philosophical, spiritual, and historical framework. In public tragedy it offers an interpretation of the event. Schwartz (1991) reminds us that the funeral rituals that accompanied Lincoln's death transformed a controversial president to a symbol of national unity.

RITUALS IN PUBLIC TRAGEDY

Spontaneous Ritual

Ritual is a powerful and longstanding way to deal with significant events, especially those involving transition and loss. It is not surprising to see their immediate use soon after a public crisis or tragedy. The first rituals usually are spontaneous—the result of a sort of collective impulse. They arise from the public's need both to symbolically master as well as define the tragedy. Often they take place on or near the site of tragedy, but in tragedies that are larger in scope, they may occur throughout a region.

Beyond initial definition of the tragedy and a symbolic mastery—there is a collective sense of doing something. These spontaneous rituals can have other roles. First, they can be sources of information and action. At these rituals information about what occurred can be shared and processed. Collective actions can be encouraged or even initiated. For example, at the ritual, persons may be encouraged to give blood or volunteer. In some rituals, clothing and money may be collected. Naturally, the one potential difficulty is that these spontaneous rituals can spread misinformation and encourage unnecessary or even unhelpful or violent activities.

A second value of these spontaneous rituals is their inclusiveness. Everyone can attend and participate. These rituals reaffirm a collective stake in the crisis, and they remind individuals personally touched by the tragedy of the social recognition and support of the larger community.

Planned Rituals

Following the immediate, spontaneous rituals, there are planned rituals. These are of three types: private, organizational, and public.

Private Rituals. Private rituals of individuals personally touched by the tragedy have their unique challenges and issues. Many public tragedies are characterized by periods of disorganization, uncertainty, ambiguous loss, and multiple losses. In the absence of a body, it may be difficult to decide when to have a funeral or memorial service. Where there is widespread destruction of property or social disorganization, it may be difficult to select meaningful places for ritual or to gather mourners together. Where there are numerous deaths, the very timing of rituals may be contingent on the practical difficulties of managing multiple losses.

Counselors, funeral directors, and clergy should be sensitive to these difficulties as they work with families in planning these rituals. Family and friends clearly need to decide when and where rituals should be held. When the needs of family members differ and compromises fail, counselors may suggest that individuals create their own rituals to meet their needs.

In conducting private rituals, there are important points to consider. Because private rituals are likely to be supplemented by public rituals, it is important to personalize the private ritual. Public rituals will define losses in collective terms—what these deaths mean for the community. By contrast, the purpose of private ritual is to commemorate not the collective deaths but the death of that unique person. Effective rituals are personal, noting the many facets and identities of the individual who died. In addition, in contemporary American society, mourners may not share the same faith tradition or cultural contexts. Inclusive rituals do well when they express the significance of readings, actions, symbols or music. For example, at a recent funeral, the song "Singing in the Rain" was played. Since only a few close friends knew of the personal significance of the song, it was explained to the larger group.

Many public tragedies pose an additional problem. There may be tragedies where body parts will continue to be found. In such situations, families should have options about whether they want to be informed of future finds as well as whether they want additional rituals to accompany the disposition of the part.

There is one further concern. Since public tragedy often involves multiple deaths, intervention plans should address the needs of ritual leaders. Conducting numerous rituals will likely take a heavy emotional toll, possibly leading to the vicarious traumatization of funeral directors and clergy.

Organizational Rituals. In addition to private family rituals, there may be rituals conducted in workplaces, schools, voluntary and fraternal associations, and places of worship. When organizations have experienced the death of a member or members, there is great value in a collective ritual. This ritual, in addition to any family rituals, acknowledges the role the lost member or members had within that organization. Beyond recognizing the loss in the setting, it gives the members both unique opportunity and permission to grieve. It reaffirms the care and sensitivity of management and administration. Even in public tragedies where the organization is not directly affected, such rituals offer opportunities to educate about grief and trauma, frame a definition of the event, and offer collective action.

Public Rituals. Public rituals are necessary interventions in public tragedies. Just as private and organizational ritual validates and structures grief, so does public ritual—but on a larger scale. Public ritual offers reassurance and support, reaffirms community, shows solidarity, structures grief, and offers a narrative of what happened and how we should respond. Because of these roles, these rituals should come soon after the tragedy, but not so early that the dimensions of the crises are yet undefined. These, too, should be timed so as to be liminal, on the threshold between reaction and response, between what we experienced and what now can and will be done. Public rituals have the centering role of holding societal attention and suggesting collective meaning and action. In a time of mass media, these rituals can be extensive and inclusive, truly binding a nation together in grief.

Ongoing Ritual

Grief does not cease with the last funeral or the centering public ritual. Just as grief continues, effective rituals should continue as well, making cycles and events as the public grieves. This may take many forms. Rituals may and should accompany significant events such as the cleanup of a site, recovery of additional bodies, or other significant changes that are likely to engender public notice and renewed signs of grief.

Anniversary rituals are very significant. As an anniversary approaches, there are seasonal and chronological cues. The days take on added significance for survivors, reminding them of events that preceded the tragedy. Grieving family or friends may think or say, "This was the last time we saw him." Seasonal cues such as the weather, other occasions, or even regular events also prompt memories and renew feelings of loss in both survivors and the general public.

The anniversary ritual can play critical roles. First, it can educate the public about grief—reminding them that grief follows no timetable. This is important since many survivors and other members of the public may still be experiencing significant grief. Ritual validates that grief. Second, the anniversary ritual offers the opportunity to reframe the significance of the tragedy. Sometimes in national disasters, the ritual is a time to reflect on lessons that have been learned. In other cases, it is a renewed commitment to a cause. For example, at the first anniversary of 9/11, President Bush declared that "though they died in tragedy, they did not die in vain" as he called for renewed and continued efforts against terrorists (*The New York Times*, 9/12/02). In other cases, the tragedy may be a warning. On the sixth anniversary of the Oklahoma City bombing, fire department Chaplain Ted Wielsen challenged would-be terrorists to "see through the eyes of those present today, or those who are not here, or those who can never be here" as they contemplate the havoc they would wreak (*Canadian Press*, 4/19/01).

Third, anniversary rituals serve as rites of intensification, strengthening unity within and between groups. The anniversary rituals allow survivors, family members, rescuers, and the community at large to renew the bonds between them. Sometimes they can build bonds between victims of other, similar, tragedies. For example, some families who suffered the deaths of loved ones on September 11 attended the seventh anniversary rituals for Oklahoma City. They found and expressed unity in their shared losses.

Finally, the passage of time allows us to contemplate the enormity of the loss and acknowledge the individuals who died. In the immediate aftermath of loss, the individual dimensions of the tragedy may not be completely known or fully felt. At the first anniversary of 9/11, former New York City Mayor Rudolph Giuliani read the names of those who died. In Oklahoma City, a traditional part of the ritual is to observe 168 seconds of silence, one for each victim who died.

Different communities may observe these anniversary rituals in other ways. The immediacy of mass media allows inclusion. Rituals also may be designed by organizations such as places of worship, schools, or workplaces. Especially in areas where populations are deeply affected, rituals may be opportunities for education, solace and support.

Therapeutic Rituals

Rituals can offer powerful therapeutic interventions both for individuals and groups struggling with tragedy. These rituals can have a number of uses. Rituals of continuity are rituals that reaffirm that the person is not forgotten. Moments of silence or lighting a candle are simple examples of such ritual. Rituals of transition reflect changes, points in the journey of grief or collective response to tragedy. For example, officials of one company that had to vacate offices near the World Trade Center decided they needed a ritual as they moved back. Participants entered the now clean and empty space, sprinkled water to represent cleansing, and placed plants to represent the renewal of life in a place they had vacated because of the carnage nearby. After that, they retired to a brunch to rebuild a feeling of community after having been scattered to other offices.

Rituals of reconciliation allow individuals to finish business interrupted by tragedy. It provides opportunities to say a final goodbye or to give or accept forgiveness. In one school where a number of children were killed in a bus accident, students were given the option of writing notes that would be burned, the ashes then placed around a tree in their dead classmates' memory.

Rituals of affirmation complement rituals of reconciliation. Here, others may simply wish to affirm the person who died, celebrating that life, and offer thanks for the legacies that person left. In a grade school where a popular fourth grade teacher died, one therapeutic ritual was for each child to have the opportunity to write the most important lesson they had learned from the teacher. These were then read to the family as part of a school-based memorial ritual.

In designing therapeutic rituals, counselors need to keep in mind several points. First, it is important to be clear about the purpose of a ritual. Some rituals might combine purposes, for example, affirmation and reconciliation. In other cases, separate rituals may be necessary to meet varied interventive goals. Second, rituals should have elements that are both visible and symbolic. Rituals need to focus on something external such as water or plants, or objects that have special meaning. Often, powerful rituals make use of primal elements: fire, water, earth (plants), or wind (chimes). Third, the goal, audience, and elements must arise from the narrative or collective experience of the group. Effective therapeutic rituals arise from the shared story and are fully owned by the participants. This means that participants must have a key role in planning. Finally, therapeutic rituals should allow participants time to discuss and process the experience.

Rituals have no set ending point. They may continue on individual, collective, or therapeutic levels until they are no longer necessary or meaningful. There are still rituals marking Pearl Harbor more than 60 years after that attack. Perhaps as that war fades into distant memory and as the last survivors die, such rituals may gradually cease. In other cases, rituals will be incorporated in special holidays or days of remembrance. The designation of September 11 as Patriots Day demonstrates, among other meanings, a desire that the day never be forgotten and the rituals never cease.

MEMORIALIZATION AND PUBLIC TRAGEDY

While a ritual is an act invested in meaning, a memorial is a space invested with meaning. That space may be a permanent section of ground, set aside to commemorate an event such as a tragedy. Sometimes it is a more portable space such as a memory box or quilt. In other cases it may even be a space in time such as Oklahoma City's 168 seconds of silence.

Memorials are spaces *set aside* to remember. This distinguishes them from rituals. While the two are conceptually different, there are clear relationships. Rituals may consecrate a space as a memorial. Likewise, the sacred ground of a memorial is a powerful place for rituals to be enacted.

Spontaneous Memorials

As in ritual, the first memorials are spontaneous. After the death of Princess Diana, individuals brought offerings of flowers and stuffed toys to Buckingham Palace and to British consulates and embassies throughout the world. Similar offerings were brought to the remains of Oklahoma City or sites of other public tragedy.

The nature of spontaneous memorialization attests to the public nature of the tragedy. Haney, Leimer, and Lowery (1997) describe these spontaneous memorializations as inherently inclusive. They allow for the public to express their grief in their own individualized ways. Since they are individual, eclectic, possibly anonymous, and otherwise uncontrolled, they can allow the expression of a variety of feelings such as anger, guilt, or revenge that may not be publicly expressed at a public ritual or in a permanent memorial. Because these spontaneous rituals represent public expression, they do create a policy issue. Plans for public tragedy may need to include rituals to acknowledge these memorials and respectfully dismantle or otherwise deal with them.

Permanent Memorials

Public tragedies often need permanent acknowledgment. Both the site and type of memorial may generate considerate debate. In some cases, such as a natural disaster, there may not be a single site representing a tragedy. Even when there is a single site, there may be other activity at the site or other projected uses. For example, there may be questions about placing a memorial in a school. Often, such concerns reflect a desire to return to a sense of normalcy, a denial that significant loss and death occurred. In the case of the World Trade Center, the emotional and economic value of the property has created controversy about any redevelopment plans. A large question in that controversy is what type of space on that site, the place where so many died, will be set aside for a memorial.

A second issue is the nature and design of the memorial itself. At the Pentagon, there was some concern raised that a memorial holding the known remains of those killed in the attack would mix victims with hijackers. In other cases, design itself is an issue. A sculpture titled "Dark Elergy" commemorates the tragic destruction of Pan Am Flight 103 over Lockerbie, Scotland, by a terrorist bomb. Yet the design, which depicts the grief of mothers who lost children on the flight, has been criticized for ignoring the grief of fathers. Rockefeller Center in New York City has draped one of the first memorials to 9/11, a statue of a tumbling woman, because of complaints that it trivializes the attack.

The problem with such controversies is that they may complicate the grief of survivors and dissipate public concern about the tragedy. Sometimes these controversies can be avoided by creating memorial committees that include a wide range of stakeholders. In upstate New York, a court eventually resolved complaints about a proposed memorial for schoolchildren killed in a tornado. In the immediate aftermath of the tragedy, only parents who had lost children were named to the memorial committee. A more inclusive committee, one that included school administrators and other parents, might not have finalized a design that polarized the community. The fact remains, however, that in large public tragedies there may be numerous stakeholders and little consensus even within each group.

Other Memorials

Technology now makes possible virtual memorials. Much like spontaneous memorials, Internet memorials permit greater public participation, unbound by location, as well as opportunities to express a wide range of emotions.

There may be nonpermanent memorials as well. These can include "moving memorials" such as the HIV Names Project, popularly called the AIDS Quilt, that can travel to different locations. Other memorial events such as races, runs, or community drives mark an event. For example, one food pantry holds a memorial food drive, reminding its community that in a previous tornado, contributions were overwhelming. This provides an opportunity for the community to come together each year to remember and to act. In another community, there is an annual run for a state trooper near the anniversary of his tragic death. Such events reinforce the community and public ownership of a tragedy. They hallow a space, no matter where that space may be.

CONCLUSION

Public tragedies demand public ritual and memorialization. These twin processes of ritual and memorialization are powerful. This is attested by both the ancient and spontaneous use. Yet readers, counselors, and individuals can marshal and harness that power to soothe and unify a public coping with tragedy. ■

Kenneth J. Doka is a Professor of Gerontology at the Graduate School of The College of New Rochelle and Senior Consultant to the Hospice Foundation of America. Dr. Doka has written or edited 16 books and published more than 60 articles and book chapters. He is editor of both Omega *and* Journeys: A Newsletter for the Bereaved. *Dr. Doka was elected President of the Association for Death Education and Counseling (ADEC) in 1993. He was elected to the Board of the International Work Group on Dying, Death and Bereavement in 1995, and served as chair from 1997 to 1999. ADEC presented him with an Award for Outstanding Contributions in the Field of Death Education in 1998. In 2000 Scott and White presented him an award for Outstanding Contributions to Thanatology and Hospice. Dr. Doka is an ordained Lutheran minister.*

REFERENCES

Aron, D., & Livingston, S. (1999). A media event interrupts the global soap opera. *Psychologist, 10,* 501-502.

Gennep, A. von (1960). *The rites of passage.* Chicago: Chicago University Press.

Haney, C.A., Leimor, C., & Lowery, J. (1997). Spontaneous memorialization: Violent death and emerging mourning ritual. *Omega, 35,* 159-172.

Rando, T.A. (1984). *Grief, dying and death: Clinical interventions for caregivers.* Champaign, IL: Research Press.

Schwartz, B. (1991). Mourning and the making of a sacred symbol: Durkheim and the Lincoln assassination. *Social Forces, 70,* 343-364.

CHAPTER 16

A Healing Ritual at Yankee Stadium

David Benke

The day was clear. The sun was bright. Sunday, September 23, 2001, was a day in New York like so many others that autumn. It was much like September 11. But rain was about to fall through the dappled sunshine. For it was to be a day when God released in all of us a torrent of tears to bring us healing.

Coming out of the dugout into the sunshine at Yankee Stadium in the middle of the afternoon, I joined a host of religious figures in procession to our seats out on the field around second base. After the destruction of the Twin Towers just 12 days before, we had been invited to speak and to pray for healing by New York City Mayor Rudy Giuliani. Only two days after the attack he had structured a planning committee that understood both the enormous scope of the task and the city's and the nation's incredible need for such an event. As described by John Hiemstra, "The event planned and carried out was nonreligious by design, although religious leaders were included in the service, which was intended to help the general public deal with the grief and pain that was everywhere" (personal communication, January 2002). We accompanied James Earl Jones, emcee Oprah Winfrey, and guest singers, including Marc Anthony, Bette Midler, Placido Domingo, the Boys and Girls Choir of Harlem, and Lee Greenwood, among others who came as soon as they were asked. Twenty thousand at Yankee Stadium and a worldwide television audience sang, wept, prayed, mourned, listened, and held onto one another for two and a half hours on September 23.

The event was called A Prayer for America. As conceived by the mayor and carried out by all of us, it was exactly that. I sat and stood next to Admiral Natter of the United States Navy, the Commander of the Atlantic Fleet, who spoke of the strength and resolve of the government of the United States in continuing the vision of the hope connected to the American dream with rock-solid determination. A Prayer for America was a lesson in the civic ritual of healing as important as any in the recent history of the United States. It also marked a profound turning point in my own life.

WE ALL WEPT TOGETHER

We all wept together. Openly. All afternoon. In public—in fact, in the most well-known public baseball arena in the world. The admiral and the actress; the cop and the boxing impresario; the kid from Queens and the matron from Long Island; the social worker from Brooklyn and the socialite from Manhattan; the imam and the rabbi; the priest and the pundit; the violinist and the groundskeeper; the mayor and the governor; all of us were filled and emptied and filled again. The sign was our tears. Song by song, prayer by prayer, speech by speech we were moved and transported. We were taken by words and music to and from the location of our distress in lower Manhattan where rescue workers still plunged into the debris, then to the neighborhoods and homes of victim families where terrible truth was unfolding, then to the firehouses wreathed with flowers and tributes masking (failing to mask) the deadly silence at the empty stalls of colleagues, then to the inner rooms and secret places of our souls where the cries of anguish reverberate with unceasing intensity, then to the halls of heaven where those cries are finally heard.

We were transported thus *together*, as a group. Separated day by day through the usual means by race, clan, neighborhood, religious upbringing, size of wallet, age, and activity, we were for one afternoon at least a common humanity. We all wept together.

Listen to this description of the experience of our host, Mayor Giuliani, as described in *Time* magazine: "[Yankee Stadium was] the first major public event after the attack. Giuliani spoke briefly, but mostly he sat near second base, looking into the sea of grieving faces—the families of the dead and missing cops and firefighters who filled the infield, sobbing and clutching photographs of their lost loved ones. He had met many of them at the Family Center or during gatherings over the past 12 days, so 'in some cases I could put them together with a name,' he recalls. 'In some cases, I couldn't help but remember the faces. And listening to the beautiful music and the religious leaders, and Bette Midler singing the hero song, I just lost it'" (Pooley, 2001).

We all "lost it" there together. At the same time, we were granted that wondrous discovery that we were *finding* it again. The strength to go on was the gift received from our common mourning, our common humanity, our commonly shed tears.

A REPRESENTATIVE PRAYER

What was my personal role at Yankee Stadium on September 23? As a delegate through the mayor's committee, selected by the Protestant leader Dr. John Hiemstra, Executive Director of the Council of Churches, City of New York, I was asked to offer a one-minute prayer. The prayer would come late in the program, just before Lee Greenwood sang "Proud to be an American" and just after what I knew would be a ringing and powerful speech by Dr. Calvin Butts, Pastor of Abyssinian Baptist Church in Harlem.

The sweep of the ritual of healing happening through the day was in this way compacted into the mini-unit of speech, prayer, and song there at the end. My own emotions and spiritual vulnerability were at the raw and open edge after two hours.

I was introduced by Dr. Butts and made my way to the podium. This is what I said and prayed:

> Oh, we're stronger now than we were an hour ago.
> And you know, my sisters and brothers, we're not nearly
> as strong as we're going to be. And the strength
> we have is the power of love. And the power of love you have
> received is from God, for God is love. So take the hand of one
> next to you now and join me in prayer on this
> "Field of dreams" turned into God's house of prayer:

> O Lord our God, we're leaning on You today.
> You are our Tower of Strength, and we're leaning on You.
> You are our Mighty Fortress, our God who is a Rock;
> in You do we stand. Those of us who bear the name of Christ know that
> You stood so tall when You stooped down to
> send a Son through death and life to bring us back together,
> and we lean on You today.

O Tower of Strength, be with those who mourn the loss of loved ones;
bring them closer to us day by day.
O Heavenly Father, we pray at this time that
You might extend Jacob's ladder for those who ascended
the stairways to save us, as others escaped the fire and flames.

O Tower of Strength, open innocent and victimized hearts
to the sacrifice of the Innocent One; pour Your consolation
upon the traumatized, especially our children.

O Heavenly Father, un-bind, un-fear, un-scorch, un-sear our souls;
renew us in Your free Spirit. We're leaning on You,
our Tower of Strength.
We find our refuge in the shadow of Your shelter.

Lead us from this place—strong—to bring forth the
power of Your love, wherever we are.
In the precious name of Jesus. Amen.

I had made up my mind on the way to the podium to return only after personally embracing four people: Mayor Giuliani, Governor Pataki, Police Commissioner Bernard Kerik, and Fire Commissioner Nicholas Von Essen. These civic leaders had been front and center in the lives and hearts of all New Yorkers for 12 straight days. On a tour of Ground Zero in the middle of the week, I had met Governor Pataki. We were at the nadir of our journey, at the morgue outside the World Financial Center. His presence to those of us on that tour was a sign that somehow death in its full horror was being wrestled to the ground. Fire Commissioner Von Essen had the most difficult duty of all, dealing with the loss of 342 firefighters, the greatest such tragedy in the history of the United States.

I returned to my seat to harmonize with Lee Greenwood as he sang "Proud to Be an American." The line "I'd gladly stand up next to you and defend her still today" remains with me for this reason—next to me stood Admiral Natter. Yes, we all wept together on September 23, 2001.

LESSONS FROM THIS CIVIC RITUAL OF HEALING

The points I wish to make are primarily personal and experiential. They cannot and could not be clinical. By the same token, because what happened in New York during September, 2001, will become paradigmatic and symbolic for our nation and even for the world for some years to come, lessons from the experience can be parsed and used in other times and places.

Civic Leadership and its Religious Rationale

The most critical ingredient in the civic ritual of healing that took place on September 23, 2001, at Yankee Stadium was the leadership of the mayor of New York City. This cannot be overemphasized. Given the diversity of opinion and belief in our country, the unifying factor in developing a program that is civic, religious, and patriotic is the community leader exercising his or her office.

What leadership did Mayor Giuliani provide between September 11 and September 23? The list would include, in no particular order:

- *Unifying tasks.* There was a common reporting and organizing function that the mayor's office performed from the very beginning.

- *Access.* For example, the location of the event changed, due to the tremendous increase in security processes, from Central Park to Yankee Stadium. The mayoral team could coordinate this enormous task, specifically, assigning police and security forces, getting necessary legal permissions, and communicating to the public through local police precincts.

- *Civic, patriotic, and religious coordination.* The divergent worlds of celebrities, entertainers, politicians, religious leaders, and the general public all coalesced on September 23. Could the preacher deliver the actor? Could the entertainer tell the priest what to do? None of that would have worked in the least, and yet the mayor and his staff were able to arrange all of these "divisions of labor."

- *Specific religious coordination.* For those of us in the religious realm, there was great, real tension in our interrelationships in September 2001. The terrorists were uniformly Muslim, the targets indiscriminately American yet centered on our towers of strength. The ability to speak and conduct ourselves religiously was greatly aided by the influence of the mayor's office. We were neither kept at arms' length from one another nor locked in argument. Through the mayor's leadership, we were able to focus on a single purpose: bring the city together to heal.

■ *Moral civic leadership.* Mayor Giuliani exerted all due influence to encourage healing at a time of strife and crisis. Since the mayor's behavior on and after September 11 was not only exemplary but heroic, his influence to call for a ritual of healing became enormous. He not only had a political instinct to do so, he had a personal burden to deal with from his extensive contact with victim families, rescue workers, and all New Yorkers. He was truly a representative person in those days.

Given these insights, my recommendation is that city by city and hamlet by hamlet, civic leaders should be trained and encouraged to use their influence to convene representative groups of religious, civic, and public leaders at times of crisis. The extraordinary, common-sense steps and inclusions offered by Mayor Giuliani, former Mayors Dinkins and Koch, and by Mayor Giuliani's designees made the September 23 civic ritual possible.

Religious Rationale

From a Christian and Lutheran perspective, the role of the civic leader in such enterprises is dictated by reading and understanding the Apostle Paul's words to the Roman Christians 20 centuries ago: "Everyone must submit himself to the governing authorities, for there is no authority except that which God has established. The authorities that exist have been established by God... Therefore, it is necessary to submit to the authorities, not only because of possible punishment but also because of conscience" (Romans 13:1,5).

As a Lutheran I appreciate the specific theological rationale for appropriate participation in the civic arena under the doctrine called the Two Kingdoms (Atlantic District Pastors, 2002). For me, God's Kingdom of Grace, which is the church, and God's Kingdom of Power, which is the world, place me in a tension that is ever present. In the world I present myself with integrity as a witness and am privileged to participate in the activities of a free society within the limits of justice and forbearance. This is a truly liberating concept. Other religious traditions have greater or lesser or different insights from the same or totally different texts.

Yet in the United States there is something more. Our country does not operate under the auspices of a state church, such as the Anglican tradition in Great Britain. We do not operate the United States as a theocracy, as in some Muslim states. We possess not partial but full religious freedom. The fundamental civic truth is that we are one nation *"under God."* This civil use of "God" in times of crisis allows civic leaders to encourage all religious leaders, irrespective of denomination or belief system, to participate specifically as *representatives of their tradition* at events such as rituals of civic healing. Yankee Stadium was simply a very visible and internationally necessary example of that principle.

The integrity of prayer or speech to religious tradition cannot in our society be specified by a governmental agent. Mayor Giuliani did not tell us how to pray. The civic leader knew that prayers were needed and that we would pray them as we represented our various constituencies. I informed my own national, regional, and local leadership that I would be representing the Lutheran Church-Missouri Synod. Poignant to me were comments from many Lutheran Christians around the country saying, "Thanks for representing me. Your prayer helped me to heal." Most especially, Lutheran victim family members present at Yankee Stadium and watching at home wrote and called to say, "You represented me before God when I could not even begin to pray. You let God lift my spirits for the first time." That was the task of the religious leaders who prayed on September 23. It was the leadership of the civic leader, the mayor of New York City, which gave us the opportunity.

Expediting Ritual in a Crisis

As the crisis in New York unfolded, every minute of every day for the first several weeks was taken up in reaction and fresh revelation. Shock, grief, new pictures, different information, threats from unknown sources, incredible difficulties in transportation—all of it became hammer blow after hammer blow. Mayor Giuliani's estimate of the death total—"It will be more than we can bear,"—was on everyone's lips and hearts (Pooley, 2001). To have delayed the civic ritual of healing would have been to deny it. The magnitude of civic fear, anger, and grief contained in metropolitan New York cannot be emphasized enough. Millions of us were eyewitnesses to the horror of the destruction of the Twin Towers. The ongoing social, emotional, economic, and spiritual impact of the event will remain for years.

The process of healing had to begin in the midst of the grief in order for New Yorkers to believe that healing was even possible. It had to be public, and it had to be quick. It is not insignificant that the first public event in New York City after 9/11 was A Prayer for America at Yankee Stadium on September 23. The effect on the populace was enormous and immediate. In my role as President of the Atlantic District and Chairman of the Lutheran Disaster Response of New York, I received correspondence from literally thousands of people around the country. In precinct after precinct, neighborhood after neighborhood, from the city through the suburbs people wrote to express their release. There was an exhalation, a fresh breath taken. People telephoned friends and shared tears as they watched, and hope breathed anew (personal correspondence, 2001-2002). My strong encouragement and advice is for civic and religious leaders not to delay in bringing citizens together at a time of crisis, so that the hope of healing can begin.

The Importance of Commemoration

The most memorable features of the Yankee Stadium event were the tear-stained faces of those in attendance lifting aloft pictures of missing loved ones while holding tight to comrades or family members. At that early date, many of these people, who eventually came to be known as victim families, were living in the hope of miraculous recoveries by rescue workers at Ground Zero. People came to Yankee Stadium with the full soul-force of dreading what they most feared while at the same time grabbing onto a thin thread of hope.

In this context the encouragement to bring and lift up those pictures as songs were sung and prayers were prayed was the first commemoration of the dead, even before the death notices had arrived. It was apparent to me that the process of remembering, of "fleshing out" the memory of the dead, was a critical component of the civic ritual healing that took place on September 23. And the most critical aspect of this fleshing out is that it was done in the open air, in public.

The 20,000 of us were specifically *not* in our homes or our churches or our neighborhoods. The public act of lifting up the pictures of the dead and missing was the most appropriate commemorative act possible because it was accomplished not by word, song, or representative, but by those directly affected themselves. For many people, only by such a public, defiant, and at the same time pleading act of commemoration can the process of healing be initiated. The act is defiant because public remembrance *will not allow* the departed person to be removed from view; it is pleading because it asks us to see that the hand holding the photograph belongs to a person who loved the missing individual and asks us to grieve with them.

My advice and strongest encouragement is to the civic leaders in New York or anywhere such a crisis and death toll might occur. Do not spare the time, energy, money, and space necessary to create an appropriate memorial. Its creation is the direct connection to the person behind the hand holding the photo. It would be inhuman and inhumane not to grant the space and context for commemoration.

INTEGRITY, NOT EXPLOITATION

The culture of commercialism and celebrity that pervades in the United States often makes a mockery of noble purpose. To conduct a ritual of civic healing appropriately and meaningfully from the standpoint of political and entertainer involvement, there could be no incursion of the promotional, venal, or, in the worst-case scenario, the self-promotional. Conversely, the participation of religious leaders had to be designed to be representative and not proselytizing. These are some pretty choppy waters!

The fact that the event was designed to be A Prayer for America and was conducted under the auspices of the civic government set the table for its success in maintaining integrity and excluding exploitation. None of the public figures or entertainers was anything more or less on that day than a participant in a public ritual of healing. Participation was painful, personal, and meaningful. This is the difference between a public event and a game or spectacle. The professional and political people involved were there in service of a public seeking healing and holding their emotions aloft. And those leaders knew and respected it.

From the point of view of religious participation, the issue is the integrity of the witness. First of all, as explained above, there were no restrictions placed on the witness to be offered by any faith community representative. Secondly, the various representatives spoke to their constituencies passionately and appropriately. From my personal Lutheran and Christian perspective, I have availed myself of the words of St. Peter, "In your hearts set apart Christ as Lord. Always be prepared to give an answer to everyone who asks you to give the reason for the hope that you have. But do this with gentleness and respect" (I Peter 3:15).

September 23, 2001, was the first visible and public occasion when New Yorkers saw their religious leaders gathered across the boundaries of their convictions, Jew and Muslim, Christian and Hindu, to give witness together. What they heard were songs and words and prayers for healing. The dynamic tension inherent in the religious impulse is both dangerous and beneficent. Particularly because of the nature of the exclusive claims of adherents, the religious enterprise is fraught with difficulty. A Prayer for America was one of the most beneficent exercises of the religious impulse I have witnessed or served as a participant. This civic ritual of healing produced genuine personal and communal healing for the citizenry. It could not have happened had dangerous religious impulses been at work.

I must also state, however, that since September 23, as a result of my prayer, I have been brought up on charges of heresy and suspended from the clergy roster of my denomination for praying in the midst of people of other religions (St. Peter's Lutheran Church, 2002). I have received death threats and been called a murderer and a terrorist for the prayer you read above. I am well aware of the dangerous aspects of the religious impulse.

The final lesson I am learning, therefore, is that the process of human grief and healing is uneven and continual; its religious dimension at the depths is both most powerfully alleviative as well as most powerfully explosive.

Dr. David H. Benke has served as President of the Atlantic District of the Lutheran Church-Missouri Synod since 1991. He is currently suspended from that post following charges against him for heresy upheld on June 25, 2002, for his prayer at Yankee Stadium on September 23, 2001. He serves under suspension as the Pastor of St. Peter's Lutheran Church, Brooklyn, New York. He is also the Chairman of the Lutheran Disaster Response of New York (LDRNY), founded on September 13, 2001. LDRNY has an annual budget of some $5 million to alleviate suffering as a result of the events of September 11, 2001. Dr. Benke also serves during 2002 as the Interim Chief Executive Officer of Lutheran Social Services of New York, which conducts programs, including "Project Life," designed to assist those affected by the events of September 11, 2001.

REFERENCES

Atlantic District Pastors. (2002). That we may be one. Sent to all parishes in the Lutheran Church-Missouri Synod. Retrieved September 7, 2002, from http://www.stpeter-brooklyn.org

St. Peter's Lutheran Church. (2002). Pastor's prayer for America: 9/23/01. Retrieved September 7, 2002 from http://www.stpeter-brooklyn.org

Pooley, Eric. (2001, December 31). Mayor of the World. *Time*. [Electronic Version]. Retrieved January 3, 2003 from http://www.time.com/time/poy2001/poyprofile.html

CHAPTER 17

Public Tragedy and the Arts

Sandra Bertman

Believing in the concept of world trade, Japanese architect Minoru Yamasaki designed New York's World Trade Center to be a living symbol of humankind's dedication to international cooperation and peace. "The World Trade Center should," Yamasaki said, "because of its importance, become a living representation of man's belief in humanity, his need for individual dignity, his belief in the cooperation of men, and through this cooperation his ability to find greatness" (Heyer, 1966).

Though he intended the 110-story steel-frame, glass, and concrete-slab towers to be more than commercial office space, Yamasaki could never have envisioned what the World Trade Center has come to signify since the events of 9/11. This public tragedy stunned Americans and left us groping and searching for explanations. The scale of the horror—the numbers who died when the towers fell, the destruction of two mighty skyscrapers, the strategy of using airplanes fully loaded with fuel as weapons, the suicides of the terrorists, the murder of the other passengers—all add to the chaos, conundrum, and soul pain.

Artists are missionaries, shamans, magicians of their crafts, expressing, in many modes and in various media, the inexpressible. The inexpressible happened on that perfect, cloudless morning—September 11, 2001—when these towers, along with the Pentagon, became the symbols of a devastating attack on democracy and freedom.

ART HELPS US COPE

What can we learn from the way people—both recognized artists and their audience—turn to the arts in times of public tragedy? In every era, artists—whether poets, dancers, musicians, architects, sculptors, painters, cartoonists, filmmakers—have created art in response to tragic events.

Thankfully, artists, both professionals who make art for a large audience and nonprofessionals who make art primarily for themselves, have already responded and will continue to respond to the 9/11 attack. Bruce Springsteen released an album, *The Rising*, urging his listeners to transform shock and grief into fortitude: in the song "My City of Ruins," the lyrics exhort, "Come on, rise up!" (Tyrangiel, 2002). Aidan Fontana, the six-year-old son of a trapped fireman, spent the months following the attack in kindergarten where he built and rebuilt the twin towers out of wooden blocks and told a story about how he might have saved his father if he had been with him (LeDuff, 2002). An elderly friend, not directly connected to the tragedy, spent several months at her computer, drawing and printing pictures of the towers—towers in night and towers by day, as if to make them stand again. She had never before shown any interest in drawing skyscrapers. There is a creative gene in each of us (Bertman, 1999), and we turn to it, and want to use it, particularly in times of perplexity.

What happened on 9/11 is unspeakable. What happened at Ground Zero initially is beyond words. We're talking now about the morality of killing—correction, murdering—so many unknowing, unprepared, innocent victims: firemen climbing endless stairs to rescue people, police responding quickly to the emergency, restaurant workers going about their daily tasks, office workers who had no idea what they represented to the terrorists. How dare the arts—normally the purveyors of words, color, sound, joy, wit, and irony—attempt to minister to such horror, emptiness, and tragedy? The half-Jewish Marxist Theodor Adorno objected to what he thought of as art's glossing over: "To write poetry after Auschwitz is barbaric" (Adorno, 1949).

Immediately after 9/11, all forms of entertainment, concerts, Broadway shows, museum openings, were cancelled. The Smithsonian museums in Washington, D.C., reported an almost 50 percent drop in attendance in the aftermath. How could any film or drama be "relevant"? At first the nation paid respect appropriately—with silence—and then with communal mourning: makeshift shrines of teddy bears, candles, photographs of the missing, messages, bouquets of flowers, flags. On these shrines, scribbled prayers referencing, indeed transcending, all religious traditions appeared

9/11 Building Block Memorial. In lower Manhattan, architects placed wooden blocks, colored markers and other art supplies on the sidewalk outside their offices and invited passersby to help design and construct the block sculpture evolving in the lobby.

spontaneously. "On Monday, we e-mailed jokes. On Tuesday [9/11], we did not…. On Monday, politicians argued about surplus budgets. On Tuesday, grief-stricken on the White House steps, they sang in unison 'God Bless America'" (adapted from a number of websites, including NATCA, 2001, quiltweb.com, 2001, Motorsports Ministries, 2001).

Within a short time, media coverage, memorial services, many kinds of music, which Leo Tolstoy called the shorthand of emotion, moved us outward to the public and collective, providing consolation and community. We began to listen to and sing along with "Amazing Grace," Barber's "Adagio for Strings," "America the Beautiful," African-American spirituals, "Ave Maria" in several versions, Sousa's marches, the national anthem, taps, as well as recordings of various requiem masses. We also continue to observe many moments of respectful silence. Art, symbol, and prayer all emanate from and minister to the same source—the human soul.

ART IS RELEVANT

In a televised interview, Bill T. Jones (2001), dancer and choreographer, was asked how dance could be relevant as a response to 9/11. Was he, himself, in fact able to dance? Could he envision himself going back to the site, to Ground Zero, and dancing? Yes, he could, was the reply, "I could dance with respect . . . I could dance with grief . . . I could dance and invite grieving people to dance, and we'd dance together." A few decades earlier, the playwright Samuel Beckett expressed his own deep-seated need to write: "one writes not in order to be published; one writes in order to breathe" (Mitchelmore, 2000). In addition to manmade disasters, public tragedies can be the result of natural catastrophes—earthquakes, hurricanes, tornadoes, floods—often sudden and terrifying. These also take their toll on the human psyche, and artists respond. A recent book of short stories by the Japanese writer Haruki Murakami, titled *After the Quake*, centers on the 1995 earthquake in Kobe. In addition to 4,000 dead, another 300,000 people lost everything, homes and all. Murakami's parents were among the homeless. A reviewer, Jeff Giles, wrote in *The New York Times*: "What makes the book so moving is the sense that on some level it is Murakami's deeply felt get-well card" (2000). Murakami writes about those who survived the quake, their dread, their fear of another similar disaster. With natural disasters, however catastrophic, the survivors do not have to deal with the evil or madness of fellow human beings; their questions involve the impersonal forces of nature or the mysteries of God.

In dealing with 9/11, most of us are just not struggling with our many emotions—shock, disbelief, surprise, horror, sadness, anger at the perpetrator—we are rediscovering and reformulating exactly what we value. In times of tragedy we desperately seek out those among us who can see beyond logic, analysis, reasons, ideologies, politics, and minister to our broken spirits. We need artists of all descriptions who can arouse our numbed or raw emotions and provide insight, catharsis, sanity, connection, even consolation.

ART IS RESISTANCE AND PROTEST

Artists have responded to public tragedies throughout the ages. In some cases, only a work of art, often a masterpiece, remains to remind us of a public tragedy, particularly after time and successive tragedies have pushed the event itself from public consciousness. Who knows about the massacre at Chios? But the painter Delacroix teaches us in his *Massacre of Chios*, hanging in the Louvre.

In 1937, Picasso painted a 26-foot-long mural as a tribute to the Spanish town of Guernica. The Basques, a minority population in Spain, were opposed to the Spanish fascist Franco, who called in his German allies to bomb one of their towns to ashes. Approximately 1,700 unarmed men, women, and children were slaughtered in a sneak raid, with no warning they were about to be shot down from the air—a relatively unknown form of attack at that date. A few days after the bombing, Picasso made his first, very rough, still existing sketch (8 by 10 inches), compelled by his feelings of outrage, and continued to develop his ideas with more finished sketches in the following weeks. Three months later, a memorable visual image, speaking of mass slaughter of innocent people and the singling out of a minority group, was brought to the world's attention by a painter already celebrated in his own lifetime.

Picasso allowed himself only black, gray, and white—paradoxically, a colorless painting. The recognizable details, a mother holding her dead child, a screaming horse, a burning house, a bull, a lamp, a broken sword, and so forth, are only schematically drawn and act as complex symbols. Picasso later said they were perhaps unconscious symbols; he was not aware of creating specific political symbols. The Norwegian painter Edvard Munch wrote of this mural: "This painting is not cruel at all—imagine how Goya would have done it—and yet it represents war" (Boeck & Sabartes, 1957). Another critic, Herbert Read, called it a "monument to disillusion, to despair, to destruction" (Barr, 1946).

A century earlier, Goya, another Spanish painter, responded to the suppression of a popular revolt by painting a monumental canvas now hanging in the Prado in Madrid, titled *Executions of the 3rd May, 1808—*

Guernica. *Pablo Picasso's huge work was inspired by an event that occurred during the Spanish Civil War. For four hours on April 26, 1937, the German* Luftwaffe *bombed and machine-gunned the Basque village of Guernica, leveling its homes and businesses and*

a historical event barely recalled. Goya shows well-equipped soldiers who put an end to a popular uprising by shooting unarmed, shabbily dressed men. The painter depicts viscerally the fear visible in the enlarged white eyes of those still alive and the profuse blood seeping from the dead lying all over the ground. Whereas Picasso uses symbolic flat images, Goya explicitly and graphically illustrates the scene. Both, however, use their art to express outrage over great wrongs done by and to fellow human beings. In diverse ways these artists document, they do not censor. One speculates that painting these massive works brought some relief to the artists themselves, in their efforts to make clear to viewers what they must know about the human capacity for brutality. The words attributed to Pastor Marin Niemoller carved in the granite base supporting an eternal flame in the Hall of Remembrance at the United States Holocaust Memorial Museum in Washington, D.C., do the same:

decimating the population. The painting aroused world opinion against fascism. Sixty-six years later, Guernica *remains one of the best-known anti-war statements of all time.*

First they came for the socialists, and I did not speak out—because I was not a socialist. Then they came for the trade unionists, and I did not speak out—because I was not a trade unionist. Then they came for the Jews, and I did not speak out—because I was not a Jew. Then they came for me—and there was no one left to speak for me. (Littell, 1986)

Art Is Consolation

Another form of healing is offered by architect Maya Lin's Vietnam Veterans Memorial located in Washington, D.C. (1991). The then young and unknown Lin won the competition to design the monument. The visual restraint of the simple wall, the aesthetics of abstraction, the endless listing of names of those lost, speak in a meaningful way to untold numbers of visitors. Vietnam veterans hold reunions at the wall, touching the names of their lost buddies, leaving offerings, and embracing tearfully. A simple, inscribed marble sculpture in a V-shape helps them, and us, acknowledge the waste and loss of war (58,158 American soldiers dead), and helps us find our way, eventually, back to humanity and hope.

Memorial Hall, now familiarly called Mem Hall, in Cambridge, Massachusetts, was erected by Harvard College to honor the young Harvard classmen who had perished in the Civil War. Harvard now uses the sizable building for lectures, concerts, and examinations. A precedent for Maya Lin's Vietnam Memorial, the names of the dead were listed high on the walls of the central hall—now easily overlooked unless one looks up. The names, from well-known New England families, along with the birth and death dates of the students—and the hallowed names of battlefields on which they died— are moving. Those killed all died at a very young age, cheated of their lives and of fathering the next generation.

The healing power of art is not a rhetorical fantasy. Somehow the pain of loss is reduced as the evidence is preserved and the event is shared. These shared human connections remind us of the fakeries of "clock" time. The past, present, and future are acknowledged and consoling in the world of now.

ART ASKS QUESTIONS

On being asked to write a poem early in World War I, Yeats did not feel personally moved by the event and even seemed emotionally detached in his reply. He responded with a very short poem of six lines, titled "On Being Asked for a War Poem" and argued in it that the poet has "no gift to set a statesman right." He further wrote, in a letter to Henry James, that this was "the only thing I have written of the war or will write" (Jeffares, 1968).

Surprisingly, he had a much stronger poem to write before the war was finished. Yeats was deeply touched when people he knew personally, Irish nationalists who were fighting for Irish independence, were quickly executed by the English after mounting a revolt around the Dublin post office. "I had no idea that any public event could so deeply move me—and I am very despondent about the future" (Jeffares, 1968). This painful situation moved Yeats to write at length; the resulting poem, "Easter 1916," frequently anthologized, is considered among the very best of his many fine poems. He memorialized several of the executed men as well as a woman friend who was imprisoned, speaking of personal qualities, not always flattering—one showed "ignorant good will," another was "a drunken, vainglorious lout." But his earlier opinion of them had been changed by their willingness to die for their passionate cause of freedom: "What if excess of love/Bewildered them till they died?" he asked. Of another dead Irish nationalist, he wrote sympathetically:

> He might have won fame in the end,
> So sensitive his nature seemed,
> So daring and sweet his thought.

Yeats was too untouched by the impersonal war to write about it until he was personally assaulted by his friends' sacrifice. In "Easter 1916," he asks himself, and us, a significant question: "Was it needless death after all?" And we respond by asking ourselves: Are all war deaths needless deaths?

ART OFFERS ANSWERS

Michael James Cotton, owner of Michael's Liquor Store in Waltham, Massachusetts, had never written a book before, but 9/11 prodded him to begin, and in four months he completed 200 pages. He then found a publisher and his book became available on Amazon.com. "After September 11," he said, "I wanted to make sure to get the point across to people that something had to be done. I never thought I'd write a book, but once I started punching out the words, I kept going" (Stern, 2002).

Cotton feels that "aggressive" methods must be used to make sure America remains safe, and his book is about a small group of American soldiers sent to find the Al Qaeda terrorist organization. He drew upon his own war experiences in Vietnam. His book, entitled *9/11: The Day the Call Went Out Around the World,* had a goal: Through his writing he wanted to urge all Americans, rather than feeling vulnerable and powerless, to take necessary steps to make sure America remains secure. His strong desire to get his message out turned him into a published writer.

We may not agree with Michael Cotton's retaliative aggressive "answers." We do not look to creative expressions simplistically for "right or wrong"— but for insight. Respecting the act of art-making for clarifying life and its meaning for each of us, we welcome the uncanny ability of others' creative products to put us in touch with ourselves and our own beliefs in authentic ways.

ART PROMPTS RECOVERY

Many artists, both professionals and nonprofessionals, have responded to the events of 9/11. Newspapers have reported record numbers of concerts, exhibitions, and sales of photography to raise money for victims. The Internet continues to spill over with websites dealing with the attack—in the categories of theater, writing (poetry), conversations with artists, sound, and music— to name just a few that were indexed (PBS, 2002; Americans for the Arts, 2002; Hauck, 2001). At the Theatre Development Fund's online newsletter for teens, *Play by Play*, high school students were invited to submit original dramatic monologues, scenes, even complete plays (2002).

Detroit's Museum of New Art rotated photography exhibits, such as "Photography Now, Beyond Narrative"; the Museum of Modern Art in New York offered "From the Ashes." *The New York Times* reports on endless books published on every aspect of the attack and estimated that as many as 150 books were published to commemorate the first anniversary of 9/11.

Students at the Stuyvesant High School, who were three blocks from the World Trade Center on that Tuesday morning, interviewed one another and wrote monologues about their experiences after their teacher noticed how eager they were to tell their individual stories of what happened to them during that day. The results were collected in a book, *With Their Eyes*, and published by HarperCollins for other young readers. Elementary school students' drawings from Lotspeich School in Cincinnati, Ohio, were used to illustrate a simple yet honest book, *September 11, 2001*, portraying the facts, stressing patriotism over assault (Poffenberger, 2002). Children's books on the subject include *New York's Bravest* (Knopf) and *Fireboat* (Putnam).

CAN ART BE INAPPROPRIATE AND TRIVIALIZE?

Public tragedies are of such magnitude that, to some critics, art dealing with them seems trivial, inappropriate, sentimental, unworkable, even offensive. Explaining what he meant by "writing a poem after Auschwitz is barbaric," Adorno later said, "something of the horror is removed" (Adorno, 1982). A more moderate position is surely that Auschwitz is not unimaginable, not inexpressible. Nor is it morally repugnant to write about it. The questions it raises deserve to be faced by every human conscience: How could human beings have done what they did at Auschwitz? Murdering women, children, whole families, because one group had decided another group should be wiped out.

The moving account, *Anne Frank: The Diary of a Young Girl,* is widely read and records the terrible forces gathering, as witnessed and recorded by a girl in hiding with her family. Her writing, her art, clearly must have helped this perceptive, acutely alive youngster who died as a teenager in a concentration camp, make sense of what was going on around her. That Anne Frank was not allowed to live out her life is indeed barbaric. Her journal writing, describing her family's attempt to survive and avoid deportation—and worse—is not, despite Theodor Adorno's dictum against art after Auschwitz. It is more illuminating to understand Anne's situation, and her fear, by reading her diary entries than to understand the phenomenon by studying statistics of how many died in camps. Art is a peaceful means of teaching about human failings and inhumanity, in the hope that the lessons of vigilance, responsibility, tolerance, and compassion can be learned before it is too late.

After 9/11, a series called "Terror Widows"—in a pop-culture comic book format—began to appear in newspapers and on the Internet. One cartoon by Ted Rally showed two panels: a widow of one of the victims laments, "I keep waiting for Kevin to come home, but I know he never will." And another widow responds: "Fortunately, the $3.2 million I collected from the Red Cross keeps me warm at night." This strip was pulled from *The New York Times* website when feedback indicated many readers found it inappropriate, feeling that it might cause gratuitous pain to victims.

The cartoonist refused to apologize, saying, "pushing the envelope of polite criticism is what editorial cartoonists do." The implication that some women prefer money to anything else might be in some circumstances amusing, but it seems highly insensitive and hurtful to women survivors trying to cope—and questionably amusing even to those not directly affected. What is the "polite criticism" that the cartoonist is trying to get beyond? Humor at the expense of people grieving is worse than tasteless. On the other hand, some pop culture creations, *The New Yorker* magazine cover at Halloween (October 29, 2001) showing youngsters going trick-or-treat dressed as firemen and policemen, or the special Marvel comic book edition, *Heroes* (2001), including works by superhero creators Alex Ross, Sam Kieth, Stan Lee and Joe Quesada (proceeds to the Twin Towers Fund), are heartwarming. Quoting from the back cover:

Comic book universes are populated by colorful characters that possess fantastic powers. But on September 11, 2001, an untold number of real men and women amazed the world with their phenomenal acts of bravery. When others ran away, they charged forward. When others reached out for safety, they offered a helping hand. When others cried out, they responded with a soothing voice. And, tragically, many of them died . . . but in doing so taught us all how to live.

They can't stick to walls.
They can't summon thunder.
They can't fly.
They're just HEROES.

After 9/11, the nation gradually recovered some of its equilibrium, but the shock and aftereffects lingered for months, and many were still feeling uneasy, approaching the first anniversary of the attack. According to *The New York Times*, survivors, witnesses and nonwitnesses, continue to seek psychiatric care and psychologists predict they might need it for years to come. In *The New Republic*, the drama critic Robert Brustein mused on the "relevance" of three new plays that had the bad luck to be mounted on Broadway in the months directly after the attack. Brustein expressed what continued to bother him and others: "Through no fault of their authors, none is really 'relevant' to what has been lacerating our souls this season." The plays Brustein wanted to see in the aftermath had to attempt to answer the large, difficult, and perhaps unanswerable questions—about evil, terrorists, human behavior—about why.

Some thoughts have been expressed about the commercialization of the event, Springsteen's album, in particular. Charles Cross, publisher of Springsteen's fan magazine, said, "they're really marketing it as a September 11 album. I think we need art that can deal with it, but . . . it's still pretty fresh. Frankly the commercial element of it really scares me" (Tryangiel, 2002).

Some critics worry that enough time and distance must pass. Whether the artist needs time and distance or not seems best left to the artist. Benjamin Britten waited, and his much admired Requiem on World War II was composed 16 years after the end of the war. But Wilfred Owen did not wait and wrote his war poems, including "Anthem for Doomed Youth," beginning with the line "What passing-bells for those who die as cattle?" in the middle of World War I, which he did not survive.

So where are we? We need the arts to help us cope and to find our way back to belief in humanity. They arm us with specific and practical strategies relevant to young and old whatever their background, culture, or beliefs. They ask the soulful and spiritual questions, offer answers and call us to action—resistance, protest, witness, and prayer. They can and do prompt recovery, but they can be inappropriate and trivialize. In *Zorba the Greek*, Zorba asks the questions, "Why do the young die? Why does anybody die? . . . What's the use of all your damn books if they can't answer questions like that? What the hell can they do for you?" The young scholar answers him: "Well, they tell me about the agony of the man who can't answer questions like yours" (Kazantzakis, 1952).

Naj Wikoff, president of the Society for the Arts and Healthcare, puts it well: "The terrorists used very simple things like matte knives to cause great destruction. We too can use very simple things like tape, pencils, crayons, a song, movement, and yes, even matte knives, to help the healing process, to bring light into this terrible darkness" (Wikoff, 2001).

We will let the poet Theodore Roetke (1964) have the final word: "In a dark time, the eyes begin to see . . ." ▪

ACKNOWLEDGMENT

The author wishes to acknowledge the support of the Dana Project, National Center for Death Education, Mount Ida College, Newton, Massachusetts.

Sandra L. Bertman, Ph.D., is Professor of Palliative Care at Boston College Graduate School of Social Work. Formerly professor of Humanities in Medicine at University of Massachusetts Medical and Graduate Schools of Nursing, she was founding Director of the Program of Medical Humanities and the Arts in Health Care. She continues to curate the Staying Soulful column for the American Academy of Hospice and Palliative Medicine, introduce "Other Ways of Knowing: Using the Arts and Humanities to Teach End-of-Life Care" into the EPEC curriculum for physicians, and train professional caregivers and communities overwhelmed with the multiple loss and AIDS pandemic in Botswana, Africa.

REFERENCES

Adorno, T. (1974). Minima moralia: Reflections from damaged life. (E.F.N. Jephcott, Trans.). New York and London: Verso.

Adorno, T. (1982). *Against epistemology: A metacritique : Studies in husserl and the phenomenological antinomies.* (W. Domingo, trans.). Cambridge, MA: MIT Press.

Americans for the Arts. (2001). Arts healing America. [Online]. Available: http://www.americansforthearts.org/arts_healing_america/programs

Barr, A. H. Jr. (1946). Picasso: *Fifty years of his art.* New York: MOMA.

Bertman, S. (2000, Summer). Volts of connection: the arts as shock therapy. *Grief matters* Australian Journal of Grief and Bereavement.

Bertman, S. (Ed.). (1999). *Grief and the healing Arts: Creativity as therapy.* New York: Baywood.

Boeck, W., & Sabartes, J. (1957). *Picasso.* New York: Harry W. Abrams.

Brustein, R. (2001, November 12). Robert Brustein on theatre: The new relevance. *The New Republic.*

Giles, J. (2002, August 18). A shock to the system. *New York Times Book Review,* 5.

Hauck, R. (2001, September 15). The Wall. *Re: Constructions.* [Online]. Available: http://web.mit.edu/cms/reconstructions/representations/thewall.html

Heroes, (2001 December). New York: *Marvel Comics, 1.*

Heyer, P. (1966). Architects on Architecture: New Directions in America. New York: Walker and Company.

Jeffares, A.N. (1968). *A commentary on the collected poems of W.B. Yeats.* Stanford, CA: Stanford University Press.

Jones, B.T. (2001, September 20). *Moyers in conversation,* televised interview, PBS.

Kazantzakis, N. (1952). *Zorba the Greek.* Quoted in Bertman, S., (1991). *Facing Death: Images, Insights and Interventions,* Philadelphia, PA: Taylor and Francis.

LeDuff, C. (2002, August 9). A hard year without dad. *New York Times,* A-14.

Little, F. (1986). Foreword in H.G. Locke (Ed.), *Exile in the Fatherland, Martin Niemoller's Letters from Moabit Prison.* Grand Rapids, MI: William B. Eerdman's Publishing Company.

Mitchelmore, S. (2002). After the disaster [Online]. *Spike Magazine.* Available: http://www.spikemagazine.com/0900celan4.htm

PBS. (2001). America responds: Classroom resources. [Online]. Available: http://www.pbs.org/americaresponds/educators.html

Poffenberger, N. (2002). *September 11th, 2001.* Cincinnati, OH: Fun Publishing.

Roethke, T. (1964). In a Dark Time. *The collected poems of Theodore Roethke.* New York: Doubleday.www.palace.net/~llama/poetry/darktime.

Stern, S. (2002, August 26). His pen is mightier than terrorism. *Daily News Tribune* (Waltham, MA), p. 1.

Theatre Development Fund. (2002). *Play By Play.* [Online]. Available: http://www.tdf.org/PlaybyPlayOnline

Tyrangiel, J. (2002. August 5). An intimate look at how Sprinsteen turned 9/11 into a message of hope. *Time,* 52-59.

What a difference a day makes, (2001). Numerous websites, including: Motorsports Ministries, Weekly Inspiration, www.motorsportsministries; National Air Traffic Controllers Association AFL-CIO, http://september11.natca.org/Poems; www.quiltweb.com/yellow/day.htm.

Wikoff, N. (2001, December). Quoted in *ArtsLinks.*

CHAPTER 18

Victim Advocacy in the Aftermath of Tragedy

Marlene A. Young

I believe that man will not only endure: he will prevail.
He is immortal, not because he alone among creatures has
an inexhaustible voice, but because he has a soul, a spirit
capable of compassion and sacrifice and endurance.
—William Faulkner, Nobel Prize speech, December 10, 1950

The compelling words of William Faulkner speak to the hearts of advocates on behalf of victims and survivors of life's most terrible crises. Survivors of individual and community tragedies often face additional challenges that are experienced as second assaults from society. These may come from social institutions, health services, educational institutions, or the legal system. While victims or survivors are facing major losses due to an event of historical significance in their lives, they are compelled to respond to demands of social congruence or feel the need to proactively fight for rights or services. Survivors may be their own advocates; at times, this may become a way of reconstructing their lives. At other times, it is useful to have an organization or another person speak for them. In either case, understanding the role of advocacy and the legal or advocacy issues that often face survivors in the aftermath of a catastrophe is critical.

THE ROLE OF ADVOCACY

Advocacy in this context refers to focused efforts to accomplish specific goals on behalf of victims or survivors either by themselves or their representatives. Advocacy usually addresses practical problems that the victims or survivors face. Often, the second assaults perpetuated in the aftermath of catastrophe force survivors or their advocates to fight back. They may run into problems with the criminal justice system such as the lack of information or notification about a case. They may confront roadblocks in obtaining just compensation through insurance agencies or state compensation programs. They may face issues with the medical system in which they find themselves confused by differing diagnoses or treatments. Advocacy may be the only avenue to solving problems faced by victims or survivors. Two kinds of advocacy—case advocacy and system advocacy—are described below.

Case Advocacy

Elements of case advocacy include working with individuals on a specific issue or, typically, on a tangible conflict with another individual or agency because of attitudes, values, traditions, regulations, policies, or laws that adversely affect the individuals involved. Whatever effect advocacy has in this instance, it is restricted to this case with no effect on other cases. If, on the other hand, it can be used as precedent, then it serves the goals of system advocacy.

In case advocacy, the advocate's purpose may be to change behaviors, attitudes, values, traditions, or laws through specific actions that apply to this one specific case. The purpose can also be to ensure that victims receive their just due after their victimization. For example, the case of *David Jacobsen versus the Government of Iran*, after Jacobsen was taken hostage in 1985, was adjudicated on his behalf with an award of monetary compensation for his and his family's suffering as well as his loss of productivity and wages during the time he was a captive. It was an individual case brought by his attorney (his advocate) to hold the government of Iran accountable for his suffering and to reimburse him for his losses. It also had a critical element of system advocacy, for to get his day in court, Jacobsen led a successful lobbying campaign in Congress to make Iran's frozen assets available to satisfy such judgments, thereby opening that door for other victims of such crimes.

System Advocacy

Elements of system advocacy include working on behalf of classes of individuals or society as a whole; seeking changes in the system after an actual conflict and prior to the repeat of a similar conflict; and working in a legislative, legal, programmatic, or educational arena. The advocate's purpose is to change behaviors, attitudes, values, traditions, or laws through actions that apply to the class of cases that are invoked on behalf of society as a whole. System advocacy may merge with case advocacy after general change has occurred.

Over the last two decades victim service providers, in partnership with victims and survivors, have worked to establish and expand victim rights legislation. In most states, victims have rights to information, participation, and restitution in criminal cases. A federal constitutional amendment is now being sought to provide victims of all crimes—state or federal—such rights in adult, juvenile, administrative, and military criminal proceedings. The importance of such an amendment was underscored when Marsha Kight, a survivor of a daughter killed in the Oklahoma City bombing, testified in a hearing before the U.S. Senate Judiciary Committee: "In my mind, there were only three other times when the need for constitutional change was so pressing: when the Bill of Rights was written; when slavery was abolished; and when women were granted the right to vote" (Kight, 1997).

Victims' self-advocacy helps them to find some degree of resolution of their traumatic experience within their own personal experience. That personal experience is used as a basis for social or personal change; their activism gives meaning to their pain. In addition, social action offers survivors a source of power that draws upon their own initiative, energy, and resourcefulness and magnifies these qualities far beyond their individual capacities. It offers them an alliance with others based on cooperation and shared purpose. Participating in organized, demanding social efforts calls upon mature and adaptive coping strategies of patience, anticipation, and altruism.

Social action can take many forms, from concrete engagement with particular individuals to abstract intellectual pursuits. Survivors may focus their energies on helping others who have been similarly victimized; on educational, legal, or political efforts to prevent others from being victimized in the future; or on attempts to bring offenders to justice. Public truth-telling is the common denominator of all social action. (Herman, 1992)

Activism may be a part of case or system advocacy but does not need to be limited to it. Charlotte and Bob Hullinger became activists when they founded Parents of Murdered Children as a system of peer support groups. Many victims and survivors become activists when they choose to tell their stories at forums or conferences to help others learn about trauma. Some people employ activism as a basis for choosing new vocations or avocations in life.

The "FIRST RIGHT" plan for victim advocacy and activism has been helpful to many survivors of tragedy. The elements of the plan are as follows:

- *Focus.* For many survivors, advocacy and activism can help to restructure their understanding of order through a focus on specific functional activities. Some studies have shown that women become more active in social relationships and men may become more involved in their professional work. Survivors of both genders who have worked with advocates at the National Organization for Victim Assistance (NOVA) have often talked of new activities that they took on as a result of their personal tragedies. One man wrote of his experience after the death of his son, "I became a wood-carver. I carved wood in the shapes of birds, butterflies, squirrels and chipmunks … my son was a naturalist. I carved and carved—my wife almost left me, but she realized that I was a carver because of my son. It was all that was left to me. I sold my carvings and donated all of the profits to a victim assistance organization" (NOVA Reports, 1997).

- *Insight.* Advocacy and activism provide a way to hear from others who have suffered similar traumas or losses as well as from people who have studied or done research about such tragedies. Hearing other people's experiences can help clarify one's own experiences.

- *Relationships.* Many victims and survivors lose touch with once-close friends and family. Those friends or relations may be afraid of the emotional upheaval in the victim's life, may not know what to do or say, or may blame the victim. Victim activism often gives survivors a chance to form new "families" and relationships bound together by trauma and commitment.

- *Self-esteem.* After the death of a loved one, it is not unusual for survivors to suffer a loss of a sense of identity. Self-esteem and identity can be based upon how the loved one perceived the individual. If death or loss is also accompanied by trauma or victimization due to crime, the trauma or victimization may have been a humiliating, degrading experience. Activism can give victims tangible evidence of their accomplishments and self-worth. It is not unusual for there to be social acknowledgment of the survivors' courage or strength in their efforts to accomplish social change or to provide support to others. Achievements such as helping to change public policy or establishing groups to help others may help survivors establish new identities.

- *Testimony.* Victims or survivors not only need to tell their story but to have it acknowledged by others. Public testimony forms the basis for a historical record that can continue through time. The suffering of one or many is recorded, recognized, and legitimated through that recognition.

- *Repetition.* A vital part of reconstructing a life after tragedy is the ability to develop and organize the story of what happened. Victim impact panels, legislative testimony, speak-outs, and support groups all provide opportunity for telling and retelling a story so that survivors can begin to gain perspective and interpretation.

- *Integration.* An important therapeutic goal for many is to be able to incorporate the story of their tragedy into their lives. Advocacy and activism allow victims to restructure their lives and recognize how their victimization and survival have altered them forever. Loss and victimization are violation of a person's life. They might be construed as a violation of the plot in the novel of one's life. This means that the plot and novel must change. The ultimate integration is for the author (the survivor or victim) to be the narrator of the change in plot.

- *Generation.* For many, the impact of crime or tragedy shatters their sense of meaning and purpose in life. Their plans are thrown asunder. For example, a mother whose life has been centered on her child dies a special kind of death when the child is murdered. Advocacy and activism can be the key to generating a sense of triumph over tragedy and providing meaning for both that parent's life and the deceased child.

- *Hope.* Advocacy and activism may provide survivors with hope. Victims often need to take time before they become involved in activism. When victims take up activism immediately after a major disaster, they often unconsciously use it to delay mourning their losses or confronting the tragedy. It is often best if victims or survivors take some time to try to process their experience and think about it privately before trying to translate it to the world.

Mothers Against Drunk Driving invites recently affected victims of that crime immediately into their local chapters and support groups, but it also holds to a policy that requires a number of months to pass before the new members can join in that chapter's advocacy efforts. There's an ironic footnote to this sensible policy—Candy Lightener, MADD's founder, says she never took time out to grieve her daughter's homicide until she watched the made-for-television film, *The Candy Lightener Story.*

Victims and survivors should also be cautioned that their activism does not necessarily mean that their position or work or policy will succeed. There may be no "victory" over what a perpetrator or a society does. Still, advocacy and activism are useful to affirm in the mind of survivors that horrible things can be confronted, they do not have to completely destroy lives, and there is hope.

- *Triumph.* The ultimate goal of survival is triumph. For most survivors and victims such triumph is based on constructing a new life. Advocacy and activism can provide a way to express intensely frightening emotions in a safe and socially acceptable way. Many survivors are able to triumph over life's perils without outside assistance, but, many can use additional help even if they are able to withstand emotional challenges. Because survivors and victims may face institutional or legal challenges that seem overwhelming, it is useful to know some of the issues and obstacles that face them.

CRITICAL ISSUES IN THE AFTERMATH OF TRAUMA AND DEATH

It is impossible to predict all of the problems that victims or survivors will face in the aftermath of tragedy. Such problems vary depending upon the nature of the tragedy and the environment in which the survivors exist. Just as the problems vary, so do the possible solutions. The eight most common advocacy issues and legal questions for victims or survivors that arise after death and disaster are discussed below.

Notification of Death or Injury and Related Proceedings

Despite the increasing number of courses that include instruction in how to notify survivors about the injury or death of a loved one, notification often is done carelessly and callously. Advocates who are working with survivors should be prepared with complete information about the steps taken to determine the identity of the deceased or injured. They should be prepared to describe the crime or disaster situation without trying to explain the cause of death or injury. All advocates must be prepared to refer individuals to spiritual counselors without passing judgment on their spiritual beliefs.

The police will often interview survivors of loved ones who have been injured or who are deceased due to crime or terrorism. Advocates should let survivors know that police need to investigate sudden, violent, or unexpected deaths. In most cases, surviving family members or close friends will be interviewed. In some cases, survivors will be considered as possible suspects (in the great majority of homicide cases, the victim and the murderer had a prior relationship), so it may be useful to have an advocate accompany them to such interviews to help them cope with intrusive or inappropriate questioning.

The law in most jurisdictions requires autopsies in cases of sudden or unexpected death. Examples of such cases include when the deceased was not recently seen by a physician, when a violent death has occurred, when a person dies alone, when there is a motor vehicle death, and other special circumstances. If autopsies are required, the medical examiner requires no consent for an autopsy, and if not required by law, they still may be ordered by a local health officer, judge, district or county attorney, or director of a state mental hospital. Survivors often are uninformed about autopsy proceedings and the circumstances that mandate autopsy. Advocates should be ready to explain such policies.

Survivors also should be informed that when autopsies are required, they will be paid for by the local jurisdiction. Autopsies that are performed at the family's request may be paid for by the jurisdiction if the death ends up being determined a criminal matter. Any autopsy may delay the release of the body for a funeral.

Some survivors unexpectedly learn that their loved ones have signed organ donor directives or that medical personnel request organ or tissue donation. Advocates should inform survivors that federal law *requires* medical personnel to request organ and tissue donation. Advocates should be aware of the Uniform Anatomical Gift Act that governs organ donation and has been adopted by all states, Washington, D.C., and Puerto Rico (National Conference of Commissioners on Uniform State Laws, 1988).

Communicating with Injured Victims or Viewing the Deceased

It is not unusual for family members or loved ones to be denied the opportunity to speak with victims who are injured. The denial may be based on policies that focus on investigation by law enforcement or emergency responses of medical professionals. In most cases, loved ones should be able to communicate with injured victims unless medical interventions are being administered. It is often helpful for crisis responders to help to defuse the emotional responses of victims at an early stage after an injury prior to law enforcement interviews. This may help to provide law enforcement with better interviews because victims may have a more complete and comprehensive story of what happened after a defusing.

Sometimes, survivors are prevented from viewing their deceased loved ones by policies of the medical examiners or law enforcement officers. These policies are often purportedly dictated by the need to preserve evidence. It is rare that this need would not allow survivors from seeing their loved ones. They may not be able to touch or hold their loved ones, but they should be allowed to view the deceased. Advocates should make it clear to governing authorities that the right to view is clear. In all cases of communication or viewing, victims or survivors should be offered support before and after such contact and should be provided with escorts and transportation to and from hospitals or morgues.

Financial Assistance

One of the key issues that survivors face after the sudden death of a loved one is how to handle their financial affairs. Even when the deceased has left a will that disposes of property, financial issues still arise. It is not unusual that the costs of funeral arrangements, burials, or memorials are burdensome to survivors. It is important for advocates to talk with survivors about their options. If a loved one has died due to a crime or an act of terrorism, there may be financial assistance available through state or federal victim compensation. If a loved one has died while at work or in the workplace, there may be financial assistance available through worker's compensation. Advocates may also be able to find financial resources through reviewing insurance policies of the deceased or through funds that have been created by charitable organizations.

Arranging Disposition of the Body and Memorials

Often, survivors are faced with decisions about the disposition of the body of their loved one. This is particularly true in cases where the deceased has not designated what might be done and the deceased or the survivors have no religious beliefs that affect the determination of disposition. Advocates should be aware of the possible choices. Survivors may consider direct or immediate cremation or burial with no embalming, funeral, or other rituals. This is usually done within the first 24 hours after death or discovery of death. Survivors who wish to have a funeral may want to have the deceased embalmed prior to cremation or burial. All survivors should be well informed about the costs associated with disposition. Such costs can include fees for funeral directors, the use of funeral home facilities and equipment, the cost of caskets, urns, or vaults, the costs of ministers, flowers, obituaries, clothing for the deceased, transportation to and from the services, cemetery costs, cremation costs, costs for storage in a mausoleum, and so forth.

If a loved one dies overseas there are additional issues to be addressed. After notification of the death, survivors must consider how to bring the deceased home. If the deceased is already buried, there may be a need for an exhumation request. This may or may not be handled in an expeditious manner. In most cases, the deceased is shipped by common carrier, however, each state has its own rules about transportation. The requirements of the country where the deceased died can be complicated. It takes about 10 to 15 days for a body to be returned from European countries and longer from other parts of the world. This may be expedited in cases of people who die when they are serving in the military or with the U.S. State Department but not for ordinary citizens.

If survivors are willing to have their loved ones cremated, the retrieval is not as complicated. They need only ensure that a marker on the container states that it holds the remains. This must be accompanied by a copy of the official death certificate and a certificate from the crematorium that states that the container holds only the cremated remains of the decedent. A permit to export the remains may also be required.

Advocates should also be aware that survivors need to know about forms authorizing the release of the deceased's body and itemization and acknowledgment of receipt of the deceased's clothing and personal effects if released by a hospital or a law enforcement agency.

Death certificates are needed for transportation, burial, or disposition of the deceased's body, filing for life insurance, death benefits, or, in some cases when requests are made for family leave. In some states, documents may be required that pertain to the disposal of the deceased's body.

Time Off from Work to Handle Family Affairs

Many employers allow one to three days leave for designated next of kin to attend funerals and participate in memorial services. However, often such leave must be deducted from sick leave or vacation leave. If a person dies due to crime or terrorism, many states have victim assistance programs that provide employer intercession so that advocates can work with employers on behalf of survivors to obtain or expand the duration of such leave. In most cases, such time off is given to only parents or children of the deceased.

Travel Arrangements

Many people are aware that airlines offer bereavement fares that are much lower than regular fares to assist survivors of someone who has died to attend funerals or memorials. The problem is, once again, that these fares are usually offered only to parents or children of the deceased. Advocates for the survivors can be very useful in persuading airline agents or travel agents to extend these fares to other loved ones.

Media Intrusion

In situations involving crime or terrorism, it is not unusual for survivors to be inundated with requests from the media to make public statements. The media may also cover funerals or memorials. It is critical for advocates to be available to assist survivors with media management and to protect the rights of survivors when they have encounters with the media.

In most cases there are very few legal rights that survivors can rely upon to protect their own privacy, however, there are a number of guidelines that can be used to help mitigate the impact of such media intrusions. The National Organization for Victim Assistance (NOVA) has published a Media Code of Ethics that includes suggestions for compassionate media coverage. The media itself is assuming more responsibility for urging the members of its professions to treat victims with dignity. This is reflected in the Code of Ethics of the Society of Professional Journalists. NOVA also has published a manual to guide advocates who work with the media. (Offen, Stein, & Young, 1996)

Criminal Justice Involvement

Probably the most difficult legal issues facing victims or survivors are raised when they have been subject to criminal attack. The criminal justice process of investigation, prosecution, and appeals can take months or years to complete. During that time, the survivors may be inundated by constant reminders of their injuries and loss. They often are confused by the system and have little knowledge about how the law actually works. Virtually all jurisdictions in the United States have victim and witness assistance programs to provide survivors with support and aid as their cases are handled. All 50 states have laws that address rights for victims in the justice system. These rights include the right to accurate and timely information about case status, the right to participate in the system by attending court proceedings and providing input at sentencing, and the right to restitution from the offender.

Despite these laws, it is not unusual for victims to be unaware of their rights or for their rights to be ignored during the process. There is also considerable controversy over the extent to which the constitutional rights of defendants take precedent over victim rights. Due to these issues, there is currently a national movement to try to enact an amendment to the U.S. Constitution that would make such rights consistent throughout the country and give them additional legal status. It is critical that case advocates work to ensure the implementation of the laws protecting victim rights as they exist and that system advocates work to ensure the passage of the constitutional amendment.

While these eight issues are the ones most commonly confronted by victims and survivors, it is difficult to predict all problems they might face. For instance, NOVA worked on behalf of one survivor to help ensure that a grave marker was installed in a timely manner after the burial of her father. In another case, NOVA served as an advocate to help devise a protection plan for a survivor of a homicide victim who feared that he might be targeted for reprisals after testifying against a perpetrator when the case went to trial. Because of the wide array of concerns with which victims and survivors may become involved, it is critical that those who work with them are well trained not only in the tools of advocacy but also the resources available for them. ■

Marlene A. Young, Ph.D., J.D. is the Executive Director of the National Organization for Victim Assistance (NOVA). She has served in that capacity since 1981. She is the author of The Community Crisis Response Team Training Manual (3rd edition), which is the foundation for the NOVA National Crisis Response Training that has been presented to more than 1,000 organizations throughout the world. In addition, she is the author of some 300 articles and chapters on crisis response, death and dying, restorative justice, and victim rights.

REFERENCES

Kight, M. (April 16, 1997). Testimony before the U.S. Senate Committee on the Judiciary.

Herman, J. (1992). *Trauma and Recovery*. New York: Basic Books.

Uniform Anatomical Gift Act. (1988). National Conference of Commissioners on Uniform State Laws, Chicago, IL.

NOVA Reports. (1997). National Organization for Victim Assistance, Washington, DC.

Offen, E.N., Stein, J.H., & Young, M.A. (1996). Washington, DC: National Organization for Victim Assistance.

CHAPTER 19

Lessons from Combat Veterans

Alfonso R. Batres

*The lessons learned in Vet Centers have helped
ordinary Americans touched by trauma.*
—Anthony J. Principi, Secretary of Veterans Affairs
August, 2002

INTRODUCTION AND OVERVIEW

In the immediate aftermath of 9/11, several Veterans Service Centers operated by the U.S. Department of Veterans Affairs (VA) deployed mental health disaster workers to the New York City area to provide crisis counseling to VA clients and staff who lived and worked in or near lower Manhattan. They counseled professional colleagues at the Manhattan Vet Center and at two other centers across the Hudson River in Newark and Jersey City, New Jersey. One of the volunteer disaster workers, a staff psychologist from the Philadelphia Vet Center, went to Jersey City and reported later:

> Vet Center staff watched as people jumped from the upper floors and the World Trade Center buildings collapsed. Vet Center employees were so close they could see men's ties and women's dresses blow up as they fell. They could hear the sounds and smell the fire and smoke from the disaster. They were all clearly traumatized by the horrific events they witnessed. (Kingsley, 2002, p. 44)

As part of the VA's national disaster response team, Vet Centers have responded to other public tragedies, including earthquakes, plane crashes, urban riots, hurricanes, and the Oklahoma City bombing. Their expertise derives from nearly a quarter-century of learning how to recognize and treat post-traumatic stress disorder (PTSD) in combat veterans.

Administered by the VA's Readjustment Counseling Service, the Vet Centers are small, non-hospital, community-based facilities that provide mental health services and other "help without hassles" to combat veterans. The program was authorized by Congress in 1979 after years of study and debate. The goal was to fashion a compassionate and effective response to what was becoming recognized as a major social issue—the profoundly disabling, service-connected psychological problems experienced by many veterans who had seen heavy combat in Vietnam.

The landmark National Vietnam Veterans Readjustment Study, mandated by Congress in 1983, found that nearly one-third (30.6 percent) of male veterans (more than 960,000 men) and over one-fourth (26.9 percent) of female veterans (more than 1,900 women) who had served in Vietnam had experienced PTSD at some point (Kulka, Schlenger, Fairbank, Hough, Jordan, Marmar & Weiss, 1990). The same study found that nearly half a million Vietnam veterans—15.2 percent of the men and 8.5 percent of the women—still suffered from PTSD at least 15 years after their military service.

The literature on Vietnam veterans and PTSD is vast; studies of veterans have been essential in developing and extending the concept of PTSD (Knox & Price, 1996; Shay, 1994; Kulka, et al., 1990). It is fair to say that much, if not most, of what is known today about normal responses to catastrophic events, to fear, and to the threat of being killed, has been learned from combat veterans.

The purpose of this chapter is to sketch a brief history of PTSD in terms of the contributions and experiences of combat veterans, particularly Vietnam veterans, and their advocates in the mental health professions, Congress, and the VA. The chapter includes a snapshot of the Vet Center program, which was (and still is) one of the federal government's primary responses to PTSD among Vietnam and all other combat veterans. In the view of many observers, it is the gold standard of federal programs.

Combat Veterans and PTSD

PTSD did not emerge for the first time during or following the war in Vietnam. Although the term is relatively new, the condition itself "has been around ever since man has been on earth" (MacPherson, 1984, p. 190). In Vietnam and in earlier wars, what came to be called (if not understood) as PTSD was known variously as soldier's heart, battle fatigue, shell shock, combat neurosis, combat exhaustion, and even pseudo-combat fatigue.

A 1998 report describes the case of a World War I veteran whose combat-related traumatic stress persisted for 75 years—from the time he returned home in 1918 until his death in 1993 at the age of 94 (Hamilton & Workman, 1998). Published references to combat-related trauma date back at least to the 1940s, some based on clinical cases first seen in the 1920s. Delayed stress also was observed in many World War II combat veterans.

In literature, if not in published case studies, full-blown PTSD apparently was described long before that. Jonathan Shay (1994), a psychiatrist who treats Vietnam veterans suffering from severe and chronic PTSD, was struck by the similarity of their war experiences to Homer's account of Achilles in the *Iliad*. Writing 27 centuries ago about soldiers at war, Homer saw "things that we in psychiatry and psychology have more or less missed." Homer's epic emphasizes two common events of heavy, continuous combat—betrayal of "what's right" by a commander, and the onset of what Shay terms the berserk state.

Similarly, Shay (1994) and Grady (1990) found in Shakespeare's *Henry IV* an account of what seemed very much like the symptoms of PTSD. The soliloquy of a combat veteran's wife ("O, my good lord, why are you thus alone?") described her husband's symptoms: social withdrawal and isolation; unwarranted rage; sexual dysfunction; incapacity for intimacy; somatic disturbances; inability to experience pleasure; insomnia; depression; hyperactive startle reaction; peripheral vasoconstriction, autonomic hyperactivity; sense of the dead being more real than the living; fragmented and vigilant sleep; traumatic dreams; and reliving episodes of combat.

If signs of combat-related traumatic stress have been observed in many wars over much of human history, then why has it taken so long to come to grips with the condition now known as PTSD? One possible answer lies in the historic tenacity of an alternative explanation.

In her award-winning book, *Long Time Passing: Vietnam and the Haunted Generation*, Myra MacPherson (1984) traces the history of an idea that persisted from colonial times through the Civil War to the Vietnam era. The idea was that a soldier's "breaking" in response to exposure to continuous heavy combat was due to predisposing factors of one sort or another, such as bad character, cowardice, unstable family backgrounds, or "pathological failure in the self-control of fear."

Ultimately, however, the concept of predisposing factors could not stand up to serious scientific study. "In all wars," MacPherson concluded from her review, "there have been countless numbers from strife-torn, unstable families...who have indeed fought, not only without breaking down, but heroically" (p. 198).

READJUSTMENT

In 1936, the concept of readjustment—helping combat veterans make it through the transition from military service to civilian status—was articulated in a letter written by Major General Smedley Butler, United States Marine Corps, a two-time recipient of the Congressional Medal of Honor (Knox & Price, 1996):

> Then, suddenly, we discharged them and told them to make another "about face!" This time they had to do their own readjusting, sans mass psychology, sans Officers' aid and advice, sans nation-wide propaganda. We didn't need them anymore. So we scattered them about without any speeches and parades. Many, too many, of these fine young boys were eventually destroyed, mentally, because they could not make the final "about face" alone.

Erik Erikson (1945), a non-physician lay analyst, spent much of his clinical practice during World War II seeing returning combat veterans at the Veterans Rehabilitation Clinic of Mount Zion Hospital in San Francisco. He used his clinical work with war veterans to reintroduce environmental factors (including traumatic experiences) into the psychological equation for understanding adult adjustment. Erikson's comments from his work with war veterans validate the importance of an informal trusting therapeutic relationship and the value of veterans treating veterans:

The administration of the help given should be locally centralized so that the veteran will not feel "pushed around" and "up against red tape" when asking for a little assistance. The assistance should be handled, not by the personal representative of organizations, but by specially selected people who have a direct, informed, and resourceful approach and preferably are themselves veterans of this or the First World War. (p. 121)

VIETNAM VETERANS AND PTSD

By 1971, Vietnam veterans were returning in large numbers from a divisive war. Society had difficulty separating the war from the warrior, and Vietnam veterans found they would not be getting an enthusiastic welcome from a grateful nation.

In the VA and in Congress, concern emerged about Vietnam veterans' ability to re-enter civilian life. Government-funded survey research (U.S. Senate, 1972) found that veterans were having difficulty finding jobs. College graduates among them fared no better than those with far less education. Moreover, various government programs designed to help veterans find jobs appeared to be ineffective, and only 18 percent of returning veterans took advantage of their rehiring rights. Reports of substance abuse and disturbed and violent behavior contributed to a negative stereotype of Vietnam veterans.

Misdiagnosis

By the mid-1970s, it appeared that many returning Vietnam veterans who wanted help were not getting it. A 1976 study suggested that 77 percent of the veterans who sought psychiatric services and were admitted to VA hospitals were wrongly diagnosed (Brende & Parson, 1985):

Their flashbacks or hallucinations of being in combat were often so real that psychiatrists unfamiliar with the nature of postwar symptoms diagnosed the veterans as suffering from acute schizophrenic episodes. Hence, patients were primarily drugged with heavy doses of antipsychotic medications. Though these medications temporarily proved helpful in many cases, they were too often the only treatment provided. (p. 102)

A big part of the problem was that PTSD can mimic virtually any condition in psychiatry. Shay (1994) suggested that combat veterans first seen in the early 1970s were almost always diagnosed as paranoid schizophrenic. If they were first seen in the late 1970s, however, they were invariably diagnosed as manic-depressive. And if they were first seen in the mid-1980s, they were found to be suffering from PTSD. Shay complained that even the official definition "almost totally fails to convey the ease with which PTSD can be confused with other mental disorders."

Taboo Subject

For many Americans, the Vietnam War remained a taboo subject until nearly a decade after it ended (Brende & Parson, 1985). In his Pulitzer Prize-winning autobiography, *Fortunate Son*, Lewis Puller, Jr. (1991) recalled that his law school classmates were so clearly discomfited whenever he mentioned his Vietnam service that he felt obliged to help them change the subject. Worse, his military psychiatrist did not seem to want him to talk about it either. Puller, a decorated Marine who had lost both legs and part of one hand in Vietnam, was in therapy because of depression, alcoholism and a failed suicide attempt. On a few occasions over the course of his therapy, Puller brought up the subject of his war service. Unable to elicit a response, he soon gave up.

> Having fought a war that cost me so dearly while leaving virtually all my new acquaintances untouched, I was now told in countless subtle ways that I could not vent my grief and frustration by talking about the war because it made society uncomfortable. (p. 253)

Rap Groups

Vietnam veterans wanted to talk, and they would not be denied. Out of this determination was born the rap group. Initially, rap groups were spontaneous and undirected. Brende and Parson (1985) quoted a severely wounded veteran who was hospitalized for 21 months:

> There were a lot of other guys from Vietnam in the hospital when I was there. The nursing staff didn't understand us, either ignored us or wanted us to stop talking about what we went through. So we would get together off in the corner and rap about what happened. After spending almost two years doing that, I got it all out of my system. I haven't had a need to talk about it since that time. (p. 99)

Veterans soon sensed the value of self-help and invited trained therapists to work with them. What evolved was a kind of innovative, customized group therapy. It was initiated by veterans, including veterans who were psychologists and psychiatrists, and aided by other, non-veteran mental health professionals recruited to their cause.

Among the first psychiatrists to become involved was Robert Jay Lifton, a veteran, renowned author, and Yale University psychiatrist. In his book, *Home from the War: Vietnam Veterans Neither Victims nor Executioners* (1973), Lifton described the genesis of rap groups. He and Chaim Shatan, a New York University psychoanalyst, met with a group of combat veterans and developed the initial skeleton of the combat rap group process.

At the time, Lifton recalled, he had a sense that he was either groping toward a new group form or being caught up in one. Although there were definite elements of group psychotherapy, he wrote, the process could more accurately be described as a dialogue between mental health professionals and combat veterans (Lifton, 1973). The groups called themselves rap groups, not therapy groups. They avoided the medical model, emphasizing that PTSD is a normal response to inordinate levels of stress and trauma. They welcomed drop-ins and maintained a casual atmosphere. All participants called each other by their first names.

Arthur Egendorf (1985), a psychologist and Vietnam veteran, coordinated some of the first-generation rap groups, which were held in New York City from 1970 to 1974. In addition to providing a place where combat veterans could talk about the horrors they could not talk about elsewhere, "we made a distinction in the rap groups that is crucial for healing: the difference between blame and responsible criticism. Blame justifies your aloofness or sense of impotence; responsible criticism involves you in constructive change" (p. 105).

The experience of the rap groups served as a blueprint for the later therapeutic groups that would become a mainstay of the services offered by the Vet Centers (Brende & Parson, 1985).

ORIGIN AND HISTORY OF THE VET CENTERS

Congress Acts

By the late 1970s, veterans' advocates in Congress had become well aware that many Vietnam veterans were feeling alienated from their community support systems and were not accessing care at VA hospitals commensurate with the utilization rates of veterans of other wars.

In mid-1979, Congress authorized and funded the new Readjustment Counseling Service (it would later become known informally as the Vet Center Program) and the VA moved immediately to implement it. By October 1, the VA was offering readjustment counseling in 87 community-based centers nationwide.

New Focus for the VA

The program's central purpose was to assist Vietnam combat veterans with their "about face" readjustment to civilian life. The program initially was called Operation Outreach and the centers were called Vietnam Veterans Outreach Counseling Centers. The idea was to help Vietnam veterans reconnect to social support systems including family, community, employment services, medical care and other veterans' benefits. The program was designed and staffed mostly by Vietnam veteran providers (Blank, 1985).

Vet Centers were community-based, storefront-type facilities housed outside of traditional VA facilities. The average-size staff of four was headed by a team leader, usually a veteran who was also a mental health professional. The style was informal and flexible, based on a veteran-helping-veteran model. The teams offered safe, welcoming places where combat veterans could talk about their experiences and participate in the rap groups as a first step toward healing. As knowledge accumulated about the devastating effects of PTSD on families (Verbosky, 1988), the centers offered rap groups and other support for wives and children (Brende & Parson, 1985) of combat veterans.

Although not without flaws and start-up problems (MacPherson, 1984), the Vet Centers soon proved to be hugely popular with veterans and a success story in the eyes of Congress. In late 1983, Congress approved funding for additional centers.

Advancing the Study of PTSD

Beyond its acceptance by Vietnam veterans and members of Congress, the Readjustment Counseling Service "created a fundamental change in the capacity of the VA to provide care, research and training regarding PTSD" according to Arthur Blank (1992), the new program's second director.

In 1980, the American Psychiatric Association (APA) included PTSD in the third revision of *Diagnostic and Statistical Manual of Mental Disorders*, known as DSM-III. Strictly speaking, this was not a new entry, but a reinstated and updated old one. The APA had recognized war neuroses under the term "gross stress reaction" in its first DSM in 1952, but then inexplicably dropped it from DSM–II in 1968. The reinstatement in 1980 was due in large part to the urging of mental health professionals who had been working with Vietnam combat veterans (Knox & Price, 1996).

By the late 1980s, the VA had become "the acknowledged experts in diagnosing and treating war-related PTSD" (Grady, 1990). Looking to the future, the VA assured Congress that it was "committed to ongoing excellence in treating the psychological as well as the physical trauma of war" (Grady, 1990). The VA could now point to PTSD inpatient units that served only combat veterans, specially trained PTSD clinical teams at VA medical centers, partial hospitalization programs, outpatient mental health clinics, and the National Center for PTSD, a resource offering scientific data and information about PTSD treatment options.

During the Persian Gulf War, the number of mental health specialists deployed by the military was four times the number deployed at the height of the Vietnam War and this time they were equipped with a sophisticated understanding of PTSD (Blank, 1992). The Readjustment Counseling Service and the Vet Centers had been the "organizational trail-blazer for PTSD programs in the VA" (Blank, 1992).

VET CENTERS TODAY

We are the people in the Department of Veterans Affairs who welcome home with honor the war veteran by providing quality readjustment services in a caring manner, assisting them and their family members toward a successful post-war adjustment in or near their respective communities.

—Vet Center Statement of Purpose

Each year, the 206 Vet Centers assist approximately 130,000 veterans and conduct at least 900,000 visits from veterans and family members. Since the program began in 1979, the Vet Centers have assisted 1.7 million veterans. Originally established to help Vietnam veterans readjust to civilian life, the Vet Centers now are open to all veterans who have served in a combat zone or area of armed hostility. They also are open to all veterans who have been sexually traumatized while serving in the military.

Over 80 percent of Vet Center staff members are veterans and over 60 percent have served in a combat zone. This enhances their understanding and appreciation of the population they serve. Staff members include psychiatrists, psychologists, social workers (the largest proportion of providers), psychiatric nurses, master's-level counselors, and allied health workers.

Services

Vet Centers offer assessment and evaluation; individual, group and family counseling; job counseling; substance abuse screening and counseling; benefits counseling; health education; and links with community health and social service agencies. Sometimes, the services provided by Vet Centers are as basic as food and shelter. Staff members occasionally make house calls. The Vet Centers' historic emphasis on reaching out to disenfranchised and unserved veterans continues.

Above all, the Vet Centers retain their focus on high-quality treatment of PTSD. In recent years, this has meant increasing emphasis on long-term intervention. Since the extension of eligibility in the 1990s to all combat veterans, the Vet Centers are seeing more veterans of World War II and the Korean War. Some of these veterans have not completed their "about face" in 50 years.

Vet Centers use a mix of peer and professional counseling. One treatment modality developed and used by the Vet Centers is combat (rap group) peer counseling, the origins of which are described elsewhere in this chapter. The rap groups continue to be a major contributor to the Vet Centers' over all success. As one veteran of the Korean War stated:

> I have been trying to forget these horrible thoughts and nightmares that I have had for so many years. I avoided talking about this, wanting to protect my wife and kids from these things, I drank like a fish to try to forget, always thinking all along that there was something wrong with me because Marines aren't suppose to have these problems. It took a while, but by talking to my counselor, also a combat Marine, and the other combat veterans in my group, I am today able to know that I am not a freak; I am doing so much better. This Vet Center and my counselor have saved my dignity, my marriage, and my life. I feel like a real person again.

Client Satisfaction

Such testimonials are not unusual. Most initial referrals to Vet Centers are by word of mouth (Knox & Price, 1996). In client surveys, the proportion of respondents who say they would recommend the Vet Center to other veterans is consistently well over 90 percent. Between 1979 and 1990, Vet Centers assisted more than one million veterans and members of their families, but received only 45 letters of complaint. What accounts for this high level of customer satisfaction? Important program attributes include these:

"Help without Hassles." More than a slogan, these words remind Vet Center staff of the value of streamlining or omitting bureaucratic processes and obstacles whenever possible. The idea is to facilitate access to care by valuing the fact that veterans who have been traumatized may already feel alienated by "the system." Readjustment Counseling Service policy is that all veterans, including new clients without appointments, will be greeted immediately and counseled or otherwise helped within 15 minutes of their arrival. Paper work and other procedural necessities come after an empathic connection has been established.

Personal service. Although personalized service plays a key role in any service delivery, this is particularly important in the delivery of services to traumatized populations. Respecting a veteran's need for personal space and confidentiality goes a long way in getting needed services to veteran clients. Vet Centers emphasize the importance of respecting the clients they serve. Vet Center clients, in turn, refer to the center they use as "my Vet Center," indicating a personal investment and ownership.

Camaraderie. Military unit identification and era of service are sources of pride for many veterans. The camaraderie between and among veterans, especially combat veterans, is a bond that transcends time. Combat veterans typically feel that few persons can understand their war-related trauma except other combat veterans.

At the Vet Centers, some groups are facilitated by counselors who are combat veterans; others are facilitated by veterans who have not seen combat or by non-veteran counselors. Virtually all counselors use the camaraderie among veterans to enhance the therapeutic process, especially in the beginning. Ultimately, however, individual progress may be measured in part by how well the veteran handles increasing heterogeneous groups and other social contacts.

Cultural competence. Vet Centers take the time to understand the cultures of the communities they assist, and to remain sensitive to issues of culture, language and spiritual and other beliefs. In providing interventions and services, cultural competence is an integral part of the Vet Centers' approach. It facilitates more meaningful interventions and is part of the emphasis on treating the whole person.

CONCLUSION

On September 11, 2001, for the first time in this country, large numbers of civilians in New York City and the Pentagon and elsewhere experienced something akin to combat trauma. "Few, I'm sure, have related their experiences to combat," the VA Secretary wrote in an essay, "but they have survived an attack by a lethal enemy" (Principi, 2002). That it may happen again cannot be ruled out.

As this book makes clear in virtually every chapter, coping with public tragedy and helping others cope require an understanding of post-traumatic stress. This is true whether the tragedy is a terrorist attack, a natural disaster or some other catastrophic event.

The VA initiative described in this chapter led to a new and innovative system for delivering care to survivors of combat stress at a time when scientific knowledge about the long-term burden of war trauma was in its infancy. The Vet Centers' track record in helping veterans with combat-related traumatic stress is relevant to the needs of the citizenry in our post-9/11 world. Their expertise is grounded in government-funded clinical and epidemiological studies, some of them ongoing, that continue to draw on the cumulative experiences of our combat veterans. ■

Alfonso R. Batres, Ph.D., M.S.W., is the Chief Officer of the Readjustment Counseling Service, U.S. Department of Veterans Affairs. He has direct oversight of the 206 Vet Centers providing trauma services to war zone veterans, including centers in Puerto Rico, Alaska, Hawaii, and Guam. He has a Ph.D. in psychology from the University of Colorado, Boulder, and a Master's in Social Work from the Kent School of Social Work, University of Louisville, Kentucky. Dr. Batres coordinated VA Vet Center mental health services at the World Trade Center and other disaster sites.

REFERENCES

American Psychiatric Association. (1980). Diagnostic and Statistical Manual of Mental Disorders (3rd ed.). Washington, DC: Author.

Blank, A.S. (1985). The Veterans Administration Viet Nam Veterans Outreach and Counseling Centers. In S. Sonnenberg, A. Blank, & J. Talbott (Eds.), *The trauma of war: Stress and recovery in Viet Nam veterans* (pp. 227-238). Washington, DC: American Psychiatric Press, Inc.

Blank, A.S., (1992). Readjustment counseling service. *NCP Clinical Quarterly, 2(2).* Retrieved December 12, 2002, from http://www.ncptsd.org/publications/cq/v2/n2/blank.html

Boscarino, J.A. (1995). Post-traumatic stress and associated disorders among Vietnam veterans: The significance of combat exposure and social support. *Journal of Traumatic Stress, 8(2),* 317-336.

Brende, J.O., & Parson, E.R. (1986). *Vietnam veterans: The road to recovery.* New York: Signet.

Committee on Veterans' Affairs. (1972). *A study of the problems facing the Vietnam era veterans on their readjustment to civilian life.* (S. prt. 7). 92nd Cong., 2nd Sess. Washington, DC: U.S. Government Printing Office.

Egendorf, A. (1985). *Healing from the war.* Boston: Houghton Mifflin Company.

Erikson, E.H. (1945). Plans for the returning veteran with symptoms of instability. In L. Wirth et al. (Eds), *Community planning for peacetime living.* Palo Alto: Stanford University Press.

Foa, E.B., & Meadows, E.A. (1997). Psychological treatments for post-traumatic stress disorder: A critical review. *Annual Review of Psychology, 48,* 449-480.

Grady, D.A. (1990). Epilogue: A self-guide for Vietnam veterans. In Kulka et al. (Eds.), *Trauma and the Vietnam War generation* (pp. 276-308). New York: Brunner/Mazel.

Hamilton, J.D., & Workman Jr., R.H. (1998). Persistence of combat-related post-traumatic stress symptoms for 75 years. *Journal of Traumatic Stress, 11(4),* 763-768.

Johnson, D.R., & Lubin, H. (1997). Treatment preferences of Vietnam veterans with post-traumatic stress disorder. *Journal of Traumatic Stress, 10(3),* 391-405.

Kingsley, R. (2002). Vet Center debriefers help out. *Vet Center Voice, 23(3),* 41-47. Retrieved January 8, 2003, from http://home.i29.net/~voice/PDFs/233/233p4147.pdf

Knox, J., & Price, D.H. (1996). *Healing America's warriors: Vet centers and the social contract.* Retrieved December 12, 2002, from http://www.vietnam.ttu.edu/vietnamcenter/events/1996_Symposium/96papers/healing/htm

Kulka, R.A., Schlenger, W.E., Fairbank, J.A., Hough, R.L., Jordan, B.K., Marmar, C.R., & Weiss, D.S. (1990). *Trauma and the Vietnam War generation.* New York: Brunner/Mazel.

Lifton, R.J. (1973). *Home from the war.* New York: Simon and Schuster.

MacPherson, M. (1984). *Long time passing.* New York: Doubleday.

Principi, A. (2002). *VA's lessons for all Americans about Sept.11.* Retrieved February 11, 2003, from http://www.va.gov/opa/pressrel/docs/911AJP.doc

Puller, L. (1991). *Fortunate Son.* Berkeley: Grove Press.

Research Triangle Institute. (1988, November 7). *Contractual report of findings from the National Vietnam Veterans readjustment study: Vol. 1.* North Carolina: Author.

Schlenger, W.E., Kulka, R.A., Fairbank, J.A., Hough, R.L., Jordan, B.K., Marmar, C.R., & Weiss, D.S. (1992). The prevalence of post-traumatic stress disorder in the Vietnam generation: A multimethod, multisource assessment of psychiatric disorder. *Journal of Traumatic Stress, 5(3)*, 333-363.

Shay, J. (1994). *Achilles in Vietnam.* New York: Touchstone.

SSM Online. (2002). *August 8, 2002: Top 10 veteran centers of excellence.* Retrieved on December 12, 2002, from http://www.ssmonline.org/News/ViewRelease.asp?ReleaseID=2385

Stellman, J. (1985, September). *Experience of American Legion Vietnam veterans with veterans administration recognition and treatment of PTSD and other mental disorders.* Paper presented at the meeting of The Society for Traumatic Stress Studies, Atlanta, GA.

Verbosky, S.J. & Ryan, D.A. (1988). The female partners of Vietnam veterans: Stress by proximity. *Issues in Mental Health Nursing, 9(1)*, 95-104.

Wiess, D.S., Marmar, C.R., Schlenger, W.E., Fairbank, J.A., Jordan, B.K., Hough, R.L., & Kulka, R.A. (1992). The prevalence of lifetime and partial post-traumatic stress disorder in Vietnam theater veterans. *Journal of Traumatic Stress, 5(3)*, 365-376.

CHAPTER 20

Workplace Interventions

Rachel E. Kaul

INTRODUCTION

The terrorist attack on the Pentagon in Washington, D.C., was both a public tragedy of immense proportions and a traumatic event in the lives of those individuals who experienced it. The Pentagon Employee Referral Service, the employee assistance program for civilian employees in and attached to the Pentagon, was faced with meeting the immediate needs of workers in the building. Anticipating future needs and preventing long-term adverse psychological reactions became a major focus for those of us providing mental health services to this population in subsequent months.

Throughout the first year following the attack, workers' traumatic stress and their complicated grief reactions required mental health professionals to expand existing services and develop new approaches. This chapter presents an overview of interventions that may be used in a workplace setting in the wake of a tragic and public event. The focus is on addressing workers' immediate, crisis-related concerns, anticipating and meeting their emerging needs following the crisis phase, and facilitating access to ongoing treatment for anyone who requires it.

PROVIDING SERVICES TO EMPLOYEES AFTER THE PENTAGON ATTACK

The attack of September 11, 2001, affected large numbers of employees. It occurred at the workplace, during business hours when many people were there. Many workers returned to the building and to their job duties the very next day, while rescue and recovery efforts were still under way and the building was still on fire. Services were established on site to assist people in managing acute stress and grief reactions and to prevent the emergence of more serious psychological disorders such as post-traumatic stress disorder (PTSD). The Pentagon's employee assistance program (EAP) became a central focus for civilian workers seeking counseling and support.

In the weeks immediately after the attack, early intervention strategies were used to assist people. In the months following the acute crisis phase, an outreach program was developed to identify workers with persistent or delayed reactions that continued to interfere with their ability to function at work or home. The primary goal was to provide workers with appropriate short-term interventions or with referrals for concrete resources or long-term psychotherapy when indicated.

EARLY INTERVENTION

Early intervention in response to a crisis has been recommended by many crisis and trauma theorists (Caplan, 1964; Everly & Mitchell, 1999; Flannery & Everly, 2000; Roberts, 2000). Crisis intervention techniques help to prevent or mitigate the disruption of healthy, adaptive functioning in people affected by an unexpected, distressing event. An event that involves sudden, tragic or multiple deaths can trigger acute psychological responses in survivors and often requires swift and targeted interventions (Caplan, 1964; Lindemann, 1944; Rando, 1994; Roberts, 2000). Clinicians have long focused on providing psychological first aid in the immediate aftermath of crisis to assist people in regaining psychological homeostasis (Caplan, 1964; Mitchell & Everly, 2001; Raphael, 1986). In recent literature, clinicians have been cautioned about relying on one-time, stand-alone interventions and are encouraged to respond to a crisis with comprehensive, multiple intervention strategies (Bisson, McFarlane & Rose, 2000; Everly & Mitchell, 1999; Everly & Mitchell, 2000).

When a crisis occurs at work, the task facing service providers can be very complex. Workers may be required to return to the actual scene where they were traumatized. They may be grieving the loss of coworkers, friends, or even family members. The workplace itself may trigger painful and disabling psychological reactions. Short-term crisis intervention can facilitate healing and help workers with their personal concerns. In addition, targeted intervention can help employees return to work sooner and can assist in minimizing the negative impact of increased absenteeism and compromised productivity as an organization moves toward recovery following a traumatic event (Friedman, Framer, & Shearer, 1988; Stein & Eisen, 1996).

Traumatic stress reactions may be widespread after a public tragedy and may include anxiety, avoidance, hyperarousal, intrusive imagery or recollection, sleep disturbance, cognitive impairment, and a change in world view or core assumptions (Everly, Lating, & Mitchell, 2000; Janoff-Bulman, 1992). These distressing reactions may negatively affect job performance and social functioning in and outside of the workplace. The additional pressure of attempting to work effectively in spite of these reactions can further aggravate the level of stress and anxiety workers are experiencing.

When an event involves the death or injury of co-workers, survivors' reactions can be complicated by emotions of grief and guilt, which create an even greater degree of anxiety and sense of vulnerability for employees (Doka, 1999; Lattanzi-Licht, 1999; Williams & Nurmi, 1997a). Survivors face an increased risk of pathological bereavement when the death they grieve results from sudden, violent or traumatic events (Rando 1996; Stamm, 1999). Normalizing reactions, educating workers about the grieving process and adaptive coping strategies, building and strengthening social support networks, and ensuring appropriate referral to higher levels of care are the primary tasks of clinicians in the workplace in early aftermath of a tragic event.

PROVIDING EARLY INTERVENTION FOR INDIVIDUALS

Recognizing that any group is made up of individuals is essential when providing crisis intervention. Group interventions can be one way to address some of the issues concerning large numbers of people; however, a focus on individual interventions must be maintained to ensure that appropriate care is available to each specific employee. Individual interventions support and complement other interventions being offered.

In the days and weeks following a large-scale event, mental health professionals in the workplace must be flexible in providing services, as demands for counseling and support may be high. Establishing drop-in services, instead of requiring scheduled appointments, and extending business hours can help meet increased needs. Additional staff may be necessary to accomplish this. Community mental health agencies and national organizations, such as the American Red Cross, are excellent sources of trained, licensed mental health clinicians who may be willing to volunteer and provide crisis counseling for an organization affected by a large-scale tragedy.

Informing the targeted population about the services in place is another consideration for providers. Posting signs in cafeterias and health care clinics, utilizing email groups, and developing web pages are very effective media for quick, widespread announcements informing workers that mental health professionals are available on-site to assist them. Further outreach may include mental health workers going to offices and work areas to talk to people informally or to attend staff meetings and make brief presentations about services available to employees.

Outreach attempts should provide people with general information about available support in a way that encourages them to access services voluntarily. Individuals recover from trauma and loss in unique and personal ways. Mental health providers should be sensitive to the fact that some people may not want any form of treatment or counseling in the earliest stages of their recovery from an event. People do not want to feel coerced or pathologized when exploring mental health services. Practitioners should encourage people to access psychological support, yet demonstrate respect for each person's personal choice. Creating a positive impression with workers who are initially reluctant to seek assistance may cause them to be more amenable to intervention at a later time.

The demand for services may be so high just after a crisis that mental health providers are severely limited in the time they can spend with individuals. This compromises the depth and nature of the assessment and intervention a clinician can provide. Developing a specific assessment tool to use temporarily can be helpful. A checklist of symptoms or a self-report questionnaire may be used to focus the session on the employee's most compelling concerns. Obtaining information, such as social and mental health history as well as previous trauma exposure, will assist the clinician in determining if further assessment or services are recommended. Brief, informational handouts about grief, traumatic stress, and available medical and psychological support services can effectively address the specific concerns of clients in an efficient manner. Generating call-back sheets and special flags for client files during the early post-crisis period will allow for appropriate and more detailed follow-up at a later point.

With the increased client flow and space and time constraints that often go hand-in-hand with large, traumatic events, client confidentiality can be a particular challenge. Medical service providers, employee assistance programs, human resource departments, and management may be providing services to many of the same people. Mental health clinicians must maintain their commitment to protecting each person's privacy. Files and documents should be kept out of view, and clinicians should be acutely aware of their surroundings during confidential conversations, especially during the chaotic post-crisis period. Obtaining written permission prior to exchanging information with other departments is common practice for mental health providers and must remain so.

Many people experience strong reactions following a tragic event. Often, during an individual session, a client simply wants to be reassured that what he or she is experiencing is normal and that symptoms should improve over time. Providing information on when and how to access more comprehensive medical or psychological services can help a worker seek assistance in the future.

A mechanism for follow-up should be agreed upon by the clinician and the client. A follow-up and referral system should be put in to place quickly. Ideally, employee assistance programs, and other providers in the workplace, have specific resource lists that are up to date and relevant to the needs brought on by a specific tragedy. Information about community organizations and agencies, trauma and grief specialists, medical professionals, and financial resources can be gathered even before a large or public event. Clinicians and their clients will be less overwhelmed when such information is close at hand and provided in a timely manner.

People accessing psychological assistance in the workplace may feel unsafe engaging in deep emotional exchanges that can affect their ability to return to their duties following a session. In the immediate aftermath of a crisis, employers and employees tend to be more tolerant of one another and job performance expectations may be altered for a period of time. In spite of the painful emotions workers are experiencing, many will want to carry out their duties as closely as possible to pre-crisis levels of ability. Some may worry that an emotional counseling session will only further prevent them from functioning in their jobs. Clinicians should be mindful of this during sessions that occur during working hours. Allowing for some ventilation of emotion is an important piece of crisis intervention, but it may need to be of a limited nature in the workplace. Clinicians can use the final portion of an individual session to teach a concrete stress management skill or to lead a client through a relaxation exercise. Workers often regain some sense of personal control during a difficult time by utilizing strategies that help them calm and soothe themselves.

PROVIDING EARLY INTERVENTION FOR GROUPS

Many clinicians rely on group interventions in the workplace following a tragedy or crisis. A group intervention can reach large numbers of employees in a time-efficient way. Social support networks within the workplace can be established or strengthened, which workers can continue to utilize as they begin to heal and recover.

Different types of group intervention should be available and applied to different groups in the immediate aftermath of a tragedy. Everly, Lating, and Mitchell (2000), writing about group crisis intervention, highlight the importance of employing a comprehensive and multi-intervention programming approach that combines large group, small group, and individual interventions to meet the broadest spectrum of needs following a crisis. At the Pentagon, many types of groups were available to workers throughout the days and weeks after the attack. Workers were often more willing to attend groups than to seek one-on-one services. Groups provided participants with a greater understanding of their reactions and needs as well as with information about available services. This resulted in many employees becoming more open to individual counseling than they had been prior to attending a group.

Early Intervention: Large Groups

In the early stages of recovery, large group interventions should focus on educating participants about the current state of the crisis, normal reactions people are experiencing, future reactions they may have, and services available for support or treatment. During a large group process, deeply personal and emotional reactions may occur within participants that can be difficult for group facilitators to effectively manage. Generally, however, participants can be encouraged to self-regulate their overwhelming emotions by not being asked to disclose details about themselves or about how they are feeling. Allowing for comments and questions is useful; however, facilitators of large groups should concentrate on providing information to participants instead of obtaining detailed input from them. Depending on the size of the group, additional counselors should be in attendance to provide one-on-one assistance to anyone experiencing overt anxiety or grief during a large group process.

Workers are sometimes troubled by issues related to safety and security in the work environment after a tragic event. If the event occurred in the workplace, such as at the Pentagon, these issues can be of paramount concern. Convening meetings to provide factual and current information related to the event can assist many workers in regaining some sense of mastery over their environment. Suggesting ways they can assist one another and themselves, such as by talking with each other or by incorporating some light exercise into the workday, can also be useful. The very act of bringing people together can help reduce the perception people may have that they alone are having difficulty with the event or that they are without mechanisms of support.

Early Intervention: Small Groups

Practitioners in the workplace rely on small group work to further stabilize crisis reactions and to provide information on adaptive coping with grief and trauma. Small groups are often referred to as "debriefings," although several different models exist and are utilized by mental health clinicians. One such small group intervention is the seven-stage model first developed by Jeffrey Mitchell (1983), the Critical Incident Stress Debriefing (CISD). The CISD is commonly used in workplace environments but is only one of several interventions that are included in the broader crisis intervention system of Critical Incident Stress Management (Mitchell & Everly, 2001). Other forms of psychological debriefing have been developed by practitioners responding to people exposed to traumatic or distressing events. It is important that practitioners be specific about the approach and model being applied when planning and executing small group interventions that are described as "debriefings." This generic term has led to confusion among clinicians and, more importantly, among participants referring to services provided after an event.

One effect of this confusion has been that small group work, and specifically "debriefing," has been questioned as an effective, appropriate early intervention strategy (Bisson, et al., 2000). Any intervention must be appropriately applied by a skilled provider. Everly, Flannery & Mitchell (2000) recommend small group interventions as just one part of a more comprehensive and multiple intervention approach to crisis intervention. Individual intervention, organizational and management consultation, family support, and comprehensive follow-up and referral are recommended to further meet the needs of traumatized individuals. Some factors that influence which group model mental health providers may use include the homogeneity of a group, the inclusion of supervisory staff, the number of participants, whether or not the group will be conducted by a team that includes peer support personnel, and the length of time that has passed since the tragedy.

Small group work, regardless of the specific model chosen, can be an excellent way to handle the needs of workers experiencing significant emotional distress in response to a tragedy (Williams & Nurmi, 1997b). A group intervention can stabilize individuals in acute crisis, allow for ventilation of feelings, provide targeted education, enhance social support networks, and assist people in accessing existing coping mechanisms or learning new ones. In addition, clinicians facilitating a small group can assess the group and identify individuals who may need more attention. Individual interventions can be arranged for those expressing concerns that cannot be effectively addressed within the group context.

Workplace providers may find that going to the actual office locations of workgroups increases accessibility and use of mental health services. Incorporating a process group or psychoeducational group into an existing staff meeting is one way to provide services with minimal disruption to the workday. Longer and more structured group processes can be planned for groups that are more directly affected by a tragedy or crisis. These more in-depth groups can be scheduled later in the workday so that employees can reflect on the experience without the pressure of having to return to their job duties.

PROVIDING ONGOING SERVICES FOR INDIVIDUALS

After several weeks or months, depending on the nature of the event, the acute crisis stage will wind down in the workplace, and the intense demand for mental health services will diminish. Mental health providers in the workplace are then faced with anticipating future needs of employees and providing services that will help them resolve trauma and grief reactions. Developing outreach strategies to connect with workers who have not accessed services or who are experiencing a delayed onset of reactions is also important.

Individuals who presented during the crisis phase will require follow-up. At the Pentagon, we established a plan to follow-up with everyone we saw in the immediate aftermath of the terrorist attack after three, six, and 12 months. Although we knew that most people would be feeling better without the benefit of professional mental health assistance, we wanted to ensure that anyone still experiencing a high frequency or level of distressing symptoms was contacted and encouraged to come to the EAP for further suggestions or referral.

In an effort to alert workers to the availability of further assistance, we developed new pages for our website outlining normal trauma and grief reactions and recovery and highlighting indicators for further care. We produced a brief handout alerting our population to the possibility of an increase in grief and traumatic stress symptoms over the holidays and at the six-month post-event mark. This information was sent to subscribers on our email distribution list as well as to human resource departments and agency managers.

Mental health providers should expect that workers will continue to present for services with concerns related to a large-scale tragedy months after the event. Traumatic stress reactions, whether or not they meet *DSM-IV* (American Psychiatric Association, 1994) criteria for a diagnosis of post-traumatic stress disorder (PTSD), are often intensified by complicated grieving or by previous trauma in an individual's life (Rando, 1996). Workers may also seek services for separate concerns such as substance abuse or interpersonal difficulties, not realizing that these may, in fact, be related to the difficulty they are having coping with traumatic reactions. This makes assessment and appropriate referral extremely important. Increasing the number of sessions devoted to assessment issues prior to making a referral can help ensure that the need for services, such as medical intervention and long-term or specialized forms of psychotherapy, are identified and thus made available to workers seeking assistance. As time passes, the number of new cases opened by an employee assistance program or behavioral health service may decrease while the complexity of new cases related to one specific event may actually increase.

PROVIDING ONGOING SERVICES FOR GROUPS

In the months following a public tragedy, practitioners can continue to meet the psychoeducational and referral needs of individuals with group techniques. Training sessions for managers, supervisors, and staff on posttraumatic stress reactions and posttraumatic stress disorder is one type of group intervention. Large, structured group educational interventions can be an effective way to provide support and to decrease any continuing distressing reactions (Williams & Nurmi, 1997b).

Ongoing Services: Large Groups

After the initial crisis stage has passed, many workers will hope to move past the tragedy and loss they have experienced and get back to their normal routine. In the Pentagon, this desire to move on was complicated by the fact that much of the building was under repair, requiring the relocation of offices and workgroups. Additionally, the loss of life and the reassignment of personnel to support the Department of Defense's efforts to combat terrorism created ongoing disruption in personnel and additional projects and job duties for many of the civilians working in the building. Many employees became more reluctant to devote time and effort to accessing mental health services.

To address this, and to continue to reach workers with ongoing needs, the EAP instituted an educational program that focused on providing an overview of stress and coping strategies to apply to different types of stress, including those related to trauma and crisis. Many workers were willing to spend two or three hours in a one-time workshop to learn and practice concrete stress management tactics and to better understand how traumatic stress might still be affecting them. The class was not designed to promote emotional processing of the events of 9/11; rather, participants were educated about stress, with an emphasis on when and how they should seek additional support. Individual referrals to the EAP increased following each workshop, and the demand for and interest in this class continued many months after the terrorist attack on the Pentagon.

Efforts to collaborate and consult with management included group training events for supervisory staff. This was a key factor in the success of the employee assistance program's outreach efforts in the Pentagon. Supervisory trainings following a large-scale or traumatic event can help managers identify employees whose performance and behavior may indicate ongoing trauma or grief reactions. With this in mind, supervisors are more likely to make a referral to the employee assistance program when an employee exhibits signs of compromised functioning at work. Working with supervisors from the earliest phases of response is an essential role mental health providers play in organizational recovery. Information about trauma, grief, recovery, and mental health services can be incorporated or emphasized in orientation presentations, documents and manuals designed for supervisory staff.

Some supervisors may themselves be adversely affected by a tragic event. Others may find it difficult to understand why some employees are able to recover and return to high levels of work performance and others are not. Providing group education, as well as one-to-one consultation, to supervisors is one way mental health practitioners can meet the needs of the organization as a whole and of the individual employees. Employees will be far more likely to access further care or educational opportunities when supervisors support them in doing so.

Ongoing Services: Small Groups

Small group education offered to specific workgroups can address their particular concerns. Some of these may be safety and security, relocation of office space, or workplace adjustment issues. One workgroup may desire a brief stress management presentation or a discussion regarding conflict resolution. Another may want suggestions on effectively dealing with members of the media, as the attention on the survivors of a public tragedy can be intense for many months. Shifting the focus of small group interventions from processing the trauma or tragedy to more concrete and educational topics can allow workers to develop skills to advance through the healing process with the support of colleagues and friends in the workplace.

Other small group interventions, such as support groups, can also be established after the initial crisis phase. Scheduling a weekly group over a lunch hour or at the completion of the business day will provide workers with a better opportunity to attend without taking time off. Support groups can allow participants to continue to expand their social support network and help them feel less isolated in their experience following a tragedy (Foy, Glynn, Schnur, Jankowski, Wattenberg, Weiss, Marmar, & Gusman, 2000).

Workgroups may experience additional distressing events that interrupt their healing process in the wake of a public tragedy. The death of a co-worker or an incident of workplace violence months after a large and public tragedy can further overwhelm the coping and functioning abilities of many members of a workgroup. Providing a Critical Incident Stress Debriefing or grief process group specifically in response to a new event may assist a workgroup in accessing coping skills and resources. In addition, workers can be reassured that any reemergence or aggravation of posttraumatic stress or grief symptoms does not indicate a relapse in their healing.

SPECIAL EVENTS

As time passes after a public tragedy, the attention of the media and of the community moves to other issues. In a workplace directly affected by such an event, it is important for mental health providers to continue to provide opportunities that allow recognition of or reflection on the event and its meaning to workers, their families and friends. Events can be formal or informal and may be only indirectly related to the public tragedy.

Health and education fairs in public areas can allow employees to get information on ways to take care of themselves and one another. A health fair focusing on stress management at the Pentagon included licensed massage therapists providing seated massage, handouts and activities related to stress management, and comedy shorts playing on video. Workers in the building were able to stop briefly and take a break from their daily routines. Mental health providers staffed the fair and spoke with people informally about stress, grief, and coping.

Planning and coordinating events such as special presentations by experts in the field of trauma, grief, and recovery can also provide a way for practitioners to reach out to broad numbers of people in an organization. During one such event at the Pentagon, sponsored by the employee assistance program, an expert on children and how they cope with disasters and crisis was included. In this way, workers who considered themselves less directly affected by the terrorist attack were encouraged to come to the event and learn how to meet the needs of their children in the event of a crisis. A secondary benefit of this was that employees received information about their own past or present reactions and suggestions to assist them to cope with crisis more effectively themselves.

ANNIVERSARIES

Employees will require particular support on and around anniversaries (Myers, 1994). It is natural for individuals to experience a reemergence of distressing memories, emotions or reactions brought on by the anniversary of a distressing event. Many will not understand what they are experiencing, and some will be concerned they are backsliding in their healing and recovery process. Employees who have not accessed mental health services before and others who have long ago terminated psychological support services may need such services from providers.

Providers in the workplace should be prepared for increased requests from workgroups for small group interventions related to the anniversary. Such interventions should focus on workers' present day concerns and avoid processing the original traumatic event and its aftermath. Large group educational presentations can be planned to educate employees about trauma and grief resolution and anniversary reactions. This kind of event can be a good way to help people anticipate anniversary reactions and to reassure those who are growing increasingly anxious as the date of the tragedy approaches. It can also assist workers who are not experiencing troubling reactions to better understand the feelings and behaviors of their colleagues who are troubled by the anniversary (Myers, 1994).

Mental health providers should develop written materials related to the anniversary to educate workers about what they may experience as to well as reassure them that, with time, these reactions should pass. In the meantime, coping strategies can help employees work through any difficult times near the anniversary date. They can limit their exposure to increased media coverage of the anniversary. Limiting media consumption is one way to guard against painful reactions triggered by images from the past. Employees can be encouraged to practice self-care by getting rest and proper nutrition, as well as to talk with others, to write in a journal or otherwise creatively express themselves, and to participate in activities that allow them to mark the event in ways that are personally meaningful.

The first anniversary of a disaster or tragedy is usually considered the most significant and receives the most attention. Mental health providers should be prepared to continue to provide services specifically related to an overwhelming and tragic event, such as a bombing, school shooting, or act of terrorism, even after the first anniversary. Subsequent anniversaries can produce similar reactions in certain individuals, and mental health providers may play a key role in ensuring that opportunities are provided in the workplace to commemorate the event, even after the one-year mark.

CARE FOR THE CAREGIVERS

Compassion fatigue has been written about by Charles Figley (1995) as an important consideration for professionals who work closely with traumatized and grieving people. Mental health providers working permanently or for an extended period of time in a workplace with distressed workers after a large and public event will find the work is as personally taxing as it is meaningful.

The intensity of emotion around a public tragedy and the high needs of large numbers of people can take a toll on the personal resources of a mental health provider. In some instances the mental health worker is directly affected by the tragedy by having been at the scene of the tragedy, as were many of the Pentagon mental health providers, or by having suffered a personal loss due to the event. Some mental health professionals may feel unprepared or may lack the training and experience to effectively address the intense needs of the people they are hoping to assist.

Providing for the needs of the caregivers must be a priority from the earliest possible phase of a crisis. One-on-one support for caregivers may be offered through supervision, during which the mental health worker has an opportunity to process some of the things he or she has seen and heard. Groups and debriefings can be conducted specifically for caregivers to encourage them to be mindful of their need for self-care throughout their work with others. Some mental health workers may need to be encouraged to take a break or an unplanned day off to bolster their own energy and emotional reserves. Others may require psychological services to better understand their experiences and personal reactions. Caregivers must be aware that the work following a tragedy or crisis is extremely stressful and that they will need to develop ways to protect their own physical and psychological health (Figley, 1995).

FINAL CONSIDERATIONS FOR PROVIDERS IN THE WORKPLACE

One result of large, public tragedies is that those affected have many resources available to them through community and government agencies and from generous individuals. It is essential for mental health providers and organizations to collaborate effectively when providing services and resources in response to a public tragedy (Dodgen, Ladue, & Kaul, in press). After the Pentagon attack, financial and psychological resources were offered to workers in the building from a variety of sources. An important role of the employee assistance program was learning about these resources, collaborating with other providers, and ensuring that workers had access to all that was available. Guarding against duplication of services was also an important focus.

In the wake of public tragedy, the demands on mental health service providers in the workplace are extremely high. To anticipate the needs of large numbers of people affected by such an event, mental health workers need to plan interventions that will stabilize workers in crisis, accomplish outreach and support, and facilitate access to more specialized medical and psychological services for those who require it. Before a crisis or large event occurs, mental health service providers can make preparations:

- Prioritize crisis intervention training and establish crisis response teams with specialized skills to help service providers feel more confident in their ability to respond to a large-scale event.

- Work closely with management to ensure a mental health perspective is included in organizational disaster and crisis contingency plans.

- Develop relationships with other local agencies and service providers to expand the pool of available resources.

Providers can thus be certain the psychological needs of an organization and its workers can be provided for in times of great tragedy. As an organization moves from crisis towards recovery, mental health interventions and services must continue to promote and support the individual and collective healing of workers, their families and their communities. ■

Rachel Kaul is Coordinator of Crisis Response Services for the Pentagon Employee Referral Service. She is a Certified Trauma Specialist by the Association of Traumatic Stress Specialists and a certified instructor of CISM interventions by the International Critical Incident Stress Foundation. Ms. Kaul has gained her experience working with people affected by grief, loss, and trauma in a variety of settings. She was an emergency room social worker at University of Michigan Health System's Level I trauma center before coming to the Pentagon. She has been a responder for community and EAP crisis teams and is currently Chair of the Disaster Mental Health Committee of the Arlington Chapter of the American Red Cross. She provides ongoing education and training to communities and mental health professionals on crisis intervention, stress management, and self-care.

REFERENCES

American Psychiatric Association. (1994). *Diagnostic and statistical manual of mental disorders* (4th ed.). Washington, DC: APA.

Bisson, J.I., McFarlane, A. & Rose. (2000). Psychological debriefing. In Foa, E., McFarlane, A., & Friedman, M., (Eds). *Effective Treatments for PTSD* (pp.39-59). NY: Guilford.

Caplan, G. (1964). *Principles of preventive psychiatry.* New York: Basic Books.

Doka, K.J. (1999). A primer on loss and grief. In J.D. Davidson & K.J. Doka (Eds.), *Living with grief: At work, at school, at worship.* Washington, DC: Hospice Foundation of America.

Dodgen, D., LaDue, L., & Kaul, R.E. (in press). Coordinating a local response to a national tragedy: Community mental health in Washington, D.C. after the Pentagon attack. *Journal of Military Medicine.*

Everly, Jr., G.S., Flannery, Jr., R.B., & Mitchell, J.T. (2000). Critical incident stress management: A review of the literature. *Aggression and Violent Behavior: A Review Journal, 5,* 23-40.

Everly, Jr., G.S., Lating, J.M., & Mitchell, J.T. (2000). Innovations in group crisis intervention. In A.R. Roberts (Ed.), *Crisis intervention handbook: Assessment, treatment, and research* (2nd ed.). New York: Oxford University Press.

Everly, Jr., G.S., & Mitchell, J.T. (1999). *Critical incident stress management (CISM): A new era and standard of care in crisis intervention* (2nd ed.). Ellicott City, MD: Chevron.

Everly, Jr., G.S., & Mitchell, J.T. (2000). The debriefing "controversy" and crisis intervention: A review of lexical and substantive issues. *International Journal of Emergency Mental Health, 2000, 2,* 211-225.

Figley, C.R. (Ed.) (1995). *Compassion fatigue: Coping with secondary traumatic stress disorder in those who treat the traumatized.* New York: Brunner/Mazel.

Flannery, Jr., R.B., & Everly, Jr., G.S. (2000). Crisis intervention: A review. *International Journal of Emergency Mental Health, 2,* 119-125.

Foy, D.W., Glynn, S.M., Schnurr, P.P., Jankowski, M.K., Wattenberg, M.S., Weiss, D.S., Marmar, C.R., & Gusman, F.D. (2000). Group therapy. In E.B. Foa, T.M. Keane, & M.J. Freidman (Eds.), *Effective treatments for PTSD.* New York: Guilford Press.

Friedman, R.J., Framer, M.B., & Shearer, D.R. (1988). Early response to posttraumatic stress. *EAP Digest, 8,* 45-49.

Janoff-Bulman, R. (1992). *Shattered assumptions: Toward a new psychology of trauma.* New York: Free Press.

Lattnazi-Licht, M.E. (1999). Grief in the workplace: Supporting the grieving employee. In J.D. Davidson & K.J. Doka (Eds.) *Living with grief: At work, at school, at worship.* Washington, DC: Hospice Foundation of America.

Lindemann, E. (1944). Symptomatology and management of acute grief. *American Journal of Psychiatry, 101,* 141-148.

Mitchell, J.T. (1983). When disaster strikes...The critical incident stress debriefing process. *Journal of Emergency Medical Services, 8,* 36-39.

Mitchell, J.T., & Everly, Jr., G.S. (2001). *Critical incident stress debriefing: An operations manual for CISD, defusing and other group crisis intervention services* (3rd ed.). Ellicott City, MD: Chevron.

Myers, D. (1994). *Disaster responses and recovery: A handbook for mental health professionals.* Rockville, MD: Center for Mental Health Studies.

Rando, T.A. (1994). Complications in mourning a traumatic death. In I.B. Corless, B.B. Germino, & M. Pittman (Eds.), *Death, dying and bereavement: Theoretical perspectives and other ways of knowing.* Boston: Jones and Bartlett.

Rando, T.A. (1996). In K.J. Doka (Ed.), *Living with grief after sudden loss: Suicide, homicide, accident, heart attack, stroke.* Washington, DC: Hospice Foundation of America.

Raphael, B. (1986). *When disaster strikes: A handbook for caring professionals.* London: Hutchinson.

Roberts, A.R. (2000). An overview of crisis theory and crisis intervention. In A.R. Roberts (Ed.), *Crisis intervention handbook: Assessment, treatment, and research* (2nd ed.). New York: Oxford University Press.

Stamm, B.H. (1999). In C.R. Figley (Ed.), *The traumatology of grieving.* Philadelphia, PA: Bruner/Mazel.

Stein, E. & Eisen, B. (1996). Helping trauma survivors cope: Effects of immediate brief co-therapy and crisis intervention. *Crisis Intervention, 3,* 113-127.

Williams, M.B. & Nurmi, L.A. (1997-a). Death of a co-worker: Conceptual overview. In C.R. Figley, B.E. Bride, & N. Mazza (Eds.), *Death and trauma: The traumatology of grieving.* Bristol, PA: Taylor & Francis.

Williams, M.B. & Nurmi, L.A. (1997-b). Death of a co-worker: Facilitating the healing. In C.R. Figley, B.E. Bride, & N. Mazza (Eds.), *Death and trauma: The traumatology of grieving.* Bristol, PA: Taylor & Francis.

CHAPTER 21

Public Tragedy and Complicated Mourning

Therese A. Rando

The premise of this chapter is that public tragedies inherently contain elements that tend to complicate mourning in persons bereaved of individuals who die in such tragedies. In this chapter, the term *public tragedy* refers to a calamitous event that brings death to one or more people and arouses great grief and oftentimes horror in its social audience. This chapter will first analyze how deaths in public tragedies predispose to complicated mourning and then identify selected perspectives and intervention strategies to target and address potential complications in the bereavement of the survivors. The purpose is to encourage an appreciation of the dynamics of trauma and complicated mourning following public tragedy deaths and to sensitize the reader to other aspects of public tragedy that can further complicate bereavement. The hope is that this information will help the reader to recognize, evaluate, and treat mourning that is complicated by public tragedy.

PUBLIC TRAGEDY AND COMPLICATED MOURNING

To understand how a public tragedy can predispose to complicated mourning, it is first necessary to be familiar with the phenomenon of complicated mourning and to appreciate one of its major determinants, trauma. Second, there must be an awareness of aspects inherent in public tragedy that give rise to complicated mourning. The intersection of complicated mourning, trauma, and public tragedy is compelling for most thanatologists and traumatologists.

Whenever a loss transpires, there are five possible outcomes. The first and most desirable is that uncomplicated mourning begins. This means that the mourner is able to

- Recognize the loss;
- React to the separation;
- Recollect and reexperience the deceased and the relationship;
- Relinquish the old attachments to the deceased and to the old assumptive world;
- Readjust to move adaptively into the new world without forgetting the old; and
- Reinvest (Rando, 1993).

Uncomplicated mourning is not, as might be inferred, without great pain and difficulty; it is uncomplicated only in that it can be addressed in a fashion that permits healthy accommodation of the loss into the mourner's life. Unfortunately, complicated mourning also can take place following a loss and occurs when, taking into consideration the amount of time since the death, there is some compromise, distortion, or failure of one or more of the "R" processes of mourning noted above. In complicated mourning, the mourner attempts to deny, repress, or avoid aspects of the loss, its pain, and the full realization of its implications. At the same time, the mourner tries to hold on to and avoid relinquishing the lost loved one.

Complicated mourning does not appear in just one guise. Indeed, it can be manifested in any one or a combination of four forms: (a) complicated mourning symptoms, (b) one or more of seven complicated mourning syndromes, (c) a diagnosable mental or physical disorder; and (d) death.

Not all adversity subsequent to a particular death stems directly from that death. To be indicative of complicated mourning, these manifestations must meet two criteria: They must have developed or significantly worsened since the death in question, and they must be associated with some "R" process failure, taking into consideration the amount of time since the death. When one or both criteria are absent, the manifestations should not be construed as symptoms of complicated mourning.

In an earlier work, I suggested that seven factors place an individual at high risk for complicated mourning (Rando, 1993). An individual may sustain a combination of these in a given bereavement. Each risk factor complicates one or more of the "R" processes in one or more ways, thus bringing about the complicated mourning. The first four factors pertain to the circumstances of death. They are (1) sudden and unexpected death, especially if associated with traumatic circumstances; (2) death after an overly lengthy illness; (3) death of a child; and (4) death perceived as preventable. Complicated mourning does not necessarily reflect pathology on the mourner's part; rather, it may develop because of the objective situation with which the mourner is confronted. The remaining three risk factors are (1) a premorbid relationship with the deceased that had been markedly angry, ambivalent, or dependent; (2) the mourner's prior or concurrent unaccommodated losses, stresses, or mental health problems; and (3) the mourner's perception of lack of support.

TRAUMA AND TRAUMATIC BEREAVEMENT

Stemming from the Greek word for wound, *trauma* is commonly defined as a disordered psychic or behavioral state resulting from mental or emotional stress or physical injury. From a more specific mental health perspective, trauma and its consequent, *traumatic stress,* can be understood as the result of what happens when an individual suddenly perceives himself or herself to be in a physically and/or psychologically dangerous situation. Escape is impossible and normal coping mechanisms are insufficient. The person feels threatened, overwhelmed, helpless, anxious, and fearful. These responses, when found in a mourner's bereavement reactions, can interfere with the "R" processes and complicate mourning.

There are three points to make about the intimate relationships between loss and trauma, grief, and traumatic stress (Rando, 2000). First, by definition, in all trauma there exists loss (at the very least, a loss of control); and in most major losses, there are dimensions of trauma.

Second, acute grief, even in relatively benign situations, can be construed as a form of traumatic stress reaction. It does not have to meet diagnostic criteria for posttraumatic stress disorder (PTSD). This underscores an important point that must be explicitly recognized: traumatic stress is a generic term that refers to both specific and nonspecific symptoms, disorders, or reactions. Contrary to popular misconception, PTSD is only one of several different kinds of traumatic stress responses (Rando, 2000).

Third, in cases of *traumatic death,* a variation of complicated mourning is stimulated, traumatic bereavement. In this unique intersection of loss and trauma, any one or a combination of six risk factors, delineated below, are known to have the potential to make any death circumstance traumatic for a mourner. This brings forth additional traumatic stress, above and beyond that found in uncomplicated acute grief. In situations where this traumatic stress overshadows the mourner's grief, the psychological priority for the mourner will be to attend first to the task of trauma mastery before the task of loss accommodation (i.e., grief and mourning). The six factors that make any death traumatic are

1. Suddenness and lack of anticipation;

2. Violence, mutilation, and destruction;

3. Preventability and/or randomness;

4. Loss of one's child;

5. Multiple deaths; and

6. The mourner's personal encounter with death secondary to a significant threat to survival or a massive and/or shocking confrontation with the death and mutilation of others (Rando, 2000).

Each of these factors presents the mourner with impediments to the "R" processes of mourning, thus creating, at least for a time, complicated mourning. For this reason, the experience of traumatic bereavement is typically associated with complicated mourning for the survivor.

FACTORS IN PUBLIC TRAGEDY THAT EXACERBATE COMPLICATED MOURNING

There are several factors inherent in a public tragedy that predispose to complicated mourning. Using the 9/11 terrorist attacks on the World Trade Center in New York City for illustration, these factors are classified into four problem categories: (1) problems associated with the characteristics of the death; (2) problems related to the public nature of the death; (3) specific problems following a World Trade Center death; and (4) problems associated with particular characteristics of survivors. Some of the factors discussed here may not be generalizable to other public tragedies.

Problems Associated with Characteristics of the Death

The terrorist attacks of September 11, 2001, show the interplay of public tragedy and the six risk factors that make any death traumatic and stimulate traumatic bereavement. For all intents and purposes, the attacks were sudden and unanticipated. There was much violence, mutilation, destruction, and loss of life. As in all terrorist attacks, these elements were parts of the larger goal because they are known to produce significant fear and assumptive world violation in the social audience. Preventability, randomness, multiple deaths, loss of a child (including adult children), and a mourner's personal encounter with death were all present in the bereavement scenarios with which survivors struggled and continue to struggle. All these factors are linked with public tragedies, each one contributing to traumatic bereavement and presenting the mourner with specific complications in his or her "R" processes of mourning. They account for these mourners' propensity to experience intense vulnerability, high anxiety, psychic numbing, significant anger and guilt, a strong search for meaning, and a need to assign responsibility and mete out punishment.

Other complicating factors associated with the circumstances of the death concern intentionality and premeditation. Both elements exacerbate the issues already brought about by the preventability of the death and the violent victimization of the mourners. Together, these contribute to even more assumptive world violation, particularly in terms of the existence of evil, breakdown of the moral universe, threats to meaningfulness, and, for some, loss of trust in other people (Janoff-Bulman, 1988).

Still other facts about the death circumstances bring their own demands that can interfere with healthy mourning. The fact that death by plane crash into two skyscrapers is unique and difficult to grasp adds to the difficulty in comprehending the event that took the loved one's life. The fact that some died because they followed directions to remain in the building is a source of intense rage on the parts of some survivors. The fact that this was the second attack on the World Trade Center (the first was in 1993), becomes a complicating element when mourners struggle to understand how the first attack failed to prompt sufficient changes so that evacuation could be better handled.

Opportunities to talk on the telephone with their doomed loved ones, to communicate via e-mail, or to retrieve their messages on telephone answering tapes had variable effects on mourners. For some, such a connection was positive, but for others, it added to their traumatization because they were utterly powerless to affect the fate bearing down upon their beloved person.

Finally, several of the more grotesque aspects of the deaths of some individuals may leave their survivors with complicating reactions. Concern about what their loved ones felt before death is not uncommon in general, but can be particularly prevalent among the bereaved whose loved ones jumped out of windows. The vaporization of many bodies, and the crushing and burning of others, added to the horror and unnaturalness of the deaths that the survivors struggled to mourn.

Problems Related to the Public Nature of the Death

News coverage of 9/11 was unparalleled. The enormity of the attacks and their sequelae, together with the fact that they occurred in one of the largest news centers of the world in an age when disasters of all kinds receive monumental amounts of air time and print space, made saturation coverage inevitable. From this derives one of the greatest blessings and one of the greatest curses for those who lost someone in the terrorist attacks. It points to the promise, as well as the peril of the truly "public" tragedy.

In their excellent book, *When A Community Weeps: Case Studies in Group Survivorship*, Zinner and Williams (1999) identify the role of the news media as being critical in intensifying the experience of group survivorship. They provide numerous examples illustrating the "double-edged sword" effect. On the one hand, the news media can disseminate necessary and accurate information and provide acknowledgment of precisely what has occurred. The news media can also promote healing if effectively utilized by leaders conveying messages that legitimize, normalize, enable, and provide direction for healthy grief. Who can forget former Mayor Rudy Giuliani's messages that New York City would survive despite the pain? Or President Bush's determination and encouragement, shouted through a bullhorn as he stood at Ground Zero?

The news media illustrate that others are affected, too. They report that concerned individuals, communities, and nations care about the survivors' losses and share their sorrow, shock, confusion, and outrage. The news media can help the bereaved search for loved ones and memorialize their lives when the search is finally recognized to be fruitless, as was so poignantly and effectively done by *The New York Times* in the "Portraits of Grief" series. For some, media coverage can be especially helpful. The repetitious recounting of events, presentation of images, and proffering of expert analysis can facilitate the cognitive grasping of what has occurred, thereby enabling the initial steps of mourning and, ultimately, the composition of a personal narrative of the event.

Yet the other side of the double-edged sword also slices. The media can directly and indirectly cause problems for the survivor. While news coverage can validate the significance of a loved one's death, it can also retraumatize mourners and increase their suffering. They cannot escape the trauma; they are constantly reminded of it. Because their loved ones died in an event of such national importance, survivors are sentenced to what could become a lifetime of contending with follow-up analyses and the perpetual discovery of new information. The news coverage was so extensive that it even generated vicarious bereavement (Rando, in press) in those who had lost no one.

The nature of the deaths resulted in the identification of the mourners as "9/11 persons," which can have substantial drawbacks. Some mourners do not want to bear the burden of such a designation. Some are distressed by having their behavior constantly scrutinized. Not a few have voiced concerns about having to live up to the expectations others have established for them. Many resent losing their individuality; they are lumped together with other survivors, and their loved ones are glorified as 9/11 victims. The latter action can be problematic in terms of complicating mourning if it inhibits the survivor's ability to address issues such as ambivalence or anger. It is not socially appropriate to resent the times your spouse let you down when everyone else is calling him a hero. In some instances, this can contribute to the individual becoming a disenfranchised mourner (Doka, 2002).

Survivors of those who have died very public deaths may discover that they have lost control over post-death rituals and other decisions. Their ownership of their situation can feel diluted as organizational, political, and public concerns intervene and they become fodder for news stories. Their awareness of the personal right to be free of the good will and intentions of others can become clouded, if indeed it is possessed at all.

Specific Problems after a World Trade Center Death

Some problems for mourners arose from specific issues confronted at Ground Zero. For many mourners, there was no body or body part that could be returned to them. This has happened in other disasters, of course, and the problems associated with the lack of confirmation and the inability to view the body are well documented in the literature. At Ground Zero, there was the unparalleled enormity of the airplane impacts, the inferno, and the building collapses that each contributed to leaving so few remains. There were the intensely dramatic and literal searches for loved ones that ended up fruitless, the overwhelming numbers of others in a similar situation, and the mourners' participation in locating personal items or providing samples of bodily material for DNA analyses. These all added elements that adversely affected the mourning of some survivors.

Financial issues created concurrent crises for a large proportion of the bereaved. Different mourners have been plagued with different stressors. These included struggling with bureaucratic red tape, deciding whether to file a lawsuit or accept what someone else has determined to be just, contending with others who see the search for compensation fueled by greed rather than necessity or fairness, and dealing with guilt over money that has been received.

Some bereaved persons feel that their mourning has been worsened by their observation that some 9/11 victims received more attention than others, and their perception that their loved one came out on the wrong side of the public's focus. For others, the sheer numbers of loved ones, friends, and acquaintances who perished in the catastrophe give new meaning to the terms *multiple loss* or *bereavement overload*, both of which complicate mourning. Among those who had been in one of the twin towers but managed to get out, there is often the discovery that survival of such an event does not come without its literal and figurative scars, the latter revealed by varying degrees of survival guilt and the question, "Why did I live when so many others did not?" For those lacking support, unresolved issues can compromise their mourning for those who did not escape.

Problems Associated with Characteristics of World Trade Center Survivors

Because so many of those killed in the terrorist attacks were relatively young, they left behind young families and bereaved parents—two populations believed to have particular propensities for complicated mourning. This statement in no way diminishes the bereavement of those in other roles or dismisses the experiences of those who lost older individuals; it simply highlights the risk of two cohorts. Those whose loved ones died in the line of duty may sustain additional complicating anger and bewilderment because their relatives or friends were supposed to have been rescuers, not victims.

According to U.S. government officials, the issue is not if another terrorist attack will occur, but when. Thus, those who already have been bereaved by a terrorist attack must live with the knowledge that other attacks are yet to come. To the extent that fear of future loss is a salient issue for all bereaved persons, especially if it comes from the same cause, those bereaved by 9/11 must cope with the specter of future attacks, very possibly in the same geographical area, given New York's appeal as a terrorist target. This tends to eliminate the consolation of thinking that others will be spared the fate of those who already have been taken.

MINIMIZING COMPLICATED MOURNING AFTER PUBLIC TRAGEDY

By understanding factors in public tragedy that predispose toward complicated mourning, the thanatologist or traumatologist is better equipped to intervene during the tragic event or soon afterward. Yet most clinicians dealing with complicated mourning have access to the bereaved only after a period of time has elapsed. For that reason, the information presented here is primarily for those working with individuals whose losses have occurred some time before the beginning of treatment. It may also be helpful for professionals and volunteers who provide crisis care, debriefing, or assistance in ritual construction or celebration. Space permits discussion of only a few selected perspectives and interventions. The term caregiver is used for maximum generalizability.

Perspectives

Three perspectives should be kept in mind by the caregiver and should inform all treatment decisions. These perspectives on public tragedy, trauma (including traumatic bereavement), and complicated mourning are briefly described below.

Public tragedy. The caregiver should remember that public tragedies usually generate complicated mourning. This is a consequence of traumatic bereavement and the factors intrinsic to public tragedies that complicate the "R" processes of mourning. Particularly salient are the public nature of the death and the impact of the news media.

Trauma and traumatic bereavement. The caregiver should keep in mind that along with the loss, the mourner is contending with trauma. Interventions should be those geared toward traumatic stress in general and traumatic bereavement in particular. Failure to intervene in the trauma, and to focus instead exclusively or primarily on the loss, can result in either a retraumatization of the mourner or the mourner's flight from treatment. The psychological priority of the ego of the traumatized mourner is typically on trauma mastery before accommodation of loss, i.e., relief of the traumatic anxiety before grief work and mourning (Eth & Pynoos, 1985).

Complicated mourning. The caregiver should be aware that complicated mourning represents the mourner's attempts to deny, repress, or avoid aspects of the loss, its pain, and the full realization of its implications, while at the same time holding on to and avoiding relinquishing the lost loved one. Complicated mourning is "complicated" in that it must be defined in reference to where the mourner is in his or her "R" processes and that it can be manifested in one or a combination of four forms. Finally, complicated mourning does not necessarily imply pathology on the part of the mourner; mourning can become complicated because of the objective characteristics of the death.

Interventions

In *Treatment of Complicated Mourning* (Rando, 1993), I discuss the issue of treatment of complicated mourning, including 14 points of clinical perspectives necessary for facilitating uncomplicated mourning and 18 on the treatment of complicated mourning. These are broken down into three categories: general perspectives, perspectives on the mourner, and perspectives on treatment. As a full discussion is precluded here, the reader is referred to the text for further details.

Others have covered interventions for complicated mourning, as well. In general, mourners who have lost loved ones in public tragedies will benefit from treatment for traumatic bereavement (Doka, 1996; Figley, 1999; Figley, Bride & Mazza, 1997; Kauffman, 2002; Rando, 1993). Ideally, any such treatment inherently would not only include techniques to ameliorate traumatic stress but also incorporate generic interventions for complicated mourning and expand to include tailored interventions to address the specific factors present in the particular public tragedy at hand.

At present, Wortman and colleagues are conducting research with persons bereaved by World Trade Center deaths (see Note). The goal is to develop and validate a 20-week treatment protocol for survivors of sudden, traumatic, unnatural deaths. This innovative treatment combines selected techniques from a variety of therapies and theories to address development of self-capacities, processing of trauma, processing of loss through mourning, facilitation of social support, challenging of negative automatic thoughts, and the teaching of bereavement-related coping strategies. To date, there is no other treatment of which I am aware that integrates as many diverse approaches to address the multidimensional issues presented by deaths in public tragedies.

CONCLUSION

In our contemporary world, we focus intensely upon public tragedies. The consequence is that we both help and harm the mourner who has lost a loved one in such an event. The purposes of this chapter have been to identify those aspects of public tragedy that complicate the individual's mourning and to provide knowledge and focal points for appropriate intervention. ■

Therese A. Rando, Ph.D., BCETS, BCBT is a clinical psychologist in Warwick, Rhode Island. She is Clinical Director of the Institute for the Study and Treatment of Loss, which provides mental health services through psychotherapy, training, supervision, and consultation. Dr. Rando specializes in loss and grief, traumatic stress, and the psychosocial care of chronically or terminally ill persons and their families. An internationally recognized researcher, author and lecturer, Dr. Rando's current work focuses on complicated mourning, loss of a child, the interface between posttraumatic stress and grief, and intervention techniques in the treatment of traumatic bereavement.

REFERENCES

Doka, K. (Ed.) (1996). *Living with grief after sudden loss: Suicide, homicide, accident, heart attack, stroke.* Washington, DC: Hospice Foundation of America.

Doka, K. (Ed.) (2002). *Disenfranchised grief: New directions, challenges, and strategies for practice.* Champaign, IL: Research Press.

Eth, S., & Pynoos, R. (1985). Interaction of trauma and grief in childhood. In S. Eth and R. Pynoos (Eds.), *Post-traumatic stress disorder in children.* Washington, DC: American Psychiatric Press.

Figley, C.R. (Ed.) (1999). *Traumatology of grieving: Conceptual, theoretical, and treatment foundations.* Philadelphia: Brunner/Mazel.

Figley, C.R., Bride, B.E., & Mazza, N. (Eds.) (1997). *Death and trauma: The traumatology of grieving.* Washington, DC: Taylor & Francis.

Janoff-Bulman, R. (1988). Victims of violence. In S. Fisher and J. Reason (Eds.), *Handbook of life stress, cognition and health* (pp. 101-113). New York: John Wiley & Sons.

Kauffman, J. (Ed.) (2002). *Loss of the assumptive world: A theory of traumatic loss.* New York: Brunner-Routledge.

Rando, T.A. (1993). *Treatment of complicated mourning.* Champaign, IL: Research Press.

Rando, T.A. (2000). On the experience of traumatic stress in anticipatory and postdeath mourning. In T.A. Rando (Ed.), *Clinical dimensions of anticipatory mourning: Theory and practice in working with the dying, their loved ones, and their caregivers* (pp. 155-221). Champaign, IL: Research Press.

Rando, T.A. (In press). Vicarious bereavement. In R. Kastenbaum (Ed.), *Encyclopedia of death and dying.* Farmington Hills, MI: Macmillan Reference USA.

Zinner, E.S., & Williams, M.B. (Eds.) (1999). *When a community weeps: Case studies in group survivorship.* Philadelphia: Brunner/Mazel.

Note: Development and research of the 20-week manualized treatment protocol for sudden, traumatic, unnatural death survivors have been spearheaded by Camille Wortman, Ph.D., in collaboration with Laurie Anne Pearlman, Ph.D., Therese A. Rando, Ph.D., BCETS, BCBT, Catherine Feuer, Ph.D., and Christine Farber, Ph.D. For information, contact Dr. Wortman at the Department of Psychology, State University of New York, Stony Brook.

■ PART IV ■

The Role of Hospice in Public Tragedy

This book concludes by reaffirming the constructive role that hospices can fill in times of public tragedy. Nadine Reimer Penner contributes to the effort by offering a guide to hospice for collaborating with disaster relief agencies. Many government agencies (local, state and federal), as well as private non-profit groups and quasi-governmental organizations, share responsibilities for providing disaster assistance. Understanding their roles is the first step in creating meaningful partnerships. This chapter demystifies the agencies and their mandates. It also articulates principles for collaboration.

Marcia Lattanzi-Licht offers the last word—reminding hospices of the services they can offer in times of community need. Her vision of hospice, shared by Hospice Foundation of America, is an expansive one. Hospices are community-based grief resources. They can offer support services in the immediate aftermath of community tragedy and over the long term as well. Even before tragedy strikes, hospices can offer preventive education to their communities and the news media about the process of grief.

As hospices rise to the challenge of this expanded role, taking care of grieving communities in the context of public tragedy, they need to remain mindful of the needs of their own employees. They cannot forget to offer crisis care and support to hospice workers who, even as they help others cope, may themselves be affected profoundly by community tragedy. ■

■ CHAPTER 22 ■

Collaborating with Relief Agencies: A Guide for Hospice

Nadine Reimer Penner

The first published account of disaster relief (Dunant, 1986) was written by Jean Henry Dunant in 1862. In *A Memory of Solferino*, the Swiss citizen Dunant described his efforts to help the wounded from an Italian war battle that occurred in 1859. He urged the creation of war relief societies leading to the founding of the Red Cross in 1863. In the United States, the American Association of the Red Cross was founded in 1881 by Clara Barton.

Disaster relief has changed significantly since its beginnings as humanitarian assistance during times of war. Since 1803, the U.S. Congress has repeatedly passed legislation granting authority and financial resources. Presidents can now implement disaster declarations allowing the federal government to intervene when the disaster is too large for local and state governments to manage. More than 100 national organizations, including government, business, labor unions, religious and community agencies, and other voluntary organizations are currently involved in disaster relief.

Hospices began to get involved in disaster work in the early 1990s. Early efforts were provided by Harry Hynes Memorial Hospice, formerly known as Hospice Incorporated, when a tornado ripped through Andover and metropolitan Wichita, Kansas, and when Hurricane Andrew devastated parts of Florida and Louisiana. On Hawaii's Kauai Island, Kauai Hospice has responded to several helicopter crashes by providing support to relatives whose family members died in the disasters (Slavin, 1998).

One of the biggest challenges for hospice workers is to understand the maze of organizations that come together during a disaster. The following is a summary of the major organizations involved.

GOVERNMENT AGENCIES

Federal Emergency Management Agency

The Federal Emergency Management Agency (FEMA) is the lead federal disaster coordinating agency. It had its beginnings in an Act of Congress in 1803. Many years later, President Carter signed an executive order in 1979 merging many of the separate federal disaster-related agencies into what is now known as FEMA. The legislation giving FEMA authorization to administer public relief programs comes from the Robert T. Stafford Disaster Relief and Emergency Assistance Act, Public Law 93-288, as amended. FEMA is an independent agency that reports to the President. Its mission is "to reduce loss of life and property and protect our nation's critical infrastructure from all types of hazards through a comprehensive, risk-based emergency management program of mitigation, preparedness, response and recovery" (FEMA, 2002). In order for FEMA to become involved, the president must officially declare a disaster.

FEMA can provide emergency and long-term assistance. Emergency work includes removal of debris, sandbagging, putting warning devices into place, and search and rescue. This work must be completed within six months of the date of the disaster declaration. Permanent work, which must be completed within 18 months, includes repair or replacement of roads, bridges, water control facilities, buildings, equipment, utilities, parks, recreational facilities, beaches, and cemeteries.

FEMA can also provide individual assistance to people affected by a disaster. It administers the Disaster Housing Assistance program, which provides assistance to individuals whose permanent residences are damaged or destroyed. Funds to obtain other housing, to make emergency and essential repairs, and to obtain short-term rental and mortgage assistance may be granted.

FEMA's Individual and Family Grant (IFG) program is designed to provide funds as quickly as possible to meet individual emergency expenses when assistance from other means, either public or private, has not been received. This may include housing repairs, clothing, appliances, transportation repairs, and medical, dental, and funeral expenses.

Center for Mental Health Services

The Robert T. Stafford Disaster Relief and Recovery Act also provides for mental health services. Within the Substance Abuse and Mental Health Services Administration (SAMHSA) is the Center for Mental Health Services (CMHS). CMHS has the federal responsibility to meet the mental health needs of survivors and responders and works closely with FEMA and SAMHSA. The Emergency Services and Disaster Relief Branch (ESDRB) of CMHS collaborates with FEMA to implement the Crisis Counseling Assistance and Training Program (CCP). States can apply for Crisis Counseling Program grants to provide mental health services to disaster victims when a presidentially declared disaster has occurred. Funding to provide mental health grants can be for immediate services and regular services. Immediate services provide funds for 60 days from the declaration date. Grants for regular services are for nine months from the declaration date (CMHS, 2002).

Small Business Administration

The Small Business Administration (SBA) provides a loan program to homeowners, renters, and businesses to restore or replace damaged or destroyed property. Loans may be given to repair or replace buildings, inventory, machinery, or equipment or to alleviate economic injury losses. The loan must be paid back with interest (SBA, 2002).

Disaster Unemployment Assistance

Unemployment insurance is provided to individuals whose employment has been lost or interrupted as a result of a presidentially declared disaster. The program is administered by state government as agents of the federal government. Benefits can be up to 26 weeks after the declaration of a disaster (U.S. Department of Labor, 2002).

Other Agencies

The Internal Revenue Service (IRS) states that some casualty losses can be deducted on federal income tax returns for the year of the loss or through an immediate amendment to a previous year's return (IRS, 2002). The United States Department of Agriculture (USDA) has numerous agricultural programs that assist farmers in disaster recovery (USDA, 2002).

NOT-FOR-PROFIT ORGANIZATIONS

National Voluntary Organizations Active in Disaster

The National Voluntary Organizations Active in Disaster (*NVOAD*) began in 1970 as a partnership of organizations. The initial focus was to reduce duplication of efforts and to be more effective in managing disaster activities. Today its mission is to foster a cooperative planning and preparedness environment for organizations active in disaster relief. It also facilitates the coordination of mitigation, response, and recovery services of its member organizations (NVOAD, 2002).

In 1997, a memorandum of understanding between NVOAD and FEMA was signed. The memorandum states that FEMA agrees to contribute to NVOAD by increasing public awareness of the organization, training of organizational leaders, assisting in helping its members contribute to disaster mitigation by identifying available resources, facilitating appropriate use of FEMA equipment and supplies, assisting in the development of a partnership between NVOAD and the business community, and engaging in joint efforts. In return, NVOAD keeps FEMA informed about the activities of its members; shares FEMA information within the organization; encourages collaboration between governments, businesses, and local voluntary organizations; supports an effective national donations management plan; participates in joint efforts with FEMA; reduces natural hazard risks; assists FEMA when a disaster occurs; and encourages members to share information about disaster activities (NVOAD, 1997).

American Red Cross

The American Red Cross (ARC) is an independent, not-for-profit volunteer organization that provides disaster relief and education about preventing, preparing, and responding to disasters. Although the Red Cross is an independent organization, in 1905 it was granted a charter by the U.S. Congress to provide disaster services around the world. As stated in 1918 by then-solicitor general John W. Davis:

> When any question arises as to the scope and activities of the
> American Red Cross, it must always be remembered that its
> Charter is not only a grant of power but an imposition of duties.
> The American Red Cross is a quasi-governmental organization,
> operating under Congressional charter, officered in part, at least,
> by governmental appointment, disbursing its funds under the

security of a governmental audit, and designated by Presidential order for the fulfillment of certain treaty obligations into which the government has entered. It owes, therefore, to the government which it serves the distinct duty of discharging all those functions for which it was created. (ARC, 1982, p. 1)

These responsibilities have been reaffirmed by Congress in the Disaster Relief Acts of 1970 and 1974. The Red Cross has four primary disaster functions:

- Mass Care (MC)—provides congregate shelter and fixed and mobile food service to victims and emergency workers in the disaster area.

- Disaster Welfare Inquiry (DWI)—responds to inquiries about the welfare of individuals and families within the disaster area, collects locator information about those persons, and prepares and distributes information to other Red Cross chapters about the disaster operation.

- Family Service (FS)—provides emergency assistance to individuals and appropriate referrals to government and other agencies.

- Disaster Health Services (DHS)—oversees delivery of physical and mental health care.

DHS also manages two subsidiary functions: Disaster Physical Health Services (DPHS) and Disaster Mental Health Services (DMHS). DPHS arranges for assistance in meeting individual physical health needs, ensures availability of blood and blood products, supports community physical health services with information and personnel and provides physical health care for disaster operation staff. DMHS arranges for assistance in meeting individual mental health needs, supports community mental health services by providing material and personnel, and provides mental health care for disaster operation staff. Specific crisis intervention techniques utilized by DMHS staff include defusings, debriefings, crisis reduction strategies, and referrals.

The Red Cross also has a special role in major aviation disasters. The Aviation Disaster Family Assistance Act of 1996 provides specific responsibilities for coordinating the emotional care of the families of passengers involved in airline disasters to the airlines, the National Transportation Safety Board (NTSB), and a "...designated independent nonprofit organization..." The NTSB designated the American Red Cross to be the organization responsible for "Family Care and Mental Health." The Red Cross has established Aviation

Incident Response (AIR) teams composed of specially trained staff members that respond when notified by the NTSB of an airline disaster (ARC, 1998).

National Organization for Victim Assistance

The National Organization for Victim Assistance (NOVA) is an umbrella organization of agencies providing victim services throughout the United States. Generally the services provided by NOVA include the following (2002c):

- Information about disaster response, which may include handouts, training materials, and local resource contacts.

- Telephone consultation to a local disaster site, a 24-hour crisis hotline, telephone debriefing of local staff and volunteers, and follow-up recommendations.

- On-site consultation, leadership, and training to the local Crisis Response Team.

- Crisis Response Team activation within 24 hours of an invitation from local site officials. The National Crisis Response Team usually stays from 48 to 72 hours. Its mission is to serve as a consultant to the community. It helps local leaders identify groups at risk, trains local caregivers, and leads group crisis intervention sessions. CRT members generally are licensed mental health specialists (NOVA, 2002b).

RELIGIOUS ORGANIZATIONS

Dozens of denominational organizations and other faith-based organizations provide disaster assistance. Clean-up, home repair and rebuilding, distribution of supplies and food, child care, job training and placement, and advocacy are examples of the many kinds of assistance provided. In addition to the concrete services, some denominations provide pastoral care or chaplaincy, while others, such as the Mennonite Disaster Service, prefer to have their work be their witness (MDS, 2002).

One of the largest faith-based organizations is the Salvation Army. Since 1900, the Salvation Army has provided assistance to people dealing with disasters. Providing meals has been its main service. Other services include financial aid and mental health counseling.

PROFESSIONAL ORGANIZATIONS

Many professional associations have become involved in disaster assistance. Health and mental health professional associations may post information about coping on their web sites. Some, such as the American Psychological Association and the National Association of Social Workers, have developed formal collaborative agreements with the American Red Cross. Individual professional members can become involved in other organizations such as NOVA or their specific religious organizational efforts.

TRAINING OPPORTUNITIES

Opportunities to obtain training in disaster and trauma work have significantly increased in recent years. The challenge is to determine which organization providing training best meets the hospice needs and budget. The following is a summary of some of the options:

American Red Cross

Licensed or certified mental health professionals can take the Disaster Mental Health Services I class, which is a two-day course designed to adapt existing skills to working with disaster workers and victims. Local American Red Cross chapters can be contacted for specific course information (Morgan, 1994).

National Organization for Victim Assistance

The National Organization for Victim Assistance (*NOVA*) requires a 40-hour Basic Crisis Response Team Training Institute before a person is eligible to become a member of a Crisis Response Team. Training focuses on the practical aspects of mobilizing a team, determining team responsibilities, and learning specific skills such as group crisis intervention. Training can be arranged for local communities (NOVA, 2002a).

American Academy of Experts in Traumatic Stress

This organization offers several certification programs for different aspects of traumatic stress. Board certification can be obtained in areas such as emergency crisis response, motor vehicle trauma, disability trauma, bereavement trauma, and stress management.

Association of Traumatic Stress Specialists

Three certifications in trauma can be obtained through the *Association of Traumatic Stress Specialists* (ATSS). A Certified Trauma Specialist (CTS) is the highest level, requiring a four-year college degree related to counseling, 2000 hours of trauma counseling and intervention, and a minimum of 240 hours of education and training in trauma intervention. Documentation of 50 hours of personal counseling is also part of the application process. CTS certification is designed for clinicians who provide individual, group, and family counseling.

Other certifications provided by ATSS are the Certified Trauma Responder (CTR) and Certified Trauma Services Specialist (CTSS). CTR is for those who provide immediate trauma interventions, including critical incident stress debriefing. CTSS is for individuals who provide crisis support, advocacy, and assistance to victims (ATSS, 2002).

International Critical Incident Stress Foundation, Inc.

The International Critical Incident Stress Foundation (ICISF) provides training in Critical Incident Stress Management. Individuals can obtain specialized certifications in mass disasters and terrorism, emergency services, workplace and industrial applications, schools, children, and others (ICISF, 2002).

The International Traumatology Institute

The University of South Florida (USF) through The International Traumatology Institute offers certifications in trauma work. The traumatology certifications include field traumatologist and certified traumatologist. A master traumatologist designation is being developed. Minimum requirements include education provided by the Traumatology Institute, 100 documented hours of direct work with traumatized individuals, 20 hours of supervision, and membership in the Institute (USF, 2001).

Training opportunities also exist in professional associations as well as individual religious organizations. The Salvation Army received a grant from Lilly Endowment Inc. to develop and implement a disaster training program for volunteers from faith-based organizations. The program will include basic, intermediate, and advanced courses focusing on spiritual needs and the role of congregations (Salvation Army, 2002).

GUIDELINES FOR COLLABORATION

When a disaster occurs, the primary role of a hospice program is to attend to its patients, families, and staff. Beyond that, a hospice may choose to become involved in the broader community response. Collaboration with other agencies involved in disaster response will be essential. For hospice organizations to be effective collaborators, they need to take the following steps:

- *Become informed.* Many organizations have been involved in providing disaster relief for years. Protocols for working together have been established. Relationships have been formed. Know the history of the disaster efforts in your community and what is currently being done.

- *Examine motivation.* Before committing to disaster work, the hospice must decide that disaster work will be a vital part of its mission. The decision should not be based on a particular individual's desire, but on the full commitment of the management, staff, and board. Other community agencies need to know that the hospice's commitment is serious.

- *Support needed training.* Recognize that additional training in disaster and trauma work will be needed, and be willing to provide resources for staff to obtain it. Disaster mental health is an evolving field. Debate exists about the appropriateness of utilizing debriefing as a trauma intervention (Kenardy, 2000; Raphael, Meldrum, & McFarlane, 1995). Hospice staff will need ongoing education on the latest developments in the field.

- *Address internal disaster issues first.* The hospice's primary responsibility should be to provide for its patients, families, and staff. Have a disaster plan in place and practice it. Understand that when a disaster occurs in your community, it affects hospice staff even if they are not directly threatened. Be prepared to provide appropriate support to staff.

- *Decide who will be the liaison with community agencies.* Turf issues may exist, and some community agencies may not welcome hospice involvement. Individuals must have the ability and desire to cooperate with other agencies. They must be able to promote hospice services but at the same time recognize when the needs of the larger community take precedence.

- *Understand that offered services may not be used.* Hospices will have to consider how to reach out to people affected by public tragedies. Waiting for other organizations to refer or for victims to appear will result in services not being used. Acceptance occurs more readily when disaster-related services offered by hospices are coordinated with trusted organizations that represent diverse religious, ethnic, and cultural groups in the community.

- *Get involved in voluntary organizations active in disaster.* Hospice staff can learn who the key players are in local disaster relief, what collaborative efforts have been undertaken in the past, and how they have fared.

- *Learn to work with the news media.* Hospices may fear that intrusive reporters will oversimplify complex issues, pressure distraught victims for interviews, or get in the way when there is important work to be done. Hospices need to understand the legitimate news-gathering role of a free press in a democratic society. At the very least, hospices should be able to cooperate with the news media to disseminate information about common emotional reactions, preventive recommendations, and help-line telephone numbers.

- *Offer services over time.* Consider providing services over a longer period than the usual hospice bereavement follow-up of 12 or 13 months. Individuals who have been directly affected by a public tragedy need to know that help will be available for some time. Some may not even begin to seek help until long after the tragic event has occurred.

- *Avoid "competitive guilt."* Hospices should not feel that they can be of service only if they work at the disaster site, or provide round-the-clock assistance, or assist others even though their own building was destroyed. Crises should bring about collaboration, not competition to determine who worked the hardest to meet the needs.

Disaster relief and trauma work are appropriate extensions of hospice bereavement services. Collaboration with other community organizations is the key to helping to meet the challenge of providing effective services in response to public tragedies. ■

Nadine Reimer Penner, ACSW, LSCSW, is a licensed clinical social worker and Director of Bereavement Services for Harry Hynes Memorial Hospice in Wichita, Kansas. She is a disaster mental health instructor for the American Red Cross and has served as Bereavement Section Chair for the National Council of Hospice and Palliative Care Professionals. She is a nationally recognized speaker and author on hospice bereavement issues.

REFERENCES

American Red Cross (1998). *Disaster Mental Health Services.* ARC 3043.

American Red Cross (1982). Authority and legal status of Red Cross Disaster Services. *American Red Cross Disaster Services Regulations and Procedures.* ARC 3001.

Association of Traumatic Stress Specialists. (2002). *Certifications recognitions.* [Online]. Available: http://www.atss-hq.com/certifications/index.cfm

Center for Mental Health Services. (2002). *Emergency services and disaster relief branch.* [Online]. Available: http://www.mentalhealth.org/publications/allpubs/KEN95-0011/default.asp

Dunant, H. (1986). *A memory of Solferino.* Geneva: ICRC.

Federal Emergency Management Agency (2002). *FEMA history.* [Online]. Available: http://www.fema.gov/about/hisotry.shtm

Internal Revenue Service. (2002). *Disaster area losses.* [Online]. Available: http://www.irs.gov/formspubs/display/0,,i1=50&genericId=11295,00html

International Critical Incident Stress Foundation, Inc. (2002). *ICISF Certificate of Specialized Training Program.* [Online]. Available: http://www.icisf.org/COSTProgramhtm

Kenardy, J. (2000). The current status of psychological debriefing. *BMJ,* 321. 1032-1033.

Mennonite Disaster Service. (2002). *Mennonite disaster service history.* [Online]. Available: http://www.mds.mennonite.net/history.html

Morgan, J. (1994). Providing disaster mental health services through the American Red Cross. *NCP Clinical Quarterly,* 4. 13-14.

National Organization for Victim Assistance. (2002a). *Basic crisis response team training.* [Online]. Available: http://www.try-nova.org/AB/basic_crt.html

National Organization for Victim Assistance. (2002b). *National crisis response team.* [Online]. Available: http://www.try-nova.org/N/national_crisis_responseteam.html

National Organization for Victim Assistance. (2002c). *NOVA's mission, purposes, accomplishments, and organizational structure.* [Online]. Available: http://www.try-nova.org/Victims/mission.html

National Voluntary Organizations Active in Disaster. (2002). *About NVOAD.* [Online]. Available: http://www.novoad.org/

National Voluntary Organizations Active in Disaster. (1997). *Memorandum of understanding between national voluntary organizations active in disaster and the federal emergency management agency.* [Online]. Available: http://www.nvoad.org/mou.htm

Raphael, B., Meldrum, L., & McFarlane, A. (1995). Does debriefing after psychological trauma work? *BMJ*, 310. 1479-1480.

Salvation Army. (2002). *Training program enabled by $4.66 million grant from Lilly Endowment.* [Online]. Available: http://www/salvationarmyusa.org/www_usn.nsf.vw_news/

Slavin, P. (1998). Accountable to the community. *Hospice*, 9. 15-18.

Small Business Administration. (2002). *SBA disaster assistance loan information.* [Online]. Available: m http://www.sba.gov/disaster/loans.html

University of South Florida Educational Outreach. (2001). Criteria for Traumatology Certification. [Online] Available: http://www.outreach.usf.edu/trauma/criteria.htm

U.S. Department of Agriculture. (2002) *Farm service agency disaster assistance.* [Online]. Available: http://www.fsa.usda.gov/pas/disaster/assistance1.htm

ADDITIONAL READING

Center for Mental Health Services. (1994). *Disaster response and recovery: a handbook for mental health professionals.* Washington, DC: U.S. Department of Health and Human Services; Publication No. (SMA) 94-31010.

Hodgkinson, P.E., & Stewart, M. (1998). *Coping with catastrophe: a handbook of post-disaster psychosocial aftercare.* London: Routledge.

Lattanzi-Licht, M. (2002). Hospice's evolving role in community-based bereavement services. *Hospice and Palliative Care Insights*, 1. 8-11.

Zinner, E.S., & Williams, M.B., (Eds.), (1999). *When a community weeps: Case studies in group survivorship.* Philadelphia: Brunner/Mazel.

CHAPTER 23

Hospice:
A Resource in
Community Tragedies

Marcia Lattanzi-Licht

Hospice programs across the United States have been a source of support for millions of families facing personal tragedies. Hospice professionals and volunteers witness daily lessons about the fragility and impermanence of life. "We remember countless names, and faces, families and homes that remind us how life can be forever changed in an instant" (Scuillo, 2002).

Tragedies affect us on several levels: personal, family, community, and public. There can be overlap, depending upon our relationship to the people who die in tragedies. Offering ongoing support to survivors of public tragedy is a natural extension of hospice's mission and community focus. Most hospices have made a strong commitment to the end-of-life and grief-related concerns of the larger communities they serve. As providers of continuing support for bereaved persons, hospices are well positioned to be an important part of the spectrum of services offered in the aftermath of public tragedy.

Hospice standards, bereavement care guidelines, and the reported practice patterns of hospices reflect their commitment to providing community-based bereavement services (NHO, 1995; 1996; NHPCO, 2001a).

Many hospice programs in the United States have offered community support in time of a public tragedy. For example, Lower Cape Fear Hospice in Wilmington, North Carolina, was part of a community collaboration that involved educational efforts at the outset of the 1997 hurricane season following the previous year's devastating hurricanes (Cameron & Lattanzi-Licht, 1998). Programs in Missouri and Kansas worked together following major flooding of the Missouri River to ensure care of patients and families on either side of the river. Hospices in Florida (Slavin, 1998), Colorado and other states supported families evacuated by wildfires and also transported hospice patients and families to safe locations. When a 1983 Boulder Fire Department training accident left two young firefighters dead, hospice was called in to help. Hospice of Boulder County professionals provided psychoeducational sessions on grief and trauma to all members of the fire department along with short-term individual counseling and referrals.

Hospice programs in Kansas, Kentucky, Colorado, Oklahoma City, New York, New Jersey, Virginia, the District of Columbia, Pennsylvania, Massachusetts, Hawaii, and Missouri have worked in their communities in various ways to be part of the response to public tragedies. In rural communities such as Springfield, Colorado, where a series of sudden deaths deeply affected the small population, hospice played a central role in the ongoing support offered in the community.

HOSPICE INVOLVEMENT IN COMMUNITY TRAGEDY

Most hospices and palliative care services are, like the rest of our country, unprepared for the impact and aftermath of a large-scale disaster or tragedy. The question of hospice's role in disaster and trauma reaches into some key areas. These concerns, which can represent real obstacles to hospice's involvement in community tragedy, are outlined below.

Resources: Capacity and Funding

The cost and feasibility of offering trauma- and disaster-related services is a major consideration for hospices. The primary concern of a hospice must be the patients and families it serves. Hospice and palliative care programs also are concerned with the well- being of their staff and volunteers. Recent staffing recommendations are for one full-time hospice bereavement professional for every 200 to 300 deaths per year (NHPCO, 2001). Many hospice staff members serve dual roles, working with families facing the death of a loved one and also with bereaved families (Lattanzi-Licht, 1989).

Providing bereavement services in the context of a public tragedy is an important hospice role, but it can also place significant strain on staff. Limited funding of bereavement services is an added challenge. Funding and staffing of community bereavement services should be addressed in the hospice's overall plan and budget.

Clinical Staff Expertise

While it is true that hospice and palliative care staff are ideally suited to offer support in times of public tragedy, they can benefit from education about the experience and impact of trauma. Sudden deaths routinely touch hospices— the unexpected heart attack of the caregiving wife, the traumatic circumstances under which a patient's death occurs, or the sudden death of a hospice staff member. Nevertheless, key bereavement professionals should have specific training and certification in trauma/disaster services. At the local level, this training benefits not only the community, but also hospice and palliative care patients, families, and staff.

In November 2001, when flight 586 crashed in Belle Harbor, New York, Hospice Care Network's CEO, Maureen Hinkelman, went to the airport and organized staff participation in support of families. Nurses, social workers, and pastoral care and bereavement staff members made themselves available as needs arose in the emergency room. By setting priorities, the work of caring for the hospice's families continued. Nonurgent visits were rescheduled, allowing the hospice's patients and families to feel that they were contributing to the support those affected by the disaster (Vogt, 2002).

Hospice staff members often are willing to become involved in community disaster and trauma, and many hospice programs support these involvements. For example, when a trauma-trained staff member from a Pennsylvania hospice was called to the September 11 crash site in that state, the agency allowed time off, in addition to a week's leave after her return. She then offered an in-service for staff about her experiences with families at the site (Homan, 2001).

Community Awareness of Hospice Resources

Coping with public tragedy requires the effective identification and utilization of community resources. Hospice's role in public tragedy relates to a number of variables: the nature of the community, its needs related to disaster/ trauma across time, and the hospice's position and relationships within the community. In particular, the relationships are the vehicle for involvement in community tragedy.

When terrorists struck on September 11, 2001, the Hospices of the National Capital Region were creating their annual strategic media plan. Almost immediately they decided to provide free counseling to their entire community. After logistical arrangements were complete (staffing by professionals experienced in dealing with sudden loss, adequate coverage for hospice's patients, and a toll-free telephone number), the challenge was to deliver the message that hospice's services were available and free. The hospices' media outreach strategy included e-mailing the press, making clinical staff available for interviews, keeping the website updated, and creating a 30-second public service announcement (PSA). The PSA was produced within a month, thanks to the generosity of local donors and businesses. Custom versions were made available at no cost to state hospice associations in New York and California, and a generic version to Massachusetts (Levine, 2002). Collaboration and community involvement were keys to these successful efforts.

Timing and Hospice's Support

There is an instinctive desire to go to the scene of the tragedy and to offer support during the crisis response, but we cannot all be at the scene of the tragedy. Many community members speak to the excess of help early on and the scarcity of follow-up services. There is a critical need to plan for a coordinated continuum of services for those affected by the tragedy. The American Red Cross identifies four phases of a disaster (1995) and describes them in relation to clients and activities of disaster recovery:

- Heroic phase (prior to and immediately after)

- Honeymoon phase (one week to 3 to 6 months after)

- Disillusionment phase (two months to 1 to 2 years after)

- Reconstruction phase (may last for several years after).

In the heroic phase, hospice's chief role is to support other responders and educate and work with representatives of the news media. In the honeymoon phase, hospices should help to inform others about their available services. Hospice's main activities fall during the disillusionment phase, when the reality of the impact and grieving are paramount. During the reconstruction phase there is typically a return to predisaster activities. Posttraumatic stress disorder will be apparent in some survivors at this point.

Hospices can make an important contribution during the reconstruction phase through referrals to competent private therapists in the community. The needs of people affected by tragedy in the heroic and reconstruction phases are typically met. Less effective support is available during the honeymoon and disillusionment phases. Hospice services have the greatest impact during these times.

Finally, hospices typically offer bereavement services to families for 13 months following the death of their loved one. Some hospice programs make their group or educational offerings available to families for a longer period of time, typically two to three years. Because of the complicated mourning involved in public tragedy, hospices offering bereavement services to surviving loved ones must consider extending the time frame for involvement with those services to two to three years following the tragedy.

Public Tragedy and Hospice Families

For regular hospice clients—the families preparing for or grieving the death of a loved one—public tragedies can have an unanticipated impact. There can be a magnification of grief and an intensified vulnerability for people facing the end of life and during bereavement. One woman whose husband died during the afternoon of September 11 described her response, "I felt like it didn't matter that Joe had died. His life seemed less important than the people who died in the terrorist attacks." Others can minimize their sorrow. A daughter who had cared for her mother with Alzheimer's for seven years said, "Compared to what other people have gone through with the tragedy, my grief seems small." It is important for hospice bereavement care providers to acknowledge the deep grief of surviving family members and help them cope with deficits in their support.

INDIVIDUAL HOSPICES AND TRAGEDY INVOLVEMENT

Hospice values of support during painful life experiences and community-based care form the foundation for involvement in community tragedy. The family-centered focus of hospice services, and the provision of bereavement care for at least 13 months following the death of a loved one, are unique dimensions that create both understanding and experience relevant to involvement in a community tragedy.

It is wise for hospices to focus on activities and services that are realistic in terms of staff time and resources and to prioritize those activities based on community needs. Hospices seek to offer victims of tragedy services similar to those they provide in their ongoing programs (NHPCO, 2001b):

- Delivering grief and loss presentations to responders, community groups

- Informing survivors of hospice's group offerings

- Offering or collaborating in community memorial services

- Extending individual counseling services to victims

- Consulting and delivering presentations to schools

- Making written materials, brochures available.

There is a growing number of comprehensive hospice centers (Ryndes & Jennings, 2002) in the United States. These centers offer traditional hospice care, palliative care, palliative care consultation services, life transition services, and education, research, and policy programs. For example, the Compassionate Care Counseling Center in Las Vegas, Nevada, offers counselor intervention after the suicide or traumatic death of a coworker, the diagnosis or death of a coworker from a serious illness, downsizing or layoffs, intervention for business employees following a robbery, and intervention and support following a local or national disaster (Gardia, 2002). Counselors are master's level prepared and licensed, have attended Red Cross training programs, and have a minimum of two years experience. Local Employee Assistance Programs most frequently request services, but local business often contact the center directly.

Defining the nature, timing, and level of involvement in public tragedy is a crucial task for hospice programs. In a chapter titled "Shattered Dreams: A Community Responds to a Tragic Accident" in *The Hospice Choice* (1998), I describe a community-based collaboration and plan for responding to tragedy. Hospices not only serve the long-term needs of families through their bereavement programs, they are also resources for professionals and providers. In considering the services they can provide related to public tragedy, hospice programs should address these questions:

1. How can hospice define collaborative roles in a tragedy response plan?

2. What kind of services will be offered at the time of the tragedy/disaster and in the aftermath?

3. Who will deliver tragedy/disaster services, both initially and across time?

4. How will the services be evaluated?

Hospices also need to examine the services they provide to survivors of public tragedy. Hospice's approach to bereavement, like hospice care, involves a wellness and prevention approach. Except for hospices with a full range of mental health services, grief therapy is appropriately referred to professional providers in the community. Key staff should keep current on new theoretical and research findings in traumatology. Hospices should also gather outcome information on services they provide to survivors of trauma.

While support groups may have a beneficial effect for some people, they are not for everyone. In fact, work by Herman (1992) suggests the limitations of the efficacy of group treatment. Her follow-up study showed that combat veterans who attended support groups generally felt better about themselves and more connected to others, but they also reported little change in intrusive symptoms.

Hospices should carefully consider the type of psychoeducational or support groups they offer and the populations included in those groups. A number of hospices across the country offer groups for family members whose loved one was murdered. In communities affected by public tragedy with large numbers of surviving family members, hospices should offer or cosponsor groups specifically for that population. Many community self-help groups for bereaved parents, like Compassionate Friends, successfully support parents who experience the death of a child in a wide variety of circumstances, including violent, traumatic deaths, suicides, and murders.

As recognized community experts in grief, hospice and palliative care providers have much to offer to those responding to traumatic deaths. An important area of trauma involvement for hospice and palliative care programs is educating crisis responders and other affected members of the community about the grief process. A number of hospice and palliative care programs have formal training relationships with law enforcement and victim assistance agencies, schools, local media, and others involved in community crisis responses. By the same token, hospice staff benefits greatly from knowledge and training related to trauma (Lattanzi-Licht, 1999, 2002).

HOSPICE ACTIVITIES RELATED TO 9/11

In the aftermath of 9/11, individual hospices and state hospice organizations participated in a wide range of activities (NJHPCO, 2001; HPCANYS, 2001). Services focused on all hospice stakeholders, including patients with life-limiting illnesses and their families, bereaved persons, hospice staff and volunteers, and, finally, members of the larger community. Outreach efforts extended to schools, workplaces, law enforcement, clergy, the news media, and government agencies.

Some activities focused on the immediate event. Hospice nurses and physicians treated the injured, and staff volunteered at disaster relief sites, counseling families and registering the names of missing family members. Hospice inpatient units admitted acutely ill patients to free up other acute care beds for disaster victims. Professional staff members attended statewide crisis intervention training, and training sessions on posttraumatic stress and psychiatric symptoms of postdisaster. The Hospice and Palliative Care Association of New York State (HPCANYS) set up a toll-free number so help could be accessed by those in need. Hospice contact information was listed on the state's hotline and with crisis intervention programs (2001).

Hospices also paid special attention to the needs of their families. They reinforced outreach efforts, especially to families with children. Several hospices moved up their scheduled children's bereavement group offerings or created additional groups. Most importantly, staff reassured current hospice families that they have a right to grieve, even though their own tragedy might seem less significant than the tragedies of 9/11.

It was important for hospices to pay attention to the needs of their staff and volunteers in the aftermath of 9/11. Hospices offered counseling to employees and organized prayer services. For staff who had lost a family member, money was collected to help support the families. Hospice staff also tried to support to each other; many had friends who were killed or were injured at Ground Zero.

In communities deeply affected by the tragedy, hospice programs participated in a broad range of supportive activities, rituals, and educational events. Hospices coordinated local and countywide memorial services. Staff delivered educational presentations and provided consultations to schools. They also presented several public forums titled, *Coping with Disaster: What to Tell Your Children*. Hospice professionals facilitated support groups for those coping with the tragedy, and they set up sessions at faith communities about dealing with loss during the holidays. Hospices prepared and distributed information packets about grief. They sent letters to churches, businesses, schools, police departments, fire departments, and funeral homes, offering bereavement programs for families. Several hospice programs established and publicized a special hotline for grief counseling. Others offered walk-in counseling and psychiatric referrals.

Hospice's support extended to other caregivers in the affected communities. Staff and volunteers at a New Jersey hospice wrote to 100 long-term care providers and offered the services of their bereavement staff. Several long-term care facilities asked for on-site memorial services, and two facilities asked for counselors to be available to their staff and patients on a drop-in basis. Hospice chaplains supported and counseled ministers who had to deal with multiple funerals, serving as their on-call chaplains.

Hospices also offered information and resources to workplaces. They helped educate employers about the grief process and how it affects workflow and productivity. Hospices also sent flyers about bereavement counseling to employers, asking them to urge workers to contact hospice as needed. In addition, hospices sent literature about grief and bereavement in the workplace to state crisis centers.

In New York, New Jersey, Virginia, Maryland, Massachusetts, and the District of Columbia, state and national hospice organizations worked with the news media. They helped reporters develop stories about grief and bereavement. They created television spots on helping traumatized children and on hospice's role in community trauma. One hospice was featured on the cover of the local daily's television section in connection with a program to answer common questions about grief.

NATIONAL EFFORTS AND COORDINATION

National efforts require focus, creativity, and planning. In the aftermath of 9/11, the National Hospice and Palliative Care Organization (NHPCO) compiled for its member hospices a comprehensive list of materials related to disaster and trauma. In addition, NHPCO sought advice from national experts on future activities. After the Columbine shootings, Hospice Foundation of America (HFA) donated 100 copies of Living with Grief after Sudden Loss (Doka, 1996) to the Colorado Hospice Organization, which then distributed the books to local clergy.

Both NHPCO and HFA made resources available on their web sites and in their publications. In addition, both are planning follow-up activities to address bereavement needs in communities coping with public tragedy. Organizations such as HFA and NHPCO should demonstrate continued leadership in defining standards related to hospice's role in public tragedy. Specifically, there are several suggested areas of focus:

- Establishing formal collaborative relationships with national organizations and groups who provide disaster services

- Creating educational opportunities on trauma and disaster for hospice staff and opportunities for certified trauma training programs for key hospice bereavement care providers

- Developing models and standards for comprehensive hospice disaster plans, with an emphasis on community collaborations

- Advancing the discussion of hospice and palliative care programs' role in public tragedy, together with ethical discussion of a broad range of possible scenarios, including bio-terrorism

- Encouraging U.S. hospice involvement in global tragedies like the AIDS pandemic in Sub-Saharan Africa, where more than 6,000 people die each day. Numerous hospice programs in the United States have sponsoring and supportive relationships with partner hospices in Sub-Saharan Africa.

CONCLUSION

Supporting people is a counterbalance at a time of tragedy. Effective support reminds us that "we are all on the same bus" as citizens of our communities. It also reflects the reality that there is goodness and caring in the world, as well as violence and grief. Supporting people in the aftermath of tragedies helps restore a measure of faith in each other. Support prompts us all to remember that we may not have control over violence in the world, but we can respond with integrity and compassion to heartbreaking situations.

It is time for hospice and palliative care programs to extend themselves in their communities and form strong relationships with other service providers and media representatives. The role for hospice programs in community tragedy needs to be defined, formalized, and integrated into the framework of community responses across time. We can learn together better ways to offer education and support. There is a seat for us at the table as creative partners surrounding the human responses to public tragedy. ■

Marcia Lattanzi-Licht, MA, RN, LPC, is an educator, psychotherapist, and author. An early voice for hospice care, Mrs. Lattanzi-Licht was cofounder of Hospice of Boulder County, Colorado, where her work in education and bereavement is widely recognized. She is the principal author of The Hospice Choice *(Simon & Schuster, 1998). For her work with crime victims, Mrs. Lattanzi-Licht was awarded the Boulder County District Attorney's Office Distinguished Service Award (1988). She is a winner of the NHPCO's Heart of Hospice (1995) and the Association for Death Education and Counseling's 2002 Educator Award. Mrs. Lattanzi-Licht is a consultant to several corporations and nonprofit organizations, including the NHPCO.*

REFERENCES

American National Red Cross. (1995). *Disaster Mental Health Services I,* Instructor Manual, Publication 3077-1.

Cameron, E., & Lattanzi Licht, M. (1998, November). "Hospice and community collaboration in the aftermath of disaster." Presentation at the National Hospice Organization Annual Meeting, Dallas, TX.

Doka, K.J., Ed. (1996). *Living with grief after sudden loss.* Washington, DC: Hospice Foundation of America.

Gardia, G. (September, 2002). Personal communication with the author.

Herman, J.L. (1992). *Trauma and recovery.* New York: Basic Books.

Homan, P. (October, 2001). Personal communication with the author.

Hospice and Palliative Care Association of New York State. (2001). *Healing communities in times of trauma.* Albany: NY: HPCANYS. (Ed Note: booklet)

Lattanzi-Licht, M., Miller, G.W., & Mahoney, J.J. (1998). *The hospice choice.* New York: Simon & Schuster/Fireside.

Lattanzi-Licht, M. (1999). Responding to a community tragedy. *Forum, 25,* No 5.

Lattanzi-Licht, M. (2002). Hospice's evolving role in community-based bereavement services. *Insights, 1.* 8-11.

Lattanzi-Licht, M.E. (1989). Bereavement services: Practice and problems. In M.E. Lattanzi-Licht, J.M.Kirshling, & S. Fleming (Eds.), *Bereavement care: A new look at hospice and community based services* (pp. 1-28). New York: Haworth.

Levine, S. (2002). Lessons in Media Outreach from September 11th: A Story in Two Parts. NHPCO, *Insights*, *1*, 22-23.

National Hospice and Palliative Care Organization (NHPCO). (2001a, October). Fax-back survey for bereavement professionals: Hospice's role in trauma and disaster. Alexandria, VA: NHPCO.

NHPCO. (2001b). Guidelines for Bereavement Care in Hospice. Alexandria, VA: NHPCO.

National Hospice Organization (1996). Community Bereavement Summary Results, N. Reimer Penner, *NHO Section Notes*, Vol 4, 1.

National Hospice Organization. (1995). Hospice Trauma Response Survey. National Hospice Organization *Newsline*, Arlington, VA.

New Jersey Hospice and Palliative Care Organization (2001, October). *We're there when it matters most.* Scotch Plains, NJ: NJHPCO.

Ryndes, T., & Jennings, B. (2002, April). Increasing access to hospice and palliative care. Presentation at *End of life care: A timeless model* conference, sponsored by Duke Institute on Care at the End of Life and the NHPCO, Washington, DC.

Scuillo, R. (2002). September 11 Memorial Address, NHPCO Management and Leadership Conference, Washington, DC.

Slavin, P. (1998). Accountable to the community. *Hospice, 9.* 15-18.

Vogt, K. (2002). A New York Agency's Experience with Disaster. NHPCO, *Insights, 1*, 21-22.

■ Resources ■

American Academy of Experts in Traumatic Stress
386 Veterans Memorial Highway
Commack, NY 11725
Phone: 631-543-2217
Fax: 631-543-6977
E-mail: aaets@traumatic-stress.org
Web: www.aaets.org

The Academy is a multidisciplinary network of professionals who are committed to the advancement of intervention for trauma survivors. Its goal is to identify experts among professionals and across disciplines and to provide meaningful standards for those who work regularly with survivors. The Academy offers its members Board Certification Programs, Diplomate and Fellow Credentials, and continuing education credits. The Academy publishes *Trauma Response, Academy Updates,* and *Info Sheets.*

American Psychological Association Disaster Response Network
750 First Street, NE
Washington, DC 20002
Phone: 202-336-5898
Toll free: 1-800-374-2721
E-mail: pracpr@apa.org
Web: www.apa.org

The American Psychological Association (APA) developed its Disaster Response Network (DRN) in response to the needs of those who have been traumatized and/or suffer from PTSD. More than 1,500 psychologist volunteers provide free, onsite mental health services to disaster survivors and the relief workers who assist them. APA works collaboratively with the American Red Cross, FEMA, state emergency management teams, and other relief groups to provide free mental health services to disaster victims and relief workers.

American Red Cross
Contact your local Red Cross chapter for more information
Web: www.redcross.org

The American Red Cross responds to more than 67,000 disasters each year, including fires, hurricanes, floods, earthquakes, tornadoes, hazardous materials spills, transportation accidents, explosions, and other natural and man-made disasters. Red Cross disaster relief focuses on meeting people's immediate emergency disaster-caused needs, including providing them with shelter, food, and health and mental health services. The core of Red Cross disaster relief is the assistance given to individuals and families affected by disaster, which enables them to resume their normal daily activities independently. The Red Cross also feeds emergency workers, handles inquiries from concerned family members outside the disaster area, provides blood and blood products to disaster victims, and helps those affected by disaster to access other available resources.

America's Heroes of Freedom
PO Box 18984
Washington, DC 20036
Phone: 301-570-8124
Fax: 301-570-2279
E-mail: info@americasheroes.us
Web: www.americasheroes.us

America's Heroes of Freedom is a nonprofit organization that provides educational, commemorative, and remembrance opportunities in the wake of a national tragedy. It provides recognition and support to military, law enforcement, fire and rescue service, and civil services, which have responded to a public tragedy.

Anxiety Disorders Association of America
8730 Georgia Avenue, Suite 600
Silver Spring, MD 20910
Phone: 240-485-1001
E-mail: anxdis@adaa.org
Web: www.adaa.org

The Anxiety Disorders Association of America (ADAA) is a nonprofit organization whose mission is to promote prevention and cure of anxiety disorders and to improve the lives of all people who suffer from them. ADAA disseminates information that links people who need treatment with those who can provide it. It also advocates for cost-effective treatment. The ADAA is made up of professionals who conduct research and treat anxiety disorders and individuals who have a personal or general interest in learning more about such disorders. ADAA offers a bookstore catalogue, a brochure on PTSD, PTSD Treatment Guidelines for Patients and Families, and a quarterly newsletter.

Association of Death Education and Counseling

342 N. Main Street
West Hartford, CT 06117
Phone: 860-586-7503
Fax: 860-586-7550
E-mail: info@adec.org
Web: www.adec.org

The Association of Death Education and Counseling (ADEC) is a multi-disciplinary professional organization dedicated to promoting excellence in end-of-life education and treatment, and bereavement counseling. ADEC provides its members and the general public with information, support, and resources based on theoretical and quality research.

Association of Traumatic Stress Specialists

PO Box 2747
Georgetown, TX 78627
Phone: 512-868-3677
Fax: 512-868-3678
E-Mail: admin@atss-hq.com
Web: www.atss-hq.com

The ATSS is a nonprofit organization whose mission is to organize, educate, and professionally certify its worldwide membership in order to assist those affected by trauma. ATSS offers three types of certification: Certified Trauma Specialist (CTS) for those providing clinical treatment; Certified Trauma Responder (CTR) for those responding to a traumatic incident; Certified Trauma Service Specialist (CTSS) for those offering services to survivors. Certified individuals have distinguished themselves in complying with a standard of education, training, and experience in providing services to trauma survivors. Certification demonstrates to victims, survivors, other professionals, and the general public that services will be provided in an ethical, skillful manner. It also fosters credibility, which enables organizations to recruit volunteers, gain recognition with other associations, reward employees/volunteers, and obtain supporters. ATSS holds an annual conference and offers a quarterly newsletter, *Trauma Lines,* and other materials on traumatic stress.

(The) Compassionate Friends
PO Box 3696
Oak Brook, IL 60522
Phone: 630-990-0010
Toll free: 800-969-0010
Fax: 630-990-0246
E-mail: Trish@compassionatefriends.org
Web: www.compassionatefriends.org

Compassionate Friends is a self-help organization that was formed to offer friendship and understanding to families mourning the death of a child. There are 580 chapters across the country that provide monthly meetings, phone contacts, lending libraries, and free literature on grief and loss. The national organization provides training and referrals to the local chapters.

Concerns of Police Survivors (COPS)
PO Box 3199
S Highway 5
Camdenton, MO 65020
Phone: 573-346-4911
Fax: 573-346-1414
E-mail: cops@nationalcops.org
Web: www.nationalcops.org

COPS is a nonprofit organization that provides resources and assistance to surviving family members and friends of law enforcement officers killed in the line of duty. COPS provides training to law enforcement agencies on survivor victimization issues and raises general public awareness and support for the law enforcement professions. COPS hosts a police survivor seminar and a kids camp each May and different retreats throughout the year at the national, state, and local level.

Crisis Management International
8 Piedmont Center, Suite 420
Atlanta, GA 30305
Phone: 404-841-3400
Crisis line: 1-800-274-7470
Fax: 404-841-3404
E-mail: bblythe@cmiatl.com
Web: www.cmiatl.com

With 1,300 specially trained Mental Health Professionals on standby, Crisis Management International (CMI) helps companies manage the unexpected.

CMI leads the world in helping organizations minimize the human costs of both major and minor crises. They prepare clients for foreseeable crises and volatile situations by defusing threats of violence before they become a tragedies and by helping management and employees return to precrisis levels of productivity with reduced financial impact. Qualified providers can join the CMI network through an application and training process.

Dougy Center
PO Box 86852
Portland, OR 97286
Phone: 503-775-5683
Fax: 503-777-3097
E-mail: help@dougy.org
Web: www.dougy.org

The Dougy Center is a nonprofit organization serving children ages 3 to 19 and their families since 1982. Through its National Center for Grieving Children and Families, they provide training and support locally, nationally and internationally for children who have survived the death of a parent or sibling (for teens, a close friend) through an accident, illness, suicide, or murder. The Center itself offers support groups and counseling for families that come from all over the world. It also provides a variety of information and publications for families, children and other professionals. The Dougy Center publishes the National Directory of Children's Grief Services. The Dougy Center offers professional education in order to help other communities with grieving children.

Federal Emergency Management Agency
500 C Street, SW
Washington, DC 20472
Phone: 202-566-1600
Web: www.fema.gov

The Federal Emergency Management Agency (FEMA) is an independent federal agency reporting to the President and tasked with responding to, planning for, recovering from, and mitigating against disaster. FEMA has regional offices across the country and a cadre of standby disaster assistance employees who can be called upon in the event of an emergency, such as tornadoes, hurricanes, earthquakes, and man-made crises. Often, FEMA works in partnership with other local organizations that are part of the national emergency response system. These partners include local and state emergency management agencies, 27 federal agencies, and the American Red Cross.

FEMA provides states, communities, businesses, and individuals with disaster assistance, offers training to local disaster managers, supports the nation's fire service, and administers the national flood and crime insurance programs.

Gift from Within
16 Cobb Hill Road
Camden, ME 04843
Phone: 207-236-8858
Fax: 207-236-2818
E-mail: JoyceB3955@aol.com
Web: www.giftfromwithin.org

Gift from Within is a private, nonprofit organization dedicated to those who suffer from posttraumatic stress disorder (PTSD), those at risk for PTSD, and those who care for traumatized individuals. It develops and disseminates educational material, including videotapes, articles, books, and a resource catalog and maintains a roster of survivors who are willing to participate in an international network of peer support.

Green Cross Foundation
10064 SW 182 Court
Dunnellon, FL 34432
Web: www.greencross.org

The Foundation supports the field of traumatology in humanitarian efforts, standards of practice in research, consultation, education, and the development of humane policies affecting the traumatized. The Foundation publishes the journal Traumatology and supports the activities of the Academy of Traumatology. In the event of a disaster or other emergency need, the Green Cross Projects can provide trained traumatology specialists from its worldwide membership, who will provide information, education, consultation, and treatment for traumatized individuals or communities that have been affected by natural or human-caused disaster.

Hospice Foundation of America
2001 S Street, NW, Suite 300
Washington, DC 20009
Phone: 202-638-5419
Toll free: 800-854-3402
Fax: 202-638-5312
E-mail: hfa@hospicefoundation.org
Web: www.hospicefoundation.org

The Hospice Foundation of America (HFA) is a nonprofit organization that provides leadership in the development and application of hospice and its philosophy of care. HFA produces an annual award-winning national teleconference on grief and publishes the companion book series, *Living with Grief.* HFA also provides a variety of other resources and titles, some of which are on audiocassettes. HFA offers a monthly newsletter, *Journeys.* There are also many brochures that offer guidance on coping with end of life issues and bereavement.

International Association of Emergency Managers (IAEM)

111 Park Place
Falls Church, VA 22046-4513
Phone: 703-538-1795
Fax: 703- 241-5603
E-mail: info@iaem.com
Web: www.iaem.com

IAEM is a nonprofit educational organization dedicated to promoting the goals of saving lives and protecting property during emergencies and disasters.

International Association of Firefighters (IAFF)

1750 New York Avenue, NW
Washington, DC 20006
Phone: 202-737-8484
Fax: 202-737-8418
Web: www.iaff.org

The IAFF is comprised of 2,700 affiliates in communities across America. The IAFF provides its 250,000 members, who are firefighters and paramedics, with services such as Employee Assistance and trauma counseling in the event of a line of duty death. An auxiliary helps spouses and other family members cope with the demands of fire service, and the IAFF also supports activities that aid burn victims.

International Critical Incident Stress Foundation

10176 Baltimore National Pike, Unit 201
Ellicott City, MD 21042
Phone: 410-750-9600
Hotline: 410-313-2473
Fax: 410-750-9601
Web: www.icisf.org

The International Critical Incident Stress Foundation (ICISF) is a nonprofit, nongovernment, membership organization in special consultative status with the Economic and Social Council of the United Nations. Its mission is the prevention and mitigation of disabling stress through education, training, and support services for all emergency services professions; continuing education and training in emergency mental health services for psychologists, psychiatrists, social workers, and licensed professional counselors; and consultation in the establishment of crisis and disaster response programs for varied organizations and communities worldwide. ICISF members are placed in a network of Critical Incident Stress Management teams, service providers, administrators, commercial and industrial services, researchers, and educators. ICISF publishes a quarterly newsletter, *LIFENET*.

International Society for Traumatic Stress Studies

60 Revere Drive, Suite 500
Northbrook, IL 60062
Phone: 847-480-9028
Fax: 847-480-9282
E-mail: istss@istss.org
Web: www.istss.org

The International Society for Traumatic Stress Studies (ISTSS) is an international multidisciplinary membership organization that promotes advancement and exchange of knowledge about severe stress and trauma. This knowledge includes understanding the scope and consequences of traumatic exposure, preventing traumatic events and ameliorating their consequences, and advocating for the field of traumatic stress. ISTSS members are social, behavioral, and biological scientists, professionals from mental health and social services disciplines, and individuals representing religious, legal, and other professions. ISTSS offers education, training, and information resources. It publishes the *Journal of Traumatic Stress* and a quarterly newsletter, *Stress Points.*

Last Acts

c/o Partnership for Caring, Inc.
1620 Eye Street NW, Suite 202
Washington, DC 20006
Phone: 202-296-8071
Fax: 202-296-8352
E-mail: kaplanko@partnershipforcaring.org
Web: www.lastacts.org

Last Acts is a national coalition of more than 1,000 organizations engaged in an education campaign to improve care and support for terminally ill people and their families. Last Acts serves as a national clearinghouse for sharing information and ideas at the national, state, and local levels. Last Acts also provides a forum for discussion, collaboration, and broad dissemination of new information. Last Acts sponsors national and regional conferences, publishes a quarterly print newsletter, and offers a number of e-mail discussion groups and newsletters.

National Air Disaster Alliance and Foundation

2020 Pennsylvania Avenue, NW, Suite 315
Washington, DC 20006
Phone: 1-888-444-6232
E-mail: GADunham@aol.com
Web: www.planesafe.org

In 1995, family members from 10 different air crashes who wanted to have their grievances addressed and to provide support to each other formed the National Air Disaster Alliance and Foundation (NADA). The NADA mission has been to raise the standard of safety, security and survivability for commercial aviation passengers and to support victims' families. They have advocated for federal legislation and policies that govern the National Transportation Safety Board.

National Center for Missing and Exploited Children

Charles B. Wang International Children's Building
699 Prince Street
Alexandria, VA 22314
Phone: 1-800-THE-LOST
Fax: 703-274-2222
Web: www.missingkids.com

The mission of the National Center for Missing and Exploited Children is to provide a coordinated, international response to the problem of missing and exploited children. It provide instantaneous dissemination of pictures and information on missing children through the Internet, advocates stronger laws to protect children, assists nongovernmental organizations, offers training to professionals and law enforcement agencies around the world, and works to increase public awareness. Through the International Center for Missing & Exploited Children (ICMEC), a valuable, technological resource for law enforcement is being expanded on a worldwide basis. Participation in the global missing children's website network, a key ICMEC initiative, will be offered to agencies that share the mission of finding and protecting children.

National Center for PTSD

VA Medical Center (116D)
215 North Main Street
White River Junction, VT 05009
Phone: 802-296-5132
Fax: 802-296-5135
E-mail: ncptsd@ncptsd.org
Web: www.ncptsd.org

The National Center for PTSD was created in 1989 within the Veteran's Administration (which has since become the Department of Veterans Affairs) in response to a Congressional mandate to address the needs of veterans with military-related posttraumatic stress disorder. The mission of the National Center for PTSD is to advance the clinical care and social welfare of America's veterans through research, education, and training in the science, diagnosis, and treatment of PTSD and stress-related disorders. As a leading authority on PTSD, the Center serves and collaborates with many different agencies and constituencies, including veterans and their families, government policy-makers, scientists and researchers, doctors and psychiatrists, journalists, and the lay public. The Center produces a clinical and a research quarterly and maintains the PILOTS database, which is an electronic index to the worldwide literature on PTSD and other mental health consequences of exposure to traumatic events.

National Emergency Management Association

c/o Council of State Governments
PO Box 11910
Lexington, KY 40578
Phone: 859-244-8000
Fax: 859-244-8239
Web: www.nemaweb.org

The National Emergency Management Association (NEMA) is the professional association of state, Pacific, and Caribbean insular state emergency management directors committed to providing national leadership and expertise in comprehensive emergency management; serving as a vital information and assistance resource for state and territorial directors and their governors; and forging strategic partnerships to advance continuous improvements in emergency management.

National Fallen Firefighters Foundation
PO Drawer 498
Emmitsburg, MD 21727
Phone: 301-447-1365
Fax: 301-447-1645
E-mail: firehero@erols.com
Web: www.firehero.org

Congress created the National Fallen Firefighters Foundation to honor firefighters who die on the line of duty and to offer both immediate and continuing assistance to their survivors. The Foundation has a peer support network, a lending library, and produces a quarterly newsletter and other materials on grief.

National Organization for Victim Assistance
1730 Park Road, NW
Washington, DC 20010
Phone: 202-232-6682 x 105
Fax: 202-462-2255
Web: www.try-nova.org

The National Organization for Victim Assistance (NOVA) is a private, nonprofit organization of victim and witness assistance programs and practitioners, criminal justice agencies, mental health professionals, researchers, former victims and survivors, and others committed to the recognition and implementation of victim rights and services. The four main purposes of NOVA are national advocacy, direct services to victims, assistance to professional colleagues, and membership activities and services. NOVA publishes a monthly newsletter and period information bulletins.

National Voluntary Organizations Active in Disaster
14253 Ballinger Terrace
Burtonsville, MD 20866
Phone: 301-890-2119
Fax: 253-541-4915
E-mail: jgavin@starpower.net
Web: www.nvoad.org

The National Voluntary Organizations Active in Disaster (NVOAD) is a partnership in disaster response. Many of the voluntary disaster response agencies share a mutual concern about frequent duplication of services and services that do not meet quality standards. On state and local levels, the VOAD operates the same way as the National VOAD: as a coalition of voluntary disaster response agencies who agree to adhere to the Four C's of VOAD: Cooperation, Communication, Coordination and Collaboration in disaster response. The primary activities of the VOAD are planning, training, convening and partnering. In times of disaster, the VOAD gathers brief reports from member organizations and shares information with other members, convenes meetings of VOAD members at or near the disaster site, and works behind the scenes to identify a group or groups to guide the long-term recovery. When the recovery is well underway, VOAD convenes a special meeting to determine lessons learned, revise plans, strengthen preparedness and recruit new members. VOADs at all levels also partner with government agencies, such as FEMA and their state and county emergency management counterparts, the National Emergency Management Association (NEMA), and the International Association of Emergency Managers (IAEM).

Oklahoma City National Memorial Center
620 N. Harvey Avenue
Oklahoma City, OK 73102
Phone: 405-235-3313
Fax: 405-235-3315
Web: www.oklahomacitynationalmemorial.org

The Center is located in the former Journal Record Building that was damaged during the April 19, 1995 bombing that destroyed the Murrah Federal Building and killed 168 people. The Center provides information on the background of terrorism, the events in Oklahoma City, and survivor messages of hope and healing. The Center has a collection of books and other resources related to surviving terrorism and violence.

PTSD Alliance
450 West 15th Street, Suite 700
New York, NY 10011
Phone: 1-877-507-PTSD
E-mail: info@ptsdalliance.org
Web: www.ptsdalliance.org

The PTSD Alliance is a group of professional and advocacy organizations (American College of Obstetricians and Gynecologists, Anxiety Disorders Association of America, International Society of Traumatic Stress Studies, and the Sidran Traumatic Stress Foundation) that have come together to increase awareness and promote better understanding of the prevalence, recognition, diagnosis, and treatment of PTSD as a serious, common, and treatable condition. The Alliance has established a resource center that provides consumer and professional educational materials.

Tragedy Assistance Program for Survivors, Inc. (TAPS)
2001 S Street, NW
Suite 300
Washington, DC 20009
Phone: 202-588-TAPS(8277)
Fax: 202-638-5312
E-mail: info@taps.org
Web: www.taps.org

TAPS is America's national peer support organization made up of, and providing a wide range of services to, all those affected by a death in the armed forces. TAPS provides peer support, case work assistance, survivor link, grief counseling referral, and crisis intervention, free-of-charge, to all who have lost a loved one, friend or co-worker in military service. TAPS also sponsors the National Survivor Seminar.

Traumatic Incident Reduction Association
13 NW Barry Road
Suite 214
Kansas City, MO 64155-2728
Phone: 800-499-2751
Fax: 816-468-6656
E-mail: info@tir.org
Web: www.tir.org

The Traumatic Incident Reduction (TIR) Association is a division of Applied Metapsychology International, (AMI) which is a nonprofit membership organization dedicated to providing products, services, and support to TIR trainers, facilitators, technical directors and members. These practitioners in turn bring relief to individuals suffering from PTSD and other trauma related disabilities. They also assist individuals who seek improved quality of life, increased abilities, and personal growth. TIR is a specific technique employed to help those suffering from traumatic stress. The Association offers training and certification in this methodology and an electronic newsletter.

Workplace Trauma Center
9199 Reisterstown Road
Suite 207-A
Owings Mills, MD 21117
Phone: 410-363-4432
Emergency Line: 877-661-8070
E-mail: RJO@counselingcenters.com
Web: www.workplacetraumacenter.com

The Workplace Trauma Center offers training and response service world-wide. It specializes in workplace violence intervention, violence management training services, robbery survival skills training, employee assistance, and other training services.

Jacqueline Garrick, MSW, is a certified trauma specialist (CTS) with 15 years' experience managing health and social services programs for U.S. veterans who have served in Vietnam, the Persian Gulf, Somalia, and Haiti. She has worked at the Vietnam Veterans Resource Center, Walter Reed Army Medical Center, and the American Legion. In the immediate aftermath of 9/11, Ms. Garrick served as a disaster mental health counselor and organized referral efforts from the Pentagon Family Assistance Center. At present, she runs her own consulting firm and edits Trauma Lines, *the newsletter of the Association of Traumatic Stress Specialists (ATSS). She also manages projects for America's Heroes of Freedom.*